The Forgotten FA Cup

The Competition of 1945-46

Jack Rollin and Tony Brown

A *SoccerData* Publication

Published in Great Britain by Tony Brown,
4 Adrian Close, Beeston, Nottingham NG9 6FL.
Telephone 0115 973 6086. E-mail soccer@innotts.co.uk
First published 2007

Cover design by Bob Budd.

Printed and bound by 4Edge, Hockley, Essex
www.4edge.co.uk

ISBN: 978-1899468-86-7

FOREWORDS

Sixty years on from the 1946 FA Cup Final, two players who were there kindly shared their memories with us:

ARTHUR TURNER (Charlton Athletic)

I still remember it as an amazing occasion, the first time I had ever been to Wembley, being introduced to the King and the whole atmosphere at the game. On top of that the ball bursting and a dog running onto the pitch having to be rounded up! None of us forwards played to our potential on the day, yet still we should have won. Near the end before anyone had scored Don Welsh was clean through but shot over the bar. Derby's two outstanding inside-forwards Carter and Doherty were great and in extra time our ageing defence as good as it was simply ran out of steam.

REG HARRISON (Derby County)

My first ever view of the Stadium was from the coach taking us to the ground. Wembley Way was jam-packed and we made slow progress before arriving at around 1.45pm. Raich Carter was supremely confident about the game's outcome. The previous week he had been left out against Charlton in a League game and after our 2-1 win in which I played in his position, he announced: "the cup winners are in town!" Playing with Carter and Peter Doherty was wonderful. Doherty did the individual work, Carter was the playmaker. But you had to get to his passes - or watch out!

CONTENTS

Stanley Matthews receiving a commemorative plaque in recognition of his 44th appearance for England in January 1946, overtaking Eddie Hapgood's record. He had won 17 pre-war full caps and 27 unofficial wartime and Victory International honours.

INTRODUCTION

The origin of the post-war boom in soccer attendances dates back to the latter stages of wartime regional football and more significantly during the 1945-46 transitional season when a determined attempt was made to restore some peacetime normality to the game with the return of the FA Cup.

While the Football League's War Cup had been well received in the interim period, interest was doubly rekindled and literally so, by the decision to organize the FA Cup on a two-legged basis from the first round proper until the quarter-finals. Thus more people than ever before or since watched the competition.

There were two valid reasons for this unprecedented innovation. Firstly, it gave an equal chance of a home fixture to boost cash-strapped club finances. Secondly, it was hoped that matches on successive Saturdays in the first two rounds would settle most issues and avoid the need for midweek replays with the country still recovering from the effects of six years of war.

Tragically amid the excitement which the cup generated was the disaster at Burnden Park, Bolton, where 33 people were killed and 500 injured when a gate was forced open after ten minutes of the match between Bolton Wanderers and Stoke City.

The concept of home and away cup ties might have been comparatively new to England, but not in other parts of Europe. In the 1920s the introduction of the Central European Cup, arguably the forerunner of the European Cup and known as the Mitropa Cup, had used such a device. However, for the traditionally conservative English, it was a revolution indeed. Much of the impetus given to the FA Cup's revival was due to Stanley Rous, the FA Secretary, who had masterminded the organisation of competitive football during the previous six wartime seasons.

However, in 1945 the tactic to play defensively in the away leg and attack with home advantage was at least a decade and a half away from reality! Happily the wartime focus on entertainment on the pitch and going for goals was carried on during the FA Cup.

While there had been 539 entries for the 1939-40 FA Cup (only the extra preliminary round was played before hostilities called a halt to proceedings) the fact that many non-league clubs had still not resurfaced, others had fallen by the wayside and even two Football League clubs were unable to restart at the time, meant that only 294 were mustered for parade in 1945-46.

Sunderland's inside-forward Raich Carter at work for the Auxiliary Fire Service before enlisting in the RAF. Carter joined Derby County in 1945.

THE FA CUP 1945-46

The FA Cup itself did not have such an interesting experience as the one which befell the Jules Rimet Trophy, won by Italy in their second World Cup victory in 1938, but it did have its moments of excitement during the war.

Portsmouth's metaphorical grip on it included a night of near disaster when the cup's temporary accommodation in a local bank was threatened when the building was bombed. A frantic search was called off when it emerged that Pompey's manager Jack Tinn had taken the cup to his house and sat nursing it in a cupboard beneath the stairs during the air raid!

On another occasion it was loaned for exhibition in aid of the Red Cross. Alas, someone dropped it during the parade and the Havant police took charge of the mercifully undamaged item, depositing it overnight in the cells.

Just for the record, the World Cup demonstrated that sport can often outweigh politics, because Italian FA officials, mindful that the Nazis might confiscate the gold statuette, smuggled it from the vaults of the Swiss bank in Rome, though still basically mistrusting each other. So Secretary Ottorino Barassi decided on a safer hiding place and the World Cup spent the rest of the war in a shoebox under his bed!

Of course the FA Cup was not the only competition in 1945-46 to rekindle interest and the Football League Management Committee wanted to get back as near as possible to the pre-war structure as circumstances permitted. But when it was proposed that the 1939-40 fixtures even without promotion or relegation should be repeated throughout the four divisions, the clubs objected.

Even though it was rejected by a small margin the case for something mirroring what had gone before in the wartime regional fare was more practical as there remained a shortage of players, many of whom were still awaiting release from the armed forces with the war in the Far East still coming to a conclusion. In addition with the continuing domestic travel and hotel accommodation problems, a compromise was the only sensible answer.

However, the axe fell on one wartime familiarity; football pools coupons appearing in national newspapers. On 22 June 1945 Lord Goddard gave judgment in the King's Bench Divisional Court that such pools conducted through newspapers were illegal. Unity Pools had featured in the press to save newsprint supplies. Ironically shortages actually increased in peacetime!

An unofficial Home International Championship was brought back and won by Scotland, who had been dominated during the previous seasons by one of the finest England teams in history despite the limited opposition and obvious problems existing in team selection. A series of Victory Internationals also provided continental opposition in 1945-46. And the Moscow Dynamo visit was an added, exciting attraction.

When England beat Scotland 8-0 at Maine Road on 16 October 1943, Charles Wreford Brown, the man generally considered responsible for the word "soccer" while he had been a student at Oxford University said of it: "This England team which has won such a magnificent victory showed perhaps the greatest combination and team work in the whole history of international football. I myself have never seen anything like it before."

Many of these players were fortunate to be available as PT instructors and appeared regularly together for the Army and RAF teams, a host of fund-raising representative matches as well as in League fixtures, before the invasion of Europe in 1944.

Anyway, the existing First and Second Division clubs were regionalized into North and South sections. The existing North and South sections of the Third Division were split into four. Naturally the cup rounds on successive Saturdays for the first two rounds would eat into the domestic programme as never before. Additionally there had to be a secondary competition for the Third Division to make a reasonable fixture list. The real losers were the Division Three clubs, no longer playing teams of higher quality which had improved the overall standard of play. The clubs accepted the two-legged system for the FA Cup proper on 23 July. Receipts would be divided.

Since all agreements with players had been suspended in September 1939 there was the added problem for clubs faced with some kind of compensation for those on their strength who were now six years older and no longer figured in their plans. Then as the guest player system had helped to sustain the wartime game, there would be no such continuation in the cup. Even in League matches it would be scaled down with a maximum of six. In the event, the number of guest players was further reduced (to three) from 3rd November.

However, Tottenham Hotspur wanted guests up to the semi-final, but the League, aware of the problems which had existed with clubs chasing star players during the war, knew the Football Association would never sanction it. Spurs had drafted in Portsmouth winger Cliff Parker and Reg Smith of Millwall to ensure reaching a League (South) Cup semi-final on one occasion.

On a general level, many players attached to Football League clubs at the time were to discover their only exposure to officially recognised first-class football was to be in the FA Cup that season.

THE QUALIFYING ROUNDS

Despite a far from ideal scenario, the extra preliminary round got under way on 1st September; almost to the day the last such games had been played six years earlier. Instead of 34 ties as in 1939, there were just four in one geographical area covering the North-West home counties. There was no shortage of goals; 27 in total including Uxbridge beating Lyons Club (Greenford) 11-1 and Headington United (later to become Oxford United) suffering their heaviest cup defeat by losing 8-1 to Banbury Spencer.

A week later the preliminary round opened up with 26 ties, a further avalanche of goalscoring with two more 11-1 scorelines, one of which saw Tufnell Park thrashing Welwyn Garden City. Tufnell Park were still doubtless on a high having claimed they were the only Isthmian League team to play at Wembley, after appearing there in two wartime Middlesex Red Cross Cup finals.

Protests began to emerge in the first qualifying round on 22 September. Whether the information concerning guest players had not filtered through to the outlying clubs on the periphery of the game or not is unclear. At the time it was the usual practice for clubs to play first and complain later, almost solely if they were beaten. Yet there seemed to have been an extenuating case for the Principality of Wales, as the first instances concerned ties in that country. It was understandable since Welsh clubs by tradition had to apply for inclusion months earlier than their English counterparts and the decision over guest players was not confirmed at the time. The Welsh League allowed six guests as did the Football League.

Aberaman Athletic, who had been one of three non-league clubs - the others being Bath City and Lovell's Athletic - co-opted into the Football League in later war seasons to give the isolated west country clubs more competition, had now become Aberaman & Aberdare. Alas their impressive 6-1 victory came to nought when the vanquished Llanelli team complained and were declared the winners. Similarly Ebbw Vale's 3-1 success over Cardiff Corinthians was wiped out as was Bangor City's 4-1 win over Rhyl.

Yet Barry Town's 10-0 thrashing of Clevedon Town escaped scrutiny, presumably because there were no protests. Amazingly the *Clevedon Mercury* dated 29 September 1945 reported: "Barry included several well known League players such as Ross of Sheffield Wednesday, McCarthy of Liverpool, Ferguson and Turner of Charlton and Clayton the old Wolves captain." At the time Clayton was 35.

Moreover the Turner referred to was none other than Bert of that ilk, likely to loom large in the competition as it unfolded. The *Barry Herald*, however, listed Ferguson as a Raith Rovers player. The *Wiltshire Times and Trowbridge Advertiser* confirmed Turner's appearance at right-half.

The free-scoring continued. Walton & Hersham enjoying their first cup-tie as a combined club had an 11-0 romp with Epsom Town who were forced to disband because of ground problems in 1947 and are not to be confused with the other Epsom Town (later Epsom & Ewell)! The winners had three hat-tricksters including George Hoyle who managed a foursome.

At least in some other areas there was less confusion. As the *South Yorkshire Times and Express* reported: "Frickley were unable to play four of their guest players and brought in four reserves." Despite a gale and the long grass at Guiseley, the visitors managed a last minute equaliser at 3-3. Interest in the replay at Westfield Lane was such that scouts from at least eight Football League clubs were present, several to cast an eye over Frickley left-back Jack Brownsword. Guiseley almost scored in the first minute, but were never in the hunt subsequently as Frickley rattled in seven goals without reply, former Rotherham United amateur right-winger John Cowles scoring a hat-trick.

Frickley went on to visit an old nemesis in South Kirkby, 7-1 conquerors of Meltham Mills. But in front of a healthy 1,800 crowd they emerged 2-0 to the good only to suffer a summary 4-0 dismissal against Yorkshire Amateur.

Barry Town, having survived their situation, were paired with Cardiff Corinthians, themselves of course spared by an appeal, in the second qualifying round. "Clayton did not play by mutual arrangement," reported the *Barry Herald*. But again no sanction for Turner! Barry won 6-1. For their part, Llanelli took seven goals off Monmouth Town without reply.

On 18 October the *Ormskirk Advertiser* covering the Skelmersdale United v Darwen replay noted that in the extra period: "Darwen had taken the lead for the first time. The crowd had started to drift off thinking all was lost for the home team when Skelmersdale equalised in the last minute. It was decided to play an extra five minutes each way. The light was fading when Darwen scored again with a shot which was deflected onto the crossbar and dropped behind the goalkeeper."

There was another game of 11 goals, but in it Bournville Athletic, the Cadbury outfit, just had the better of Moor Green in extra time at 6-5. The victors were also involved in a protest match of their own in the third qualifying round.

Before that event the *Nuneaton Observer* reported on 19 October that Nuneaton Borough had received a letter from the FA stating that Worcester City had protested against the inclusion of Len Bolan in the team which had knocked them out in the previous round. However, since the protest did not fall into the statutory time scale no action could be taken, save for Nuneaton's observations to be made on the subject. The club asked for a ruling, but presumably to little avail as on 2nd November the same newspaper was quoted: "Nuneaton Borough have been ruled out of the FA Cup and fined 10 guineas (£10.50) for playing guest players against Bournville." The report went on to say that since Nuneaton had received no reply from the FA, they had decided to play their full team in the cup-tie. What a shambles! Nuneaton had won 8-1.

Yet it is interesting to note that the team against Bournville was missing Bolan, a pre-war player with Southend United who was already 36 years old and unlikely to be retained by his Football League club. They did have Murdoch Dickie the Chelsea right-winger! It should also be pointed out that the club was making its first entry into the FA Cup and as such possibly unsure of the rules.

News was also filtering through from other sources of concern. On 27th October the *Leiston Observer* reported: "Leiston go into the next round of the FA Cup against Chelmsford City at Chelmsford on 3rd November due to the FA upholding their protest against the inclusion of unregistered naval players in the Lowestoft side." For their part the *Lowestoft Journal* had stated: "After considerable difficulty the team had been composed of seven from HMS Martello and four from local clubs." The game had ended 2-2.

That was not all. There was trouble on the Isle of Wight. A healthy crowd of around 2,500 paying £125 saw visitors Cowes beat Newport 1-0, but the losers protested under rule 14 which stated that at the third qualifying round stage, players must have been recognised members of the club for at least 14 days prior to the match. So Cowes were branded while Newport were steered towards the next round in their stead.

One complaint that was not upheld concerned the Bedford Avenue v Letchworth Town tie. Bedford had won 1-0 but Letchworth pleaded, unsuccessfully, although they did have their protest fee refunded.

Barry Town won 7-1 away to Llanelli with Turner about to play his last match for them as he was soon to be posted to another unit awaiting demobilisation from the RAF. His next game for Charlton was at Swansea and he did not resume at The Valley until 1st December.

The 26 zonal qualifiers were joined by 24 exempted clubs in the fourth qualifying round, played in 11 geographical zones on 3rd November, with any replays to be completed by the following Thursday. Though goalscoring was not quite as carefree as in earlier rounds, there were one or two surprising results, not the least of them Sutton United winning 9-3 away to Gillingham, who only seven years previously had been a Football League club and were about to clear the board of Kent honours in the season with five League and Cup trophies. No hint of the second half flood as Sutton led 2-1 at the break and local observers put it down to just one of those days! Consolation came from a bumper gate of 6,258 for the twelve-goal feast.

Leiston suffered the heaviest defeat losing 9-0 at Chelmsford City. Newport pulled off a surprise win 2-1 away to Guildford City, but it was the end of the road for Barry, well beaten 5-1 by visiting Lovell's. Wisbech Town inflicted a 5-0 defeat on Colchester United and the remaining reprieved team Bournville Athletic fell 6-2 at Shrewsbury Town.

There was another unsuccessful plea by Coalville Town after they were beaten 2-1 at Kettering Town, the last hiccup before the first round proper got under way. Just to emphasise the momentum which was being gained throughout, Kettering's own run with three of four ties at home had increasingly produced gates of 2,100, 2,855 and 3,498. One of their victims was Peterborough, the 9-1 away winners at Rushden Town in the previous round when Laxton scored six times.

ROUND ONE

The 25 survivors joined the other 43 exempt clubs at the first round proper stage. They were both sections of the Third Division (North and South) minus Cardiff City, Chester, Crystal Palace and Norwich City who were exempt to the third round and two who were unable to compete, Hull City and New Brighton, both because of ground problems, Newport County from the Second Division and four non-league clubs: Bath City, Bishop Auckland, South Liverpool and Yeovil Town.

The draw was made in seven regional zones. Should aggregate scores over the two legs be level, ten minutes each way extra time was to be played. If there was still no decision, the first goal scored decided; a simple, straightforward method. Pity such logic has not survived sixty-plus years!

If daylight failed a third match had to be played. It was further re-emphasised that guest players, allowed in League matches, were not permitted. Stable door? Some flexibility was allowed as to which team played at home first if there was an extenuating reason.

On 14th November three days before the start of the competition proper, it was announced that Cup Final tickets would be fixed as follows: seats 42s (£2.10), 21s (£1.05) and 10s.6d (52½ pence); standing: 17½ pence!

With the Football League clubs entering, it was necessary for some clubs to complete their teams with players often away guesting for other clubs. Bournemouth recalled three such players including Len Smart at inside-left who was to make his first appearance for the club having been playing for an unspecified team in the Birmingham League! Ernie Tagg had been guesting for Crewe Alexandra, Harry Cooke for Luton Town. It went badly for Bournemouth at Newport against Lovell's in the first leg, losing 4-1 before a disappointing crowd of about 4,000, not aided by the fact that Moscow Dynamo
were playing Cardiff City at Ninian Park on the same day - and losing 10-1 into the bargain. Lovell's were two ahead in 25 minutes but Bournemouth had twice hit the bar.

Another first leg shock saw Shrewsbury Town hit Walsall for five without reply. Jack Maund scored three from the wing. In October 1946 he was to join Walsall! Presumably his presence was only due to the licence long enjoyed by non-league clubs who could sign transfer-listed Football League players, though he was a retained Nottingham Forest player at the time. Small wonder there was a fine line between this and being an ineligible guest.

Goals were being liberally distributed. Not all 34 games were finished. The Slough coach broke down on Mitcham Common, the team arrived 40 minutes late at Bromley and eight minutes from the end, light failed and the referee abandoned it with Bromley leading 2-1. They had another try on the following Wednesday but fog nearly stopped it with Bromley leading 6-1 this time and outside-left Stan Reece causing most of the mayhem. After consultation with both linesmen the game was allowed to continue.

That was the same afternoon of the infamous "Fog Farce" at White Hart Lane. Moscow Dynamo had not only brought a list of demands to England, but their own referee Nikolai Latyshev who patrolled near one touchline while the two English linesmen operated on the far side! Arsenal, bolstered by six guests including Stanley Matthews, lost 4-3. The 54,000 plus crowd saw very little through the fog, the Russian official only what he wanted to see!

Highest away scorers were Queens Park Rangers at Barnet in a 6-2 win watched by 6,800, the visitors conceding late goals. Frank Neary scored three himself including one from the penalty spot. The clearest advantage gained by a visiting team, however, was when Bishop Auckland won 5-0 at Willington. Yet only a week before the *Northern Echo* had merely recorded the respective fourth round victories with those Moscow Dynamos capturing the bulk of the football news.

Moscow Dynamo players training at the White City Stadium in preparation for their matches with Chelsea and Arsenal in November 1945.

Yorkshire Amateur took a slender 1-0 lead over Lincoln City with Frank Melling their scorer. Spookily he had made his debut as a wartime amateur for Sheffield Wednesday in 1941 against Lincoln, scoring frequently for the Owls for a couple of seasons.

Chorley, conquerors of Workington in the fourth qualifying round, led 2-1 over Accrington Stanley, their first success against a League team, otherwise the first leg passed off without too much of a problem for the Football League contingent. Still there were slightly raised eyebrows when Sutton's hopes appeared to have vanished when Walthamstow Avenue took a 4-1 lead at Gander Green Lane with 68-goals-in-the-season Charlie Vaughan restricted to their consolation. Wisbech, despite conceding three goals to Ipswich Town had a record attendance of 4,356.

In the derby match programme for the Reading v Aldershot leg at Elm Park, there was an appeal for accommodation for returning players from the forces. Once under way, the home team scored three times in the 15 minutes before half-time, the third a dubious penalty awarded against Oscar Hold and converted by Bill Layton. The Shots had the better of the second half, Harry Brooks scored after approach work by Tommy Sinclair and Paddy Fitzgerald. Brooks also hit an upright and had another effort charged down in front of goal. But no hint of more drama to follow.

Arguably the shock exit after the return matches saw Newport eliminate Clapton Orient. Having lost the first leg at Brisbane Road 2-1, the Hampshire League side won 2-0 on the day, 3-2 on aggregate. Lovell's, too, completed the task against Bournemouth despite losing 3-2. In fact Bournemouth were 3-0 ahead after 31 minutes, wiping out the deficit, until Lovell's recovered two goals. Again the Cherries had team problems. Tagg was unable to obtain leave, Smart failed to turn up at all and had to be replaced by Paddy Gallacher, just back from India. The crowd was 8,894. Consolation for Bournemouth came at the end of the season when they won the Third Division (South) Cup, beating Walsall with a Jack McDonald goal at Stamford Bridge watched by 19,715.

Accrington were held up until the second half before goals from George Rothwell and Charlie Hudson finally overcame Chorley's resistance and Mansfield Town with a 3-0 cushion from the first game had to struggle at Gainsborough Trinity. Two down at the interval they were forced into extra time before emerging 5-4 on aggregate. Lincoln, too, recovered their composure to ease past Yorkshire Amateur 5-1. Wrexham impressively wiped out Crewe's two-goal margin advantage with a convincing 3-0 second leg victory.

Willington, trounced 5-0 on their own ground by Bishop Auckland for whom centre-forward Fred Richardson enhanced his reputation with three goals, regained some pride from the return encounter winning 2-0, one of the highlights being when a sheep escaped onto the pitch and was chased by a dog while play continued oblivious of the intrusion. The two teams had met in the last FA Amateur Cup final in 1939, Bishops winning 3-0 after extra time at Sunderland.

Jock Davie, centre-forward guesting for League North leaders Chesterfield in the season, returned to his own club Brighton for the Romford tie. He travelled down from his Army unit at Newcastle only to arrive at 1 am. Unable to find accommodation he spent the night in a Brighton police cell! Later the same day he scored twice in Brighton's 3-1 win.

Queens Park Rangers, who had enjoyed an easy first leg win at Barnet, decided to copy Moscow Dynamo's pre-match preparation of using four balls in a 20-minute warm-up. Harry Brown the Rangers goalkeeper had been a second half guest substitute for Arsenal against the Russian team three days earlier! According to the *Daily Express* reporter: "QPR's unusual exertions seemed to tire them. At any rate Barnet made them travel and only lost by the odd goal of three." Barnet actually scored in the first minute through legendary left-winger Lester Finch and only goals by Reg Swinfen (85) and Neary (87) salvaged the day for Rangers, 8-3 aggregate winners.

Finch, a pre-war fixture in the England amateur team made his 100th representative appearance in 1941 and received a suitable commendation from the FA. His inside-forward colleague Denis Kelleher, absent from the Rangers games, had been captured at Tobruk but escaped from a POW camp in Germany, arrived back in England on a Thursday and played two days, scoring two goals for Barnet!

The North London team's efforts were rewarded at the season's end in another direction when they won the FA Amateur Cup at Stamford Bridge with 53,832 paying £4483, both competition records. The 3-2 defeat of Bishop Auckland saw Kelleher scoring the clinching goal.

Romford, famous for being the only amateur club in England run as a limited liability company, drew the second leg 1-1. Brighton defender Peter Trainor who had come down from Scotland was involved in a collision which required repairs to a head injury. Swathed in bandages he returned to the fray. As the suitably impressed *Daily Mail* recalled: "Trainor played on, tackling and kicking and even occasionally heading with a quiet confidence that was an inspiration to his colleagues."

Steve Walker's four goal feat for Exeter City in the 7-2 demolition of Trowbridge Town was all the more remarkable because it was one more than he achieved in his entire Football League career with the club over more than a decade! Usually a wing-half, he did occasionally play at inside-forward. During the conflict he served on *HMS Worcester,* a destroyer which pursued the German vessels *Scharnhorst* and *Gneisenau.*

An emphatic end of the road for Sutton at the Avenue, four down at half-time and 7-2 losers on the day. Bunny Groves scored four times, Fred Davis had two and Essex cricketer Doug Insole hit the other goal. Other individual hat-tricks included Tommy

Parker in Ipswich's five goals and Cecil McCormack in the six for Gateshead against Hartlepools.

Yet it was the second leg at the Recreation Ground between Aldershot and Reading which produced an amazing turn round, in front of 6,610 spectators. Brooks opened the scoring after 13 minutes only for Tony MacPhee to equalise after half an hour. Then Archie Summerfield put Reading ahead on the stroke of half-time. Aldershot were 2-1 down on the day, 5-2 adrift on aggregate. Within ten minutes of the resumption, Sinclair crossed and Brooks forced Gilbert Glidden to put through his own goal at 2-2. Five minutes later Brooks scored from another controversial penalty only for MacPhee to level for Reading. Brooks again regained the lead for Aldershot at 4-3.

In the 70th minute a free-kick by Jim Horton finished in the goalmouth and Fitzgerald reacted quickly to make it 5-3 for Aldershot. The tie was all square. Then in the last three minutes firstly from another free-kick by Cecil Ray, Brooks made it 6-3 and then hit his fifth for a 7-3 win and an incredible 8-6 aggregate success. As the footnote in a subsequent Aldershot programme put it: "T'was a famous victory. Well done, everybody!"

A full house at Villa Park, autumn 1945. A fleet of at least 11 trams is waiting to take the crowd back to the city centre (Copyright RT Wilson/Tramway & Light Railway Society)

ROUND TWO

Seventeen ties in the second round on 8th December produced no earth-shattering surprises. Walthamstow Avenue almost beat Brighton who only equalised with a last minute goal having missed an earlier chance to go 2-0 ahead at Greenpond Road where the attendance of nearly five figures produced record receipts of £640, but perhaps the surprise was the disintegration of giant-killers Newport.

They succumbed to another five-goal effort from Brooks of Aldershot in a 7-0 demolition at the Recreation Ground. Thus the Shots centre-forward entered the record books as the only player to score five goals in successive FA Cup matches. Bromley entertaining Watford collected a club record £450 too, from a 5,092 gate, though the amateurs committed suicide in defence giving away three goals; a misunderstanding at the back, an own goal and a twice-taken penalty in losing 3-1. According to the *News Chronicle*: "Bromley were completely stage-struck." Watford, who had fielded six pre-war players in the first leg, featured amateur Bedford Jezzard on the right wing. Just turned 18 he was soon afterwards called up for his National Service in the Army.

Northampton Town with Major Buckley's Notts County as visitors had planned for a 20,000 crowd. A number of local clubs postponed their own matches in order to see the tie. In the event less than that number of spectators turned up. Roy Peskett, reporting in the *Daily Mail* after Northampton's 3-1 victory was adamant: "I must refute the claim that Northampton scored seven seconds after the kick-off. By my watch the ball went into the net from Morrall's foot in a fraction over 16 seconds from the start." Seven seconds would have been a cup record.

Bishop Auckland put up a spirited display against York City. The *Northern Echo* wrote: "They were a clever, cup fighting combination, capably led by Richardson, who, in conjunction with Humble, gave the York defence a gruelling time."

Doug Humble was the outstanding player on view, centre-forward Fred Richardson a real handful. York though missing winger George Lee who had returned after leave to Germany took the lead against the run of play in the second half through Paddy Robbins then added a second from Ian Winters shortly afterwards following a goalmouth melee. However, with an attendance of 5,657 taking receipts of £293, Bishops had some financial comfort as well as a consolation goal. Humble and goalkeeper Washington were survivors from their 1939 FA Amateur Cup success.

Only one non-league club was certain to be included in the third round as Lovell's were paired with Bath City, to renew their "on loan" acquaintance with the wartime Football League. The Newport based team took a 2-1 lead from the first leg. Centre-half Harry Clarke, stationed at Chippenham in the RAF, had played in the first round for Lovell's. Before the Bath game he asked for a weekend pass which was refused. He still played, was charged and given seven days "confined to camp".

The north-west derby involving Barrow and Carlisle United was also full of goals. Barrow took a 4-2 lead at Holker Street, with Kevin Clarke signed from Drogheda scoring a hat-trick. He repeated the feat in the 4-3 win at Brunton Park as the second legs got under way. Darlington beat Stockton 2-0 in another first leg derby the other side of the country, both goals by Harry Clarke. He was to finish the season as overall top scorer with 48 League and Cup goals.

In their return match, Walthamstow took a 2-1 lead by half-time at Brighton who had Trainor injured again and forced to play on the wing. But pushing as many as seven players in attack at times in the second half, Brighton ran the amateurs off their legs to win 4-2. Avenue skipper Jim Lewis, aged 38, had played for the club in an FA Cup tie against Southwick exactly 15 years previously. But he was not the only veteran - George Burchell had played in the 1927 Amateur Cup Final.

Veterans were also in evidence for Bromley. A supporter sent a telegram wishing "good luck to the old fellows and their sons!" Defenders Clark and Mallett were in their 40s. The plucky amateurs did themselves proud and merited a 1-1 draw at Watford, Ron Gray scoring from the penalty spot for the League side.

Newport managed to restrict Brooks to one goal, but Aldershot still took five goals off them on the island. However, a week later Newport took awesome revenge on the unsuspecting Thornycroft Athletic in a Hampshire League match; their 14-1 victory unsurprisingly a club record! The other Newport - County from Wales - completed the elimination of Exeter City 3-1 at St James Park, 8-2 on aggregate.

A dressing-room mishap caused Ipswich Town left-half Geoff Fox to miss the game at Queens Park Rangers. He split his head open on a girder and his place was taken by Jimmy McLuckie, the coach. Neary was on the mark after eight minutes, Alec Stock added a second before half-time and Addinall had two after the break for a 4-0 Rangers lead.

The Bristol derby went City's way. They had led 4-2 from the Ashton Gate leg watched by 19,295 and scored once in each half at Eastville where Rovers returned an attendance of 21,043.

York goalkeeper Bob Ferguson saved a Bishop Auckland penalty after five minutes and City retaliated with a devastating spell of three goals in a five minute spell to end the amateurs' cup hopes. Northampton lost 1-0 at Notts but went through in what was their 100th cup match.

Rochdale held 1-1 at home had established a 2-1 first leg lead at Stockport County, for whom right-half Colin Gleave played in both games. Taken prisoner in Italy, he had escaped to Switzerland where he played carefree League football before being repatriated!

ROUND THREE

Sixty-three professional clubs entered the draw for the third round with Lovell's Athletic the South Wales Business House team the sole non-league survivors. To avoid excess expense and travelling, the pairings were made in four regions with the final exemptions coming into play.

On 1 January 1946 the *News Chronicle* reported: "For the first time in the history of the FA Cup a share pool will be run in connection with the competition for the 3rd, 4th, 5th and 6th rounds. Each club will take a third of the net receipts.

"One third will go to the pool, which will be augmented by a quarter of the net semi-final and final takings. Lovell's will receive 1/64th of the total, the remainder being divided between all the League clubs entered the first round."

It was also reported that teams were unlikely to receive gold medals for winning the cup. They cost £7 to make before the war and the wartime practice of presenting Savings Certificates would probably continue as the revised medal cost had increased to £20.

Stoke's goalkeeper Dennis Herod punches clear against Sheffield United at Bramall Lane in January 1946. Note the bomb damage to the roof of the stand.

More than a third of the third round first leg ties ended in a draw. Crowds were hugely encouraging. Newcastle United had 60,384 for the 4-2 win over Barnsley. A Gordon Pallister penalty and a Joe Harvey own goal responded to two from Jackie Milburn, one each from Grenville Hair and Albert Stubbins.

Chelsea had 39,678 to see Tommy Lawton signed from Everton two months earlier for £11,500 and who had scored in the 3-3 draw with the Dynamos, register in the 1-1 affair with Leicester City, the spectators including a party of 40 from the Fighting 4th Indian Division. Four other grounds reported gates of over 30,000 and only at three venues were crowds less than five figures. Generally games had been played on heavy, muddy pitches.

Best away performance was achieved by Derby County who scored three in each half at Luton Town, with Jackie Stamps, only recently offered to Leicester in part-exchange for Frank Soo, getting four of them.

Preston North End with 15 players still serving overseas, 22 more in the UK, took a 2-1 lead over Everton. Alex Herd and Jimmy Constantine shared the six Manchester City goals against Barrow, while other treble-shooters were Don Clark (Bristol City) and Freddie Steele (Stoke City). Barrow's Clarke, responsible for both goals at Maine Road, took his total to nine in four successive cup games.

Clark helped Bristol to a 5-1 lead over Swansea Town, who replied through Trevor Ford, the hottest property in the country, destined to finish the season with 41 League goals from the same number of games and all three in the cup as the second leg was drawn 2-2.

Overall the real sensation occurred at Upton Park where West Ham United led Arsenal 4-0 at half-time - the quartet in half an hour's play - and finished 6-0 to the good, to equal the Gunners worst cup defeat. The 35,000 did not include some 3,000 who clambered over bomb-damaged walls and fences after the gates had been shut. Pre-war signs showing "Way to Covered Stand" were misleading as there was no roof! With typical blitz humour the match programme referred to the tie as "Roofless v Homeless."

This was my first FA Cup tie and can confirm paying the correct entrance money as a schoolboy! Hammers chairman Bill Cearns subsequently asked the intruders to send the admission money to the club so it could donate to the East Ham Memorial Hospital. There was no official record of the outcome.

Of the match itself the *Daily Express* also quoted Cearns as saying: "I'm jubilant, but I wish it were anyone else but Arsenal. Their spirit in losing out there - well, it almost hurt."

Arsenal were having their most difficult season of the period having to call on 65 different players including 21 guests. The legendary Cliff Bastin often dropped back to wing-half and only Joe Wade at left back seemed to escape criticism. Neither the Gunners nor their wartime landlords Tottenham Hotspur were able to field a reserve team in the Combination as they, of course, shared White Hart Lane.

Portsmouth who had held the trophy longer than any other club since winning it in 1939 made an indifferent start to defending it losing by an own goal from Reg Flewin; a gift name for a tabloid sub-editor's headline. Included in the Pompey team was left-half Jimmy Scoular who had been serving in HMS Dolphin making his fifth first team appearance.

Alas, this was his second cup exposure of the season having turned out for Gosport Borough against Salisbury Corinthians in the first qualifying round, much to the chagrin of the blissfully unaware Portsmouth manager Tinn! Scoular was left out of the return.

The 28,928 crowd at Cardiff City thought they had been cheated out of the last five minutes of the 1-1 draw with West Bromwich Albion. Thousands stayed in the ground chanting: "We want the ref!" As the *Daily Express* reported: "An official gave them a firm hint over the loudspeakers - whatever you think of the result - the game is over. They left."

Aston Villa had been enjoying their most successful period when the draw was made. Eleven consecutive wins had been followed by two drawn affairs before the game at Coventry. It came to an abrupt end in a 2-1 defeat, City snatching a late winner.

Unlike the first two rounds, the second leg matches were staggered throughout the following week from Monday. Charlton had the cushion of a 3-1 lead over Fulham from the first leg at The Valley, but Arthur Turner, the only amateur in the team, had suffered a strained hip in the game, becoming a second half passenger and missed the return leg.

He had aggravated an injury he sustained while serving in the RAF as a Coastal Command rear-gunner when his Wellington bomber was shot down after attacking a German submarine about 200 miles out in the Bay of Biscay in July 1943, but not until the aircraft had badly damaged the U-boat. She was unable to dive or manoeuvre and the captain scuttled her. The only survivor from his crew of six, Turner spent nine hours in a self-inflated dinghy before being rescued, along with what was left of the submarine's crew, by a Canadian destroyer coming to England from North Africa. Turner reached the rank of Warrant Officer during his service.

Charlton rated 14-1 to win the cup then suffered their first defeat since losing to Notts County on 13 September, going down 2-1 at Craven Cottage, but emerging with an aggregate win. Later events were to spawn the quiz question legend of a team reaching the final having lost a game on the way.

As the *Daily Express* reporter mentioned: "Records show that when a team romps away with League honours it seldom wins the cup, but I am making Charlton my favourites." All this despite his critical report which revealed: "Charlton squeezed through, panting, foot-weary and grateful for the luck that had been a co-pilot." It continued: "Fulham's Cliff Lloyd off with a fractured leg after 12 minutes inflicted Charlton's first defeat in 20 games. Lloyd tried to come out strapped up at half-time, but couldn't get out of the dressing-room."

Ronnie Rooke scored both Fulham goals, Maurice Tadman, a last minute replacement at centre-forward for his brother George, scored Charlton's crucial goal in the 11th minute.

Plenty of late strikes around: 86th minute goals by Willie Moir (Bolton), Charlie Adam (Leicester) and Willie Fagan (Liverpool); 87th: Dennis Simpson (Coventry) and George Jones (Sheffield United); 89th: Jack Mahon (York). However the last gasp went to Reg Halton of Bury - one of Arsenal's "Fog Farce" guests - who scored with only five seconds left to salvage a 3-3 draw against visiting Rochdale.

Plucky Lovell's tired after giving Wolverhampton Wanderers, the 1939 cup runners-up, a first half fright. They scored twice and even missed a penalty! But Wolves hit back with four second half goals.

Accrington Stanley did well to hold Manchester United to a 2-2 draw at Peel Park attended by 9,968, but their season's success came on 29 December when a 4-0 victory at Barrow gave them the Third Division North (West) League title. United's pivot Allenby Chilton, twice wounded in the invasion of Europe, had made his first team debut on the eve of war. This was his second officially recognised game.

Though Millwall had no difficulty in disposing of Northampton Town 3-0, the *News Chronicle* surprisingly produced this aftermath: "Millwall were so impressed with the Northampton team they beat that they have made an offer of a five figure cheque for five of their men. A separate bid has also been made for centre-forward Morrall. The offer will go before the full Northampton board but it is not expected that it will be accepted."

Sheffield United after contriving a late 1-1 draw at Huddersfield, did win the return 2-0 but needed an outstanding display from Fred White in goal as Ernest Jackson was a limping passenger on the wing.

Coventry who had surprised Aston Villa with a late first leg winner lost 2-0 at Villa Park. Former England international Charlie Buchan writing in the *News Chronicle* was highly critical. "Players took the man and not the ball and spoiled what might have been a fine cup tie," he complained. Another observer referred to it as "grim and grimy." Driving rain and a greasy ball were additionally unhelpful ingredients. Villa's Ernie Callaghan soon suffered a pulled muscle and hobbled on the wing, but after 20 minutes Leslie Smith put them ahead. Harry Parkes hit the bar with a free-kick and with 72 minutes completed Billy Goffin added a second crucial goal.

Newly-installed Manchester United manager Matt Busby introduces himself to the players at the training ground in October 1945. Left to right: Billy Redman, Johnny Hanlon, Allenby Chilton, Johnny Carey, John Aston, Jack Warner, Norman Tapken and Ted Buckle.

Even referee Salmon of Stoke had to receive attention from the trainer after a leg injury of his own and with nine minutes remaining, his patience melting away, he sent off Bob Ward the Coventry right-half, in what was to prove the departing player's sole first class fixture! From a less fraught affair, Bury who had saved themselves even later against Rochdale, managed a more convincing 4-2 victory at Spotland.

The bulk of the ties were completed on the Wednesday. Arsenal at White Hart Lane and making half a dozen changes, were at least able to record a win courtesy of a Horace Cumner goal against West Ham, but the biggest shock was in Yorkshire where Barnsley, 4-2 down on the first leg at Newcastle gave it their best shot at Oakwell. Such was the amazing local interest that neighbouring collieries put up the following notice:

"In order that the management may have knowledge of the number intending to be absent on Wednesday afternoon, will those whose relatives are to be buried on that day please apply by Tuesday for permission to attend".

Braving the pouring rain 26,000 turned up and were rewarded by persistent Barnsley attacks from on the onset when Joe "Farmer" Wilson, once a land labourer and ex-Newcastle put them ahead, Then Joe Harvey gave away a penalty, but Pallister's shot was saved by Ray King in the United goal. Yet the disappointment turned to elation when Gavin Smith scored to level the aggregate score. The second half saw Barnsley continuing to press forward for the crucial decider, which Jimmy Baxter secured sealing a memorable comeback.

Sheffield Wednesday were in hooped shirts in 1945-46 rather than their usual stripes.

There were two matches of nine goals. Middlesbrough who had drawn the first leg at Leeds 4-4, won 7-2 with Micky Fenton scoring a hat-trick. Three days later in a League game at Sheffield United, the Boro leader hit five goals. Boro's left-winger Cliff Chadwick, used to delivering pin-point crosses, had kept his eye in during hostilities as a parachute trainer, dropping saboteurs on the right spot in enemy-occupied territory!

The other one-over-the-eight affair left Lovell's punch-drunk as they crashed 8-1 to Wolves at Molineux with Tom Galley scoring a trio of his own. Thus the last of the giant-killers was eliminated, the most successful of the *ersatz* wartime Football League conscripts.

Preston North End, cup winners in 1938, took Everton to extra time having twice been a goal down. First Jimmy McIntosh equalised, then from a penalty for hands in the extra period, up strode Bill Shankly to convert for a 2-2 draw and move Proud Preston into the fourth round.

But it was the end of the road to Wembley for holders Portsmouth against Birmingham. "Not even Jack Tinn's spats, worn at the last minute request of Freddy Worrall, could inspire Portsmouth, who had seven of the players who had won the cup in 1939," reported the *News Chronicle*. "Parker's glaring miss from six yards denied Portsmouth a certain goal, though they had six changes forced on to them through illness and injury." One might add the removal of Scoular, too.

Crystal Palace and Queens Park Rangers had slogged through a total of 207 minutes without a goal being scored - and another 90 minutes at least was required. "Cold, wind, rain and mud of Selhurst Park caused the second leg to be abandoned," said the *Daily Express*. The wind was so high that the ball had to be held still for goal kicks. Both teams agreed the result to stand.

At Vicarage Road there was a similar premature ending because of bad light in extra time with Watford and Nottingham Forest level at 1-1, 2-2 on aggregate. Incredibly the following day Watford had to fulfil a Third Division (South) League fixture! They were forced to make nine changes, eight of the mostly amateur newcomers making what was to be their only appearances and they were beaten 4-0 at Clapton Orient.

York, another of the late, late showing from the first game took a 2-0 lead in an hour through an own goal and a Winters' header. But in five minutes it was level. Extra time of ten minutes each way was conducted in descending darkness but Harry Thompson's fine individual run led to Winters volleying the winner causing an upset against Chesterfield, then the League North leaders. Thompson, who had once cost Sunderland £7,000 from Wolves, had been signed just in time for the round after guesting for three seasons.

Manchester United took care of Accrington. Jack Rowley had two of their goals in the 5-1 win played, as all their "home" fixtures were at the time, at Maine Road.

Two players defied doctors' orders and played on opposing sides. Wally Ardron the Rotherham United centre-forward his head swathed in bandages which were held firm by the inside of an ARP helmet, scored one of the two goals which knocked out Gateshead for whom Bill Cassidy, in hospital with tonsillitis only four hours before, also featured! Rotherham had Mark Hooper at outside-right. He had played his first League match 22 years previously for Darlington and at 45 was the oldest Football League player in the third round.

Thursday saw the last six games. Brentford had two goals disallowed against Tottenham Hotspur but still won 2-0 to knock out their north London opponents, veteran Welsh international winger Dai Hopkins, 39, scoring both goals, the second while lying in the mud! Chelsea's second goal at Leicester was scored by fair-haired Reg Williams whose shot went in off the bar. Amazingly he had earlier hit the upright three times.

Yet in spite of the afternoon kick-offs and poor weather, attendances held up well. Goodison Park had 35,461, while at Portsmouth there were 23,716. *The Daily Express* gave overall figures of 1,254,000 for the 64 third round matches - averaging over 23,000. However, there were still outstanding replays to add to the total.

Watford and Nottingham Forest went to White Hart Lane but the game started 40 minutes late because the midland side was delayed on their railway journey. The unfortunate Forest defender Ted Blagg put through his own goal after extra time just as he had done in the first leg! At Fulham, Albert Addinall at long last scored for Queens Park Rangers to break the goal drought with Crystal Palace. Both clubs were to have a measure of League success; Rangers winning the Third Division South (North) and reaching its cup semi-final, Palace the South section version of the same fragmentation.

Charlie Wilson-Jones (far right) turns away after scoring for Birmingham City against Arsenal at their wartime White Hart Lane evacuation home in a 3-0 win on 2 February 1946 on the way to winning the League South title, watched by a crowd of 30,416. Goalkeeper George Swindin is beaten and Leslie Compton (second left) is too late to save the situation.

Two programmes from the 1945-46 FA Cup; Aldershot v Reading on November 24 1945 and Brentford v Charlton Athletic on March 9 1946.

ROUND FOUR

Before the fourth round, police announced that they could not guarantee the safety of surrounding property if Chelsea played at West Ham in the first leg. The FA allowed the match to be switched to Stamford Bridge because of fears for public safety on the bomb-damaged ground.

Chelsea took precautions of their own and according to the *News Chronicle* in order to deter would-be roof climbers, they fixed a mile of double coil wire similar to that used by wartime coastal defences around the eaves of the stand 30 feet from the ground.

The change of venue coincided with 65,726 the biggest crowd of the day, Alec Machin heading Chelsea into the lead from a retaken corner and Dickie Spence adding a second after the interval. Alas the *Daily Mail* reported that the barbed wire had failed to prevent problems as fans stormed the houses backing on to the ground.

Charlton seemed in trouble against Wolves. At half-time they were trailing after Ray Chatham had scored twice; Duffy having opened the scoring on 18 minutes. Worse, Robert Albert John - nicknamed "Sailor" because of his rolling gait - Brown had broken down only ten minutes from the start and was limping for the rest of the half.

In the break he was given two hypodermic injections in his knee and sparked an incredible revival which saw Charlton score four times! The second best crowd of the day 44,271 witnessed the turnaround. Oddly enough Brown had written to manager Jimmy Seed declaring himself unfit, but had been called in to the ground on the Friday and given all-day treatment and massage by trainer Jimmy Trotter.

Meanwhile Derby County needed an 80th minute Peter Doherty goal to give them a slender advantage against West Bromwich Albion in front of 31,795, their best crowd since 1938 and two efforts from Stan Mortensen afforded Blackpool a 3-2 edge over Middlesbrough at Bloomfield Road.

Mortensen had had his problems on and off the field, too. While on aircrew training he had escaped death by a hair's breadth when the Wellington bomber in which he was flying crashed in Scotland. Later a knee injury baffled specialists until Mortensen had a kick about on Blackpool beach with a sea-soaked football and cured himself!

Davie, the Brighton centre-forward coveted by Sunderland and an occasional wartime guest for Aldershot, scored all three goals against the Shots. Another triple marksman was Ambrose "Jock" Mulraney in Birmingham's 5-0 win against Watford while Ray Westwood with three goals of his own and Nat Lofthouse two featured in Bolton's destruction of Liverpool watched by 39,682. Another five goals saw Sheffield Wednesday with a four-goal margin over York City, the first coming after five minutes.

Raich Carter opened his Derby account with two goals in the 3-0 success with Luton. A midnight taxi dash had enabled him to be signed in December from Sunderland for a giveaway £6,000 in time for the cup round. He had almost been lost to the game in the war. Volunteering for the Auxiliary Fire Service, he liked it so much he even thought of making it his career. But after two years he resigned and joined the RAF. Both he and Peter Doherty had guested extensively for the Rams prior to both signing on a permanent basis. Doherty's former club Manchester City, 3-1 winners at Bradford Park Avenue had set up what appeared to be a formality at Maine Road. It was not to be.

Addinall kept up his away day scoring for Queens Park Rangers at Southampton with a 32nd minute goal, but only after they had conceded a penalty in three minutes for hands against Arthur Jefferson. However, Don Roper's spot kick had been saved by Reg

Allen, ex-Commando captured in North Africa, who had escaped, been recaptured and finally liberated by the Russians in Germany!

There were 37,100 to see Barnsley take on Rotherham, the biggest gate at Oakwell for a decade. Johnny Kelly scored his first ever goal for the Reds, Smith and Chilean born centre-forward George Robledo adding two more for a comfortable 3-0 advantage.

Aston Villa were the top away-day scorers, 4-2 against Millwall at The Den after taking a 2-1 half-time lead. Jimmy Jinks had both for the Lions, while Villa's leading marksman George Edwards notched a couple of their goals.

Colin Collindridge is on his knees but scores for Sheffield United at home to Stoke despite the close attentions of Neil Franklin.

Thirteen of the 16 ties resulted in home wins and there were no drawn games. Stanley Matthews was doubtful for the Sheffield United match but was prescribed pep pills similar to those used by the Luftwaffe and German paratroopers. He was made captain for the day - or should it have been *spielfuhrer*? Stoke won 2-0.

Monday saw the two teams renewing the encounter at Bramall Lane with 50,859 inside. Colin Collindridge, normally a left-winger noted for his powerful finishing on and off the ground, was switched to lead the United attack. He responded with three goals - no mean feat against Neil Franklin - in their 3-2 victory. There were four disallowed goals in the opening quarter of an hour, Matthews twice losing efforts for offside. But Stoke came through on aggregate.

United were able to shake off the disappointment and bounced back in the League North remaining unbeaten in the last 12 games. Jimmy Hagan their talented inside-forward who returned from Army service as a PT Instructor too late for the cup, was considered to have become much stronger physically and appointed team captain.

He had also benefited from guesting for Aldershot over 100 times, often playing alongside wartime England colleagues like Cliff Britton, Stan Cullis, Joe Mercer and Lawton. Of the 27 players Sheffield United used in 1945-46, only one was a guest and five others played just once.

Aston Villa with a two-goal margin to the good from their visit to South London, added another five by half-time at Villa Park and finally ran out runaway 9-1 winners on the afternoon against the luckless Lions. Six different players shared the goals, Frank Broome netting a hat-trick. There were another nine goals the following afternoon at Bury.

Sunderland with a 3-1 lead from the first game found the Shakers living up to their nickname and needed extra time before emerging 7-4 on aggregate though losing 5-4 thanks to an "outstanding hat-trick" as the *Daily Mail* put it, from Bury's Fred Roberts, a 1938 signing from Rhyl. Sadly George Davies who had registered over 150 wartime goals for Bury decided to retire a month later at 29 with a troublesome arthritic knee.

Cyril Brown the Sunderland centre-forward who scored twice in the Roker Park leg and once at Gigg Lane, was another example of a career drastically cut short by the war period. A north-east lad from Ashington, he had a southern football background. From Felixstowe he moved to Brentford in January 1939. However he managed only a handful of wartime matches for them and returned to the north-east and Sunderland, making a scoring debut at - off all places Newcastle - in a 3-0 win on 2 April 1945, to become an instant local hit.

Wednesday, a day of snow, hail and rainstorms, witnessed the upset of the round if not the tournament when after leading 2-1 at half-time at Manchester City, Bradford - 3-1 down on the first leg - won 8-2 with Jackie Gibbons, the England amateur international centre-forward who had recently transferred his registration from Spurs, scoring four times on a waterlogged pitch watched by only 15,026. Ronnie Dix the youngest Football League debutant back in 1928 for Bristol Rovers at 15 years 173 days and the youngest goalscorer a week later, weighed in with two goals. All this, too, scored against the great Frank Swift!

In his autobiography *Football from the Goalmouth*, Swift later revealed the pre-war tale of how he had given a young lad called Jackie tips on goalkeeping by doing his homework on the game. After the Bradford debacle, a smart Army Sergeant came up to Swift and said: "Do you remember me, Frank?" After a quick chat the NCO's departing remark was: "You have plenty of homework to do to-night!"

Charlie Tomlinson, a pre-war Park Avenue winger, scored a hat-trick as Sheffield Wednesday piled more misery on York at Bootham Crescent in a 6-1 win. Fenton had two Boro goals but there had to be a replay against Blackpool with 46,566 looking on as the teams finished level on aggregate 5-5; the game abandoned in poor light after 150 minutes play!

Preston, a goal adrift to Manchester United in the first leg won 3-1 at Deepdale, Addinall struck three times for Rangers in 4-3 success against Southampton and the players had to retreat temporarily because of the hailstorm. One of Addinall's goals was so fierce, too, it came back out of the net and the referee thought it had hit the bar. However, a frantically waving, eagle-eyed linesman called him over to confirm a goal. Actually Addinall had honed his goalscoring skills in a remarkable sequence of reserve team matches for Rangers in the London Combination totalling 14 goals in the opening seven fixtures of the season.

At Upton Park the gates were closed on 31,000 with safety measures in place. Chelsea with a two goal first leg lead were soon up against it. Len Goulden signed from the Hammers in August went off with broken collarbone after only eight minutes, but the ten men hung on for a 2-1 aggregate win as Almeric Hall's goal for West Ham was insufficient.

Liverpool pulled a couple of goals back but Bolton's advantage was too great as was Charlton's at Wolves, though a Bill Morris own goal gave them a 1-1 draw. Derby looked far happier 3-1 at The Hawthorns. Referee Snape from Manchester who had worn a blue and white outfit for the first leg only to receive protests from both clubs, changed into a maroon number for this one.

Davie added two more for Brighton in an easy 4-1 win against Aldershot at the Recreation Ground, taking his tally to ten cup goals. The gate of 5,226 was the lowest in the round.

Thursday saw Brentford cancel out Bristol City's slim lead with a resounding 5-0 win. Gerry McAloon, recently recruited from Wolves, had three of the goals, but the strike which caught the headlines was Ivor Guy's own goal, simply because the right-back had scored for his own team from rather longer range in a previous League game with Cardiff: an incredible 73-yard free-kick!

Though faced with a three-goal deficit, Rotherham had 19,563 (£1700) for the visit of Barnsley and brought themselves back into the tie when first Wilson with an own goal then one from Ray Shaw retrieved two of them. Pallister was injured but ironically it helped Barnsley because he went on the wing and was handily placed to seize on a loose ball with the United defenders expecting the offside whistle. He made it 2-1 and Barnsley survived.

However, Rotherham had the satisfaction of topping the Third Division North (East) table and winning the Third Division North Cup, beating Chester in the two-legged final. They were also placed top of the North's Second Championship table, though in fact played no matches in it! The vagaries of the system were baffling indeed.

This left the Boro - Blackpool replay which was scheduled for Leeds. Over 30,000 were officially logged in at Elland Road, another 10,000 broke in. George Hardwick the Middlesbrough captain settled the issue from the penalty spot in the 51st minute after Johnny Spuhler had been brought down in the area; a kind of prehistoric golden goal in extra time, the tie having taken six hours, 21 minutes to resolve.

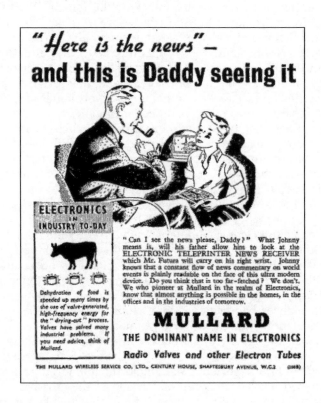

ROUND FIVE

Nine of the 16 clubs who qualified for the fifth round had lost a match already, but not one was happy about the short interval between the draw on Monday and playing ties on Saturday. The *News Chronicle* quoted the consensus as saying that it was insufficient time to arrange hotel accommodation and travel facilities.

Clearly the generosity bestowed on the Third Division clubs in the first two rounds had been eroded by the congestion of fixtures. Nothing new in the game, then or now. Anyway, Derby were installed as 3-1 favourites. Brighton, their opponents the outsiders at 500-1 according to the *Daily Express*.

Derby duly won 4-1 on the south coast with breezy braces of goals each from Carter and Doherty, but the goal which captured the attention came from amateur Stan Willemse, a 21 year old Sergeant in the Royal Marine Commandos, who infiltrated the Rams defence evading four opponents before rifling in Brighton's consolation. The gate of 23,456 was the Goldstone's best for 12 years and gave them an average in the cup run of 12,600.

Charlton's own amateur centre-forward Arthur Turner put them ahead in the 1-1 draw at Preston, but the Addicks had a Leslie Fell goal disallowed - Chris Duffy's throw-in had been taken with his feet over the line. Jackie Wharton equalised for Preston. Just before the end Jimmy Dougal and Charlton's Jack Shreeve kicked the ball simultaneously and it burst. Not the first such incident of combustion to hit Charlton.

There was yet another controversy at Loftus Road over Brentford's goal against Rangers. The home team claimed the ball had gone through the side netting. The match was delayed several minutes while the officials debated before agreeing McAloon's goal. "I examined the netting and there was no hole," said Northampton referee Barrick. But the Rangers players insisted the netting had risen up and the ball had gone underneath.

Biggest crowd was 65,307 at Stamford Bridge. Chelsea trailing from a Frank Broome goal for Aston Villa were awarded a penalty ten minutes from time, but the usually sure-shot marksman "ten-goal" Joe Payne, blasted his effort "hopelessly wide" as the *News Chronicle* reporter saw it. One of the linesmen was late arriving and a deputy wearing a sports jacket pinch-hit until the absentee appeared.

A crowd of 44,820 at Roker Park saw a Len Duns' strike give Sunderland a slender lead over Birmingham; 43,453 at Burnden Park viewed a similar result from a Ray Westwood effort for Bolton against Middlesbrough. There were 40,452 in attendance as Steele hit both Stoke goals against Sheffield Wednesday and most of the 37,770 at Barnsley were frustrated as their favourites were unable to break down the Bradford defence. Then with a quarter of an hour remaining, Len Shackleton scored his first ever FA Cup goal for Bradford, one of 167 he hit for them in these seven regional fare seasons.

Because attendances had been so good, clubs were expected to receive £1000 as their share of the pool more than the original estimate of £750.

The attendance at Hillsborough on the Monday was 62,732, but Stoke held Sheffield Wednesday to a goalless draw to become the first team to reach the sixth round. However, the *Sheffield Star* reported: "Many hold the opinion that the ball fell over the line after Froggatt had headed onto the under-side of the crossbar. Robinson was so convinced that the ball had gone over that he did not trouble to kick it in!" The following day, Aston Villa repeated their one goal effort against Chelsea, courtesy of Billy Goffin's strike in front of some 56,000.

By coincidence, both Charlton and Derby won their first leg matches 6-0. Charlton chairman Albert Gliksten on business in British Honduras as Timber Controller was cabled with the news of victory over Preston. Duffy scored two goals in two minutes, then after scoring his hat-trick he clapped himself all the way back to the centre circle! It had been goalless at half-time. Duffy, a miner, was a £330 buy from Scottish Second Division Leith Athletic in the previous September having guested for the London club during the war in which he had taken part in the Normandy landings.

Three days after this match, Charlton met Birmingham in a League game at St Andrews in front of 56,615. City were leading via a Charlie Wilson-Jones goal. In the 86th minute the visitors were awarded a penalty. Skipper Don Welsh summoned goalkeeper Sam Bartram to take the kick. He had scored from the spot on three occasions the previous season guesting for York. This time he ran the length of the field, hammered a shot which hit the top of the crossbar and sailed over. For five months Charlton had headed the table, but they fell away out of contention after this defeat. Success in the cup squeezed their other commitments to the extent they were playing three times a week. In the last four League matches, Charlton met three of the leading contenders, taking only three points and finished third, one point behind Villa.

Carter with three goals, Doherty two, delighted the 32,000 Baseball Ground crowd in the other half-dozen goal win over Brighton, while Fenton again came to Middlesbrough's rescue with the equaliser against visiting Bolton with the afternoon's highest attendance of 51,612 present, receipts £5,708. However, George Hunt, deputising for Lofthouse at centre-forward, had scored for Bolton and out went Boro.

Robledo had given Barnsley a first minute boost to lead at Bradford, but they were unable to press home their superiority and that man Gibbons managed an 85th minute equaliser in front of 29,341 supporters and the Tykes were eliminated. Then with all four goals in the second half Birmingham ousted Sunderland 3-1, their trio achieved in a lightning 11-minute spell for a 3-2 aggregate win.

Thursday wrapped up the first leg at Brentford. Both the home team and Rangers finished with several injuries. Brentford's Scottish goalkeeper Joe Crozier was hurt in a challenge with Addinall which left him with a badly lacerated thigh and his defenders had to take all subsequent goal-kicks. This tough local derby tie ended with Rangers centre-half Alf Ridyard nursing a broken nose and Brentford's inside-right Eric Jones with a head injury. There were no goals.

ROUND SIX

A small respite followed before the sixth round on 2 March. Players with winning teams would receive a bonus of £8, a full-time professional would be entitled to £17 for the game, but if a single man the PAYE figure reduced it to just over £10.

A week before the ties, Charlton manager Seed announced that placing Bert "Sailor" Brown, their England international inside-forward on the transfer list was according to the *Daily Express*: "The biggest disappointment in my career as a manager." The 30 year old was valued at £10,000, yet the reality was that the two of them did not see eye to eye, to the point of thoroughly disliking each other.

The weather was to play a part and all eight clubs delayed naming their teams because of severe fog, snow and sleet in the preceding days before the Saturday in question. Goals were plentiful - a record 22 in fact.

Nonetheless Brown was in the Charlton line-up against Brentford at The Valley with 44,060 inside braving a blizzard! Among the onlookers was the Rt Hon Herbert Morrison, Deputy Prime Minister. He would have seen the programme notes which appealed for clothing coupons for players kit, or perhaps not. McAloon put Brentford ahead in the ninth minute, but Arthur Turner equalised 14 minutes later. By the interval Charlton were 3-1 in front and it was 4-1 before McAloon's second goal in the 81st minute. Not to be side-tracked, Charlton added two more before Durrant wrapped up the scoring, the Addicks winning 6-3.

Derby produced a ground record 76,588 and receipts of £8,651 for their visit to Villa Park. The previous best there had been 75,700 in 1938 against Manchester City. In what the *Daily Express* described as "The most thrilling game of the season", the veteran Rams attack of Crooks 37, Carter 33, Stamps 27, Doherty 31 and Duncan 35 belied their combined ages. Trailing 3-2 with four minutes left, first Doherty and then Crooks in the dying seconds snatched a crucial win for the Rams in dreadfully icy conditions underfoot.

Birmingham were losing 2-0 at Bradford at the interval before drawing level and that man Westwood did the damage again with two goals for Bolton at Stoke where in contrast there was bright sunshine.

The second leg games were totally overshadowed by the tragic events at Burnden Park, Bolton where 33 people were killed and 500 injured when a crowd broke-in two minutes after the start while others were trying to get out because of the crush. Steadily mounting figures of those who had suffered came into the press box while play was continuing. There were no loudspeakers to inform the 65,419 spectators what was happening. The game ended goalless and the players were unaware of the scale of the human disaster until later.

Birmingham took a four-minute lead against Bradford through Neil Dougall and never looked in danger with the tall, fair-haired Australian born Frank Mitchell marshalling everything from centre-half. Dougall, Mulraney and Harold Bodle shared the goals in the ultimate 6-0 success.

Derby, still undefeated throughout the cup run lost Crooks with a displaced cartilage after he had been unceremoniously floored by his equally veteran opponent Ernie "Mush" Callaghan 36, continually booed whenever he subsequently touched the ball. The *Daily Mail* reported: "He had to be carried off on the shoulders of the trainer," pointedly adding: "Crooks is Chairman of the Players' Union!" He had also just been appointed Derby's chief scout. Callaghan had been awarded the BEM for conspicuous bravery as a War Reserve Policeman in the Birmingham blitz in September 1942.

Ten minutes after Crooks' departure, Rams goalkeeper Billy Townsend raced out to clear a long ball only succeeding in miss-hitting it to Broome who accepted the gift to open Villa's score. But the ten Rams battled on grimly. A minute before half-time, Vic Potts brought down Duncan. He took a quick free-kick finding Carter who headed the equaliser with the goalkeeper motionless. Carter might have scored again in the second half, but blazed over the bar.

Neither did the League South title come Villa's way. They finished as squeezed-out runners-up though George Edwards scored 41 League and Cup goals for them and the average League attendance was 32,822. Their season's profit was £18,185. Villa who only operated at this level in the last four seasons of wartime fare, called on just three guests during the period and one of those, Potts was signed in 1945-46 anyway.

At Griffin Park, any prospect of a Brentford recovery against Charlton was dampened when Duffy opened the scoring after a few minutes. Don Welsh and Arthur Turner added second half goals. Billy Scott had the Brentford reply. Absent from the home line-up was centre-forward Fred Durrant owing to the sudden death of his wife earlier in the day.

Tragedy at Burnden Park where 33 people are killed and 500 injured shortly after the start of the Bolton Wanderers v Stoke City sixth round second leg FA Cup tie in a crowd of 65,419.

THE SEMI-FINALS

Charlton were made 9-4 favourites when paired with Bolton for the semi-finals, Derby and Birmingham were both 5-2, Bolton the outsiders at 4-1. The FA declared the matches to be all-ticket; Villa Park was chosen for Charlton's game with the Derby tie at Hillsborough. Within two hours of going on sale, 24,000 tickets allocated for Derby were sold out.

In the *News Chronicle* the shrewd Charlie Buchan predicted a Derby v Charlton final. The Addicks decided to avoid the mistake of arriving too early to allow nerves to get the better of the players. They planned to travel on the 11.05 am train from Euston, relax at a Birmingham hotel and be driven to Villa Park. Police in the area were on the alert for forged tickets and pirate programme sellers. Twelve coaches of Charlton supporters carried fans to Birmingham.

Charlton's Duffy snared most of the headlines. He scored both goals after 35 and 50 minutes against Bolton. His second effort was described by his manager as: "the best goal I have ever seen." In his 30-yard run he evaded five opponents, flicked the ball past Dick Threlfall, jumped over the full-back's legs before shooting past Stan Hanson. At the back, John Oakes belied his years at centre-half for Charlton. The crowd was 70,819.

Buchan's verdict was: "As brilliant a solo effort as I have seen for many years." Duffy, who not content with his brace also hit the upright, had recently recovered from a cartilage operation to his right knee and had been discharged from the Army because of "battle exhaustion." Yet the *Daily Mail* put a different slant on the afternoon: "Bolton's defence was as shaky as a row of bean poles in a high wind."

Welsh the Charlton skipper had been led off the pitch after ten minutes with blood streaming from his head. He was patched up and returned to action. Duffy aside, the *Daily Mail* was not over-impressed: "So little was thrilling in this game." With Charlton through, the clamour for final tickets took on an earnest meaning and many supporters besieged manager Seed on the train journey back to London.

The other semi-final at Sheffield with 65,013 in attendance was considered by the *Daily Express* to be: "one of the poorest games of the season." It was a hard ground and a bouncing ball on it. Carter opened the scoring after barely four minutes, the Birmingham defence motionless expecting handball to be given against him. Later explaining what happened Carter said: "I and a Birmingham defender went forward together for the ball just outside the penalty area. He reached it first and kicked it against my arm. I played to the whistle."

Mulraney levelled it in the second half before Doherty headed against the crossbar with ten minutes remaining. As Derby pressed again, Dennis Jennings cleared off the line in the 86th minute. The replay had been pencilled in for the following Wednesday at Maine Road.

Manchester City increased the number of stewards to 50 and doubled police on duty to 80. Gates were closed 40 minutes before the kick-off. Derby were informed before the match that their cup final ticket allocation was to be 12,000!

Another record crowd 80,483 - the biggest for a midweek game outside Wembley between two Football League clubs, produced record receipts, too, of £13,202. There was no score after 90 minutes, but within five minutes of the extra period, Duncan beat Ted Duckhouse the Birmingham full-back and made ground before pulling the ball back. Duckhouse recovered, tackled Doherty as the Derby forward shot for goal, only to suffer a fractured tibia of his left leg. "Doherty's impetus carried him on and he managed to turn a complete somersault before limping back to the centre-circle," reported Roy Peskett in the *Daily Mail*.

A depleted and not unnaturally dispirited Birmingham went further behind. Doherty nutmeged goalkeeper Gil Merrick after a 40 yard run for his second goal and Stamps wrapped it up by back-heeling his own second near the close. Peskett added: "One of the most sensational periods of extra time in the history of the competition."

One of the other plusses for Derby was the performance of Jack Howe at centre-half. Back in the country only three weeks after three years in West Africa and India, he had played only once since in the reserves at Chesterfield and had never turned out at centre-half before.

Birmingham had to be content with finishing top of League South, albeit on goal average. They were fortunate to field a largely undisturbed side in several positions, four of the 24 players used making just one solitary appearance, another four turning out twice each. Centre-forward Jones was their top League scorer with 20 in only 27 matches. Inside-left Bodle and their own Arthur Turner at centre-half were absent on merely two occasions.

Though the cup attendances had been highly impressive, there were some equally crowd-filling League fixtures. On 6 April at Maine Road, the Mancunian derby attracted 62,144 for what was a Manchester United "home" match as Old Trafford was still undergoing extensive bomb-damage repairs. It proved an individual triumph for City's George Smith who had all of their goals in the 4-1 success.

While serving in South Africa during the war he had been seriously injured by a gunshot wound which necessitated the removal of the lower part of his right arm from the wrist down, though he made light of the handicap. On Boxing Day at Newcastle, he was on target again in a 1-1 draw with Jackie Milburn scoring for United in front of 54,954. A month previously St James Park had housed 50,833 for the 6-2 win against Liverpool.

Aston Villa also enjoyed some outstanding gates. Local derbies proved immensely popular of course. Over Christmas the visit of Wolves in a 1-1 draw attracted 59,970 while a month later Birmingham City's arrival pulled in 63,820.

Internationals, too, were well attended as they had been throughout hostilities and Hampden Park had two six figure crowds topped by the 139,468 for the eagerly awaited confrontation with the old enemy England.

THE FINAL

A week before the Wembley occasion, Derby and Charlton met in the League at The Valley. The Rams rested Carter and Doherty. Charlton fielded only five of what was to be their final selection but still won 2-1 with Charlie Revell, destined to miss the final, scoring both goals.

Three days before this game Charlton had lost right-back Peter Croker from a fractured right leg just above the ankle in a 1-0 League win over Tottenham Hotspur. It was the second misfortune to hit the club and that family in the season. Late in December, Flying Officer brother Ted had been the pilot of a plane which crashed in a remote part of Derbyshire. Despite suffering from two badly damaged ankles he bravely crawled five miles over difficult country to get help for his two injured crew left huddled in their parachutes for warmth. All three survived the ordeal.

Bartram, Brown, Oakes, Shreeve, Bert Turner and Welsh were pre-war Addicks. Moreover Charlton had more Wembley experience. Shreeve, Oakes, Welsh, Brown and Harold Phipps who was to take Croker's right-back berth had been in the 1943 League South Cup final team beaten 7-1 by Arsenal, Bartram, Shreeve, Oakes, Brown, Welsh and Duffy (as a guest) figured in the 1944 win over Chelsea there, while Bartram and Brown had even guested themselves for Millwall a year later when Chelsea were 2-0 winners!

Phipps had served as a bandsman in the Middlesex Regiment; Bert Turner and Welsh were cross-over servicemen! Turner had been a pre-war regular in the Welch Regiment but joined the RAF in the war, while the versatile Welsh had left the Royal Navy for a football career and became an Army PT instructor during the conflict.

Shreeve like Bartram had been a product of Boldon Villa in the north-east. Wing-half Bert Johnson had come late to the professional game, almost 23 when he joined Charlton in 1939. Oakes was of a similar age at the same career stage though a decade earlier and in a varied career had also played centre-forward.

Right-winger Fell was a part-time player previously engaged on essential war work with Shorts the aircraft manufacturers. However, the loser for Charlton was Revell, scorer of two Wembley cup final goals in 1944 and another couple on the same ground for the RAF against the Army.

Derby, too, had had their share of injures. Goalkeeper Frank Boulton was injured during the cup run and the Rams brought veteran Vic Woodley back from Bath City. Full-back Jack Parr had broken his arm and Howe was switched to his usual full-back position. Crooks, though fit again, had been replaced by then fledging Reg Harrison for the semi-final who kept his place.

Pre-war veterans were Nicholas, Howe, Duncan and Stamps, once given a free transfer by Mansfield. Carter had won an FA Cup medal with Sunderland in 1937. The Carter-Doherty partnership was the cornerstone of Derby's success. Doherty had been transferred from Manchester City prior to demob from the RAF for around £7,000 and both had served together at Loughborough. The pair had a natural and instinctive understanding on the field. Carter's strengths were his vision as a schemer and powerful shot; Doherty was the tireless box-to-box operator, quick and with a delicate touch to his game.

Skipper Jack Nicholas was a steadying influence in defence and the middle line of Jimmy Bullions, Leon Leuty and Walter Urban Musson - thankfully known as "Chick" - a varied trio of talent: Bullions the industrious former miner, Leuty a cool, commanding pivot and Musson, strong and skilful. In attack the body-swerving Duncan on the left with Stamps a forceful, opportunist leader and yet another ex-miner injured at Dunkirk and told he might never play again, completed the team.

FINALISTS HEIGHT, WEIGHT, AGE							
DERBY COUNTY				**CHARLTON ATHLETIC**			
	Ht (ft in)	Wt (lb oz)	Age (y m)		Ht (ft in)	Wt (lb oz)	Age (y n)
Woodley	5 10½	12 08	36 2	Bartram	6 0	13 02	32 3
Nicholas	5 11½	13 02	35 5	Phipps	5 11	11 12	30 3
Howe	6 0	13 03	30 6	Shreeve	5 11½	13 04	28 8
Bullions	5 10½	12 06	22 1	Turner H	5 11½	12 10	36 10
Leuty	5 11	12 02	25 6	Oakes	5 11	12 10	40 7
Musson	5 8	12 00	25 6	Johnson	5 9	11 00	29 10
Harrison	5 8½	11 06	22 11	Fell	5 6	10 03	25 4
Carter	5 8	12 06	32 5	Brown	5 7	11 02	30 5
Stamps	5 11½	13 03	27 4	Turner A	5 9	11 08	24 3
Doherty	5 10½	12 03	32 10	Welsh	6 0	12 06	35 2
Duncan	5 9½	12 02	36 6	Duffy	5 5	10 06	27 6

So to the final itself on 27 April, a humid spring day. Derby had already had a change of manager earlier in the year with Ted Magner moving abroad to work and giving way to Stuart McMillan. A players' revolt over miserly ticket allocation to wives and girlfriends, the WAGS of the era, had been averted and the gipsy's curse that the Rams would win no honours was ceremoniously lifted a few days before the final after 50 years, doubtless with silver being handed over. The omens looked good for Derby, the only unbeaten team in the competition.

The official attendance was 98,215 with receipts £43,378. Entertainments Tax took £19,840 leaving net receipts of £23,538, lower by £725 than the best pre-war. Their Majesties the King and Queen were in attendance along with Princess Elizabeth. On the same afternoon there were 33 League and other cup matches played by Football League clubs!

Tactically, Charlton probably handed the initiative to Derby. Before the match Seed in his team talk told wing-halves Johnson and Bert Turner not to come up for the square ball from Brown - known to the players as "Square-ball Brown". Seed told them to stay back and keep Carter and Doherty under control. Ultimately this played into Derby's hands and the Rams dynamic inside-forward duo had territory in which to plant Charlton's - what you could call Seed's of their own destruction! Brown himself was highly critical of his manager on this crucial point.

Alan Richards writing in *Findon's Football Handbook 1946-47* recalled: "Derby County, who gave a brilliant exhibition of ball play, defeated Charlton Athletic because they completely subjected Christopher Duffy, the goalscoring Charlton left-winger who, until the final, had scored ten goals for his club."

Duffy, the mercurial Scottish winger, was clearly nervous and off his game and even put three corners behind. Much of the threat he had posed was stifled by the

Skippers Welsh and Nicholas with referee E. D. Smith

masterly Nicholas. Derby who settled quickly had the edge in the opening 20 minutes. Carter exploited the weakness on Charlton's right defensive flank, but openings were frittered away. Even so, Carter did have the ball in the net but the goal was disallowed for offside.

Seed's half-time talk brought about a Charlton revival and Brown and Welsh came into the game and for 20 minutes they enjoyed a purple patch until fortunes took on a

Carter's first half goal, disallowed for offside

lighter shade for Derby. With ten minutes remaining, Carter took a throw-in to Harrison. He passed to Stamps who chipped the ball onto Doherty's head and from his knock-down Duncan scuffed a shot from ten yards which Bert Turner, in attempting to clear, diverted past his own goalkeeper.

From the kick-off Brown threaded his way through the Derby defence only to be brought down around 25 yards from goal. Up strode Turner whose ferocious, low drive hit Doherty's left leg before finishing in the back of the net. So Turner became the first player to score for both teams in the final and arguably the only one to have also played for a third in the same tournament!

There was still time for more drama. With five minutes remaining Duncan crossed from the left and Stamps drove hard for goal only to see the ball subside gently in front of Bartram; the ball had burst - another final first. In a pre-match BBC interview match referee E. D. Smith of Cumberland had said the odds on such a happening were a million to one. The clairvoyant strikes out.

Extra time and Welsh won the toss again, but Derby did the attacking. After two minutes Stamps tried a speculative shot from the left which Bartram could only parry. The loose ball was snapped up by Doherty who almost shoved Duncan out of the way in putting the Rams ahead. Ten minutes later Doherty laid one on for Stamps who took the ball past the tiring Oakes and beat Phipps before making it 3-1 before the end of the first half of overtime.

Within a short time of the resumption Doherty was once more the designer, Stamps the executioner in sealing a memorable 4-1 victory for the better team on the afternoon. After receiving the cup, Jack Nicholas was thrust in front of the newsreel's microphone. His words for posterity: "Well, I'm very pleased to be taking the trophy back to Derby for the first time in its history and I'm very proud to be the captain of the side that's done it. I'd like to say thanks to all the boys for taking it to Derby."

Derby County. Back, left to right: Jack Parr, Jim Bullions, Jack Nicholas, Vic Woodley, Jack Howe, Leon Leuty, Chick Musson. Centre: Sammy Crooks, Jackie Stamps, Stuart McMillan (manager), four directors, Peter Doherty, Raich Carter. Front: Reg Harrison, Dally Duncan.

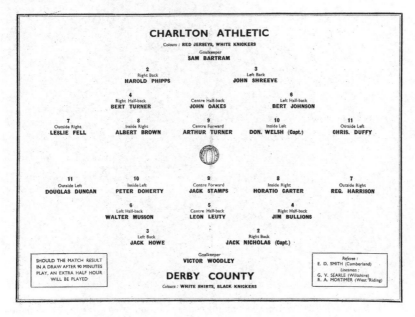

CHARLTON ATHLETIC

Colours : RED JERSEYS, WHITE KNICKERS

Goalkeeper
SAM BARTRAM

2		3
Right Back		Left Back
HAROLD PHIPPS		**JOHN SHREEVE**

4		5		6
Right Half-back		Centre Half-back		Left Half-back
BERT TURNER		**JOHN OAKES**		**BERT JOHNSON**

7	8	9	10	11
Outside Right	Inside Right	Centre Forward	Inside Left	Outside Left
LESLIE FELL	**ALBERT BROWN**	**ARTHUR TURNER**	**DON. WELSH (Capt.)**	**CHRIS. DUFFY**

11	10	9	8	7
Outside Left	Inside Left	Centre Forward	Inside Right	Outside Right
DOUGLAS DUNCAN	**PETER DOHERTY**	**JACK STAMPS**	**HORATIO CARTER**	**REG. HARRISON**

6	5	4
Left Half-back	Centre Half-back	Right Half-back
WALTER MUSSON	**LEON LEUTY**	**JIM BULLIONS**

3	2
Left Back	Right Back
JACK HOWE	**JACK NICHOLAS (Capt.)**

Goalkeeper
VICTOR WOODLEY

DERBY COUNTY

Colours : WHITE SHIRTS, BLACK KNICKERS

SHOULD THE MATCH RESULT IN A DRAW AFTER 90 MINUTES PLAY, AN EXTRA HALF HOUR WILL BE PLAYED

Referee :
E. D. SMITH (Cumberland)
Linesmen :
G. V. SEARLE (Wiltshire)
R. A. MORTIMER (West 'Riding)

The line-ups for the FA Cup final, as printed in the match programme.

Jack Nicholas introduces His Majesty King George VI to Jack Parr.
A broken right arm cost Parr his place in the final team.

A punch clear by Bartram fell at Duncan's feet on the edge of the goal area. Duncan's shot glanced off the
inside of no. 4 Bert Turner's left foot as he ran back to the goal line and into the net for Derby's furst goal.

Derby's second goal, scored by Doherty (in the centre of the three Derby players)

The King presents the Cup to Jack Nicholas. To the King's right is the Earl of Athlone, President of the Football Association. No, we don't know who the little boy is in the third row.

THE AFTERMATH

Two days after the final Charlton met Birmingham in the League, drawing 0-0. The weight of fixtures proved too much of a handicap for them. From the beginning of April until the end of the season they played 13 League and Cup games, Derby 11. Fixture congestion has its own history.

Four days after the final the fickle fixture list had decreed that the two would meet at Derby in the return. The gates were closed 20 minutes before the start with 30,000 inside the Baseball Ground, another five thousand locked outside. Derby with an unchanged team beat a Charlton with four changes 3-1. Oh yes, the ball burst again.

Carter with 12 goals was not the FA Cup's leading scorer as Aldershot's Brooks had 13. Goalscoring as a whole had been unprecedented. From the marathon 229 games in the competition proper, there had been 859 goals, for an average of 3.7. Additionally in another abandoned game after 81 minutes a further three goals had been scored. Attendances were even more staggering considering midweek matches staged with floodlighting a decade in the distance and early kick-offs. Absenteeism was clearly rife! From official and published crowd figures the total was 4,268,997.

Broken down the figures were first round 436,559; second round 271,315; third round 1,266,773; fourth round 921,580; fifth round 683,848; sixth round 374,392; semi-finals 216,315 and final 98,215.

If Duffy was the big disappointment in an otherwise excellent final, his day was just a year away as the goalscoring hero of Charlton's 1947 FA Cup triumph against Burnley, when for good measure the ball burst yet again.

THE STATISTICS SECTION

FA CUP RESULTS AND LINE-UPS

The qualifying rounds were arranged into 26 regional groups. The low numbered groups were in the North East and the high numbers in the South West. If you imagine the letter "S" superimposed on the map of England it will give you a rough idea of the sequence that the group numbers followed.

Group 19 had more than the 16 clubs that the preliminary round catered for, so 8 clubs met in an extra preliminary round. At the other extreme, only two clubs entered from three of the groups, giving these clubs byes up to the third qualifying round.

The 26 group winners of the third qualifying round were joined by 24 exempt clubs for the final qualifying round. Although the group structure was no longer used, the fourth qualifying round draw was made on a regional basis to minimise travel costs.

Group numbers are shown in the first column of the following pages. Other markers are "e" for extra time, "D" for home club disqualified, and "d" for away club disqualified. "wo/sc" indicated that the first named club was given a walkover when the second name club scratched from the competition.

Rounds one to six of the rounds proper were played over two legs. In the event of a tie at the end of the second leg, extra time was played. If games were called off in extra time because of darkness a third game was arranged on a neutral ground.

Aggregate scores in the second leg ties are shown in italics in the tables that follow.

FA CUP QUALIFYING ROUNDS 1945-46

Extra Preliminary Round (September 1 1945)

19 Aylesbury United v Chesham United	5-0
Banbury Spencer v Headington United	8-1
Pressed Steel v Morris Motors (Cowley)	1-0
Uxbridge v Lyons Club (Greenford)	11-1

Preliminary Round (September 8 1945)

2 Shildon v Usworth Colliery	7-1
9 Ossett Town v Thorne Colliery	1-3
18 Apsley v King's Langley	4-7
Edgware Town v Barnet	1-4
Harrow Town v Berkhamsted Town	8-0
Hertford Town v Enfield	3-6
Hoddesdon Town v Bishop's Stortford	0-0
Pinner v Wealdstone	1-2
St Albans City v Finchley	4-3
Tufnell Park v Welwyn Garden City	11-1
19 Aylesbury United v Osberton Radiator	5-0
Hayes v Maidenhead United	4-1
Hounslow Town v Slough United	4-4e
Marlow v Yiewsley	3-4
Newbury Town v Banbury Spencer	0-8
Oxford City v Uxbridge	4-0
Windsor & Eton v Pressed Steel	11-1
Wycombe Wanderers v Southall	0-2
20 Banstead Mental Hospital v Metropolitan Police	0-2
Epsom v Woking	1-8
Sutton United v Guildford	6-0
Tooting & Mitcham Utd v Kingstonian	5-2
22 East Grinstead v Horsham	2-2
23 Thornycrofts (Basingstoke) v Totton	1-3
24 Chippenham Town v Devizes Town	9-0
Purton v Swindon GWR Corinthians	0-6
18r Bishop's Stortford v Hoddesdon Town	4-1
19r Slough United v Hounslow Town	3-1
22r Horsham v East Grinstead	1-0

Qualifying Round One (September 22 1945)

1 Annfield Plain v Ashington	1-2
Consett v Shankhouse	6-0
Gosforth & Coxlodge v Throckley	0-2
Newburn v Amble	3-1
2 Blackhall Colliery Welfare v Seaham CW	4-2
Ferryhill Athletic v Shildon	1-3
Spennymoor United v Tow Law Town	4-1
Stanley United v West Auckland Town	5-0
5 Leyland Motors v Skelmersdale United	1-2
6 Bangor City v Rhyl	4-1 D
Hurst v Earle	9-2
Northwich Victoria v Fodens Motor Works	0-4
Witton Albion v Glossop	8-2
7 Hednesford Town v Nuneaton Borough	2-2
Hereford United v Moor Green	0-8
Tamworth v Bournville Athletic	2-5
Worcester City v Birmingham City Transport	8-0
9 East Bierley v Thorne Colliery	3-3
Goole Town v Yorkshire Amateur	0-1

Guiseley v Frickley Colliery	3-3
Meltham Mills v South Kirkby Colliery	1-7
10 Brodsworth Main Colliery v Firbeck Main Colliery	1-1
Grimethorpe Rovers v Denaby United	1-5
Monckton Athletic v Upton Colliery	6-2
Rawmarsh Welfare v Norton Woodseats	3-1
13 Kettering Town v Peterbro' Westwood Works	5-0
14 Bedford Avenue v Bedford Town	0-0
Hitchin Town v Vauxhall Motors (Luton)	3-2e
15 Abbey United (Cambs) v Cambridge Town	0-8
Chatteris Engineers v Newmarket Town	0-1
17 Eton Manor v Romford	1-1
Ford Sports(Dagenham) v Hoffmann Ath(Chelmsford)	4-2
Leyton v Grays Athletic	1-1
18 Enfield v Bishop's Stortford	8-1
Harrow Town v King's Langley	7-1
St Albans City v Wealdstone	2-2
Tufnell Park v Barnet	1-1
19 Aylesbury United v Oxford City	1-2
Hayes v Southall	1-1
Windsor & Eton v Banbury Spencer	0-3
Yiewsley v Slough United	2-2
20 Metropolitan Police v Woking	1-4
Redhill v Tooting & Mitcham Utd	1-5
Sutton United v Wimbledon	7-0
Walton & Hersham v Epsom Town	11-0
21 Erith & Belvedere v Gravesend United	3-3
Sheppey United v Bromley	1-5
Woolwich Polytechnic v Lloyds (Sittingbourne)	1-1
22 Hastings & St Leonards v Bexhill Town	wo/s
Horsham v Worthing	4-2
Newhaven v Haywards Heath	2-2
Southwick v Bognor Regis Town	4-1
23 East Cowes Victoria v Sandown	9-1
Ryde Sports v Cowes	1-3
Salisbury Corinthians v Gosport Borough Ath.	2-6
Totton v Newport (IOW)	0-4
24 Clandown v Chippenham Town	0-1
Paulton Rovers v Swindon GWR Corinthians	4-3
Pewsey YM v Trowbridge Town	1-3
Westbury United v Swindon Victoria	4-3
25 Aberaman & Aberdare v Llanelli	6-1 D
Barry Town v Clevedon	10-0
Ebbw Vale v Cardiff Corinthians	3-1 D
7r Nuneaton Borough v Hednesford Town	5-2
9r Frickley Colliery v Guiseley	7-0
r Thorne Colliery v East Bierley	1-6
10r Firbeck Main Colliery v Brodsworth Main Colliery	3-4
14r Bedford Town v Bedford Avenue	0-4
17r Grays Athletic v Leyton	0-3
r Romford (2) v Eton Manor	4-3
18r Barnet v Tufnell Park	3-1
r Wealdstone v St Albans City	3-0
19r Slough United v Yiewsley	2-2
r Southall v Hayes	2-1
21r Gravesend United v Erith & Belvedere	2-1
r Lloyds (Sittingbourne) v Woolwich Polytechnic	4-0
22r Haywards Heath v Newhaven	5-0
19r2 Slough United v Yiewsley	2-0

Qualifying Round Two (October 6 1945)

1	Ashington v Consett	1-1
	Throckley v Newburn	0-0
2	Shildon v Blackhall Colliery Welfare	6-1
	Spennymoor United v Stanley United	6-1
3	Billingham Synthonia - Bye	
	Stockton v Whitby United	4-0
4	Milnthorpe Corinthians v Kells Welfare Centre	4-5
	Netherfield (Kendal) - Bye	
5	Chorley v Wigan Athletic	5-2
	Darwen v Skelmersdale United	2-2
6	Rhyl v Fodens Motor Works	5-1
	Witton Albion v Hurst	6-1
7	Bournville Athletic v Moor Green	6-5e
	Nuneaton Borough v Worcester City	1-0
8	Lysaght's Sports - Bye	
	Scunthorpe United - Bye	
9	South Kirkby Colliery v Frickley Colliery	0-2
	Yorkshire Amateur v East Bierley	3-0
10	Brodsworth Main Colliery v Denaby United	2-3
	Rawmarsh Welfare v Monckton Athletic	2-1
11	Coalville Town - Bye	
	Gresley Rovers - Bye	
12	Grantham v Basford United	6-1
	Ollerton Colliery v Boston United	4-2
13	Rushden Town v Peterborough United	1-9
	Wellingborough Town v Kettering Town	2-5
14	Hitchin Town v Bedford Avenue	0-2
	Letchworth Town v Leighton United	3-0
15	Cambridge Town v King's Lynn	4-1
	Wisbech Town v Newmarket Town	5-0
16	Leiston - Bye	
	Lowestoft Town - Bye	
17	Leyton v Ford Sports (Dagenham)	6-2
	Romford v Crittall Athletic	7-1
18	Barnet v Enfield	5-0
	Harrow Town v Wealdstone	1-1
19	Banbury Spencer v Slough United	2-5
	Oxford City v Southall	2-1
20	Sutton United v Walton & Hersham	4-0
	Woking v Tooting & Mitcham Utd	1-2
21	Bromley v Gravesend United	2-0
	Ramsgate Athletic v Lloyds (Sittingbourne)	3-3
22	Hastings & St Leonards v Horsham	6-1
	Haywards Heath v Southwick	5-1
23	Cowes v East Cowes Victoria	4-2
	Newport (IOW) v Gosport Borough Ath.	2-0
24	Paulton Rovers v Westbury United	4-0
	Trowbridge Town v Chippenham Town	3-1
25	Barry Town v Cardiff Corinthians	6-1
	Llanelli v Monmouth Town	7-0
26	Radstock Town - Bye	
	Welton Rovers v Peasedown MW	3-7
1r	Consett v Ashington	3-0
r	Newburn v Throckley	1-2
5r	Skelmersdale United v Darwen	2-3
18r	Wealdstone v Harrow Town	6-1
21r	Lloyds (Sittingbourne) v Ramsgate Athletic	3-1

Qualifying Round Three (October 20 1945)

1	Throckley v Consett	2-4
2	Shildon v Spennymoor United	3-2
3	Stockton v Billingham Synthonia	4-1
4	Kells Welfare Centre v Netherfield (Kendal)	1-2
5	Chorley v Darwen	1-0
6	Rhyl v Witton Albion	2-2
7	Nuneaton Borough v Bournville Athletic	8-1 D
8	Scunthorpe United v Lysaght's Sports	4-1
9	Frickley Colliery v Yorkshire Amateur	0-4
10	Rawmarsh Welfare v Denaby United	5-1
11	Gresley Rovers v Coalville Town	0-7
12	Grantham v Ollerton Colliery	2-1
13	Kettering Town v Peterborough United	2-1
14	Bedford Avenue v Letchworth Town	1-0
15	Wisbech Town v Cambridge Town	3-1
16	Leiston v Lowestoft Town	2-2 d
17	Romford v Leyton	4-1
18	Barnet v Wealdstone	3-0
19	Slough United v Oxford City	3-1
20	Tooting & Mitcham Utd v Sutton United	3-3
21	Lloyds (Sittingbourne) v Bromley	3-4
22	Haywards Heath v Hastings & St Leonards	1-0
23	Newport (IOW) v Cowes	0-1 d
24	Trowbridge Town v Paulton Rovers	7-0
25	Llanelli v Barry Town	1-7
26	Peasedown MW v Radstock Town	7-0
6r	Witton Albion v Rhyl	3-1
20r	Sutton United v Tooting & Mitcham Utd	5-1

Qualifying Round Four (November 3 1945)

Barnet v Ilford	5-2
Barry Town v Lovells Athletic	1-5
Bromley v Shorts Sports	2-0
Chelmsford City v Leiston	9-0
Cheltenham Town v Peasedown MW	1-1
Consett v Stockton	2-3
Dulwich Hamlet v Romford	1-2
Gillingham v Sutton United	3-9
Grantham v Bedford Avenue	6-1
Guildford City v Newport (IOW)	1-2
Kettering Town v Coalville Town	2-1
Leytonstone v Slough United	3-3
Netherfield (Kendal) v Lancaster City	2-0
Rawmarsh Welfare v Gainsborough Trinity	1-3
Scarborough v North Shields	2-4
Scunthorpe United v Yorkshire Amateur	1-2
Shrewsbury Town v Bournville Athletic	6-2
Stalybridge Celtic v Runcorn	3-0
Trowbridge Town v Haywards Heath	6-0
Walthamstow Avenue v Clapton	4-0
Wellington Town v Kidderminster Harriers	5-2
Willington v Shildon	3-2
Wisbech Town v Colchester United	5-0
Witton Albion v Marine	2-3
Workington v Chorley	1-2
r Peasedown MW v Cheltenham Town	0-1
r Slough United v Leytonstone	3-1

ROUND ONE, FIRST LEG

Team	Score	Att.	1	2	3	4	5	6	7	8	9	10	11
Barnet	2		Powell	McCarthy	Green	Weightman	Pullen	Pymm	Finch	Jordan	Hawkins 1	Chandler	Reilly 1
Queen's Park Rangers	6		Alan AR	Rose	Swinton	Daniels	Ridyard	Farrow	Neary 3	Mallett 2	Heathcote 1	Blizzard	Whitehead
Barrow	1	5180	Phillipson	Collings	Fenny	Caine	Hall	Quigley	Dunnigan	Pitt	Clarke	Umston	McIntosh 1
Netherfield (Kendal)	0		Salisbury	Ellary	Biggs	Wilman	Baxter	Bell	Henderson	Richardson	Carswell	Woods	Hickson
Bath City	3	1500	Maggs	Owens	Eardley	Mitchell	Thompson	Caldwell	Farrington 1	Browne 1	Nuth	Dickson	Simmons 1
Cheltenham Town	2		Francis	Stokes	Hawkins	Green	Whitney	Lisle	Edwards 1	Roberts	Goring 1	Holder	Hurst
Brighton & Hove Albion	3	7423	Baldwin	Risdon	Longdon	Chase	Trainor	Darling	Hindley 1	Wilson	Davie 2	Moore	Stephens
Romford	1		Grover	Wallace	Dennis	McKenzie	Paviour	Fryatt	Brooks	Bolton	Harries	Clay	Denham

Londgon (og)

Team	Score	Att.	1	2	3	4	5	6	7	8	9	10	11
Bromley	6	6000	Barron	Mallett	Clark	Scott 2	Holder	Sheen	Coulson	Crowther 1	Ruddy 1	Viles 1	Reece 1
Slough United	1		Wakefield	Elderfield	Potter	Williams	Brown	Clements	Angell	Clarke 1	Hewitt	McKenzie	Fox
Carlisle United	5	6006	Monk	Clark 1	Hindmarsh	Reay	Wollacott	Pond	Dellow	Kirkpatrick	Cape 1	Adamson 1	Hamilton 2
North Shields	1		Johnson	Hearne	Wort	Thompson	Gledson	Dobson	Jamieson 1	Bohill	McLean	Ferguson	Rackham
Chorley	2	4019	Harper	Parr	Horrocks	A Hartley	T Hartley	Macaulay	Hastie	Wilkinson	Harrison 1	Haworth 1	Cload
Accrington Stanley	1		Hacking	Ash	Hutton	Lythgoe	Briggs	Malcolm	Conroy	Rothwell	Hudson	Keeley 1	Rotherham
Clapton Orient	2	4200	Hall	Rumbold	Farley	Froom	Bartlett	Black	Owen	Parr 1(p)	Gore 1	Merritt	Liddell
Newport (IOW)	1		Riddick	Phillips	Parkman	Hall	Smith	Knight	Miles	Holmes	B Rose	A Rose 1	Driscoll
Crewe Alexandra	4	3271	Mawson	Bainbridge	Still	Hayward 1	Cope	Hill	E Kelly	Shaw 1	Boothway 2	Chandler	Roberts
Wrexham	2		Whitelaw	Cook	Tunney	C Jones	Jackson	Bellis	Collins	Hayward	Isherwood	Lloyd 2	Wainwright
Darlington	2	9544	Dunn	Kelly	Hutchinson	Parsley	Blythe	Towers	Simpson	Harrison	Clarke 2	Varty	Stubbs
Stockton	0		Armstrong	Hewitt	Turnbull	Stephens	Oliver	Thompson	Hale	Laidman	Butler	Middleton	Pass
Doncaster Rovers	0	13055	Hardwicke	Stevenson	Wooldridge	Heydon	Archer	Eades	Mitcheson	Owens	Jordan	Todd	Gregory
Rotherham United	1		Warnes	Courts	Hanson	Mills	H Williams	D Williams	Nightingale	J Shaw	Ardron 1	Kearney	Dawson
Halifax Town	1	5849	Rayner	Allsop	Jackson	Green	Ruecroft	Wood	Doran	Gordon 1	Widdowfield	Barkas	Oliver
York City	0		Ferguson	Pinder	Poole	Gledhill	Bentall	Rodgers	Scott	Robbins	Winters	Green	Routledge
Hartlepools United	1	5148	Jarrie	Gorman	Porter	Cliff	Keeys	Troman	Morris	Robertson	Lewis	West	McMahon 1
Gateshead	2		Wilson	Robinson	Bell	J Callender	Devlin	Atkinson	McDermott	Johnson	McCormack	Cairns 2(1p)	Thompson
Kettering Town	4	4300	Ward	Tite	T Smith	Malloy	Linnell	Wragg	Dean	Starsmore	A Smith 1	Brown	Newberry
Grantham	5		Brannan	Gilbert	Cuthbert	Gregory	Taylor	Wood 1	Ranshaw 2	Searby 1	Russell	Ashton	Mitchell
Lovells Athletic	4	4000	Jennings	Slattery	Whitehouse	Prangley	H Clarke	Bye	Williams 2	Hardwicke	Holland	A Clarke 2	Morgan
Bournemouth & Bos. Ath.	1		Bird	Marsden	Cooke	Burke	Troke	Tagg	Mayes	Paton	JE Thomas 1	Smart	McDonald
Mansfield Town	3	6849	Oakley	Bramley	Chessell	Smith	Barke	Everett	Hewitt	Thorpe	Wombwell 2	Harkin 1	Poole
Gainsborough Trinity	0		Wilkinson	Walker	Bratley	Morris	Curtis	Clapham	Mills	Churms	Carr	Curry	Sampson
Marine	4	2600	Foster	Hanson	Welsby	Edwards	Dachler	Birtles	Craig	Jackson 1	Veacock	Fenton 2	Bretton 1
Stalybridge Celtic	0		Williams	Hartle	Egerton	Swindells	Phythian	Macdonald	Williamson	Dixon	Clarke	Carrick	Pye
Northampton Town	5	5000	Scott	Smalley	Barron	Lowery	Sankey	Yarker	Roberts 1	Heaselgrave	Morrall 2	Hughes 2	Fowler
Chelmsford City	1		Willsher	Thomas	Parry	Williams	Farley	Tunnicliffe	Clarke	Eaton	Foreman 1	Burley	H Marden
Notts County	2	20000	Flower	Southwell	Robinson	Harris	Corkhill	Pye	Beresford	Pye	Hubbard 1	McPherson 1	Stancer
Bradford City	2		Daniels	Hinsley	Rozier	Joyce	Noble	Cockroft	Schofield	Isaac	Murphy 2	Hastie	Broughton

ROUND ONE, FIRST LEG (Continued)

Team	Score	1	2	3	4	5	6	7	8	9	10	11	
Port Vale	4	Jepson	Smith	Pursell	Felton	Griffiths	Cooper	Allen	McDowell 2	Pointon 1	Bellis	Shore	
Wellington Town	0	E Bates	Merrington	Gannoe	H Bates	Childs	Driscoll	Phillips	Saxon	Simms	Cross	Hopley	Gannoe (og)
Reading	3	Houldsworth	Chitty	Glidden	Pattison	Wallbanks	Layton 1(p)	Fisher	Edelston 1	MacPhee	Summerfield 1	McCrohan	
Aldershot	1	Reynolds	Horton	Sheppard	Ray	J White	Hold	Hobbs	Bell	Brooks 1	Fitzgerald	Sinclair	
Shrewsbury Town	5	Streten	Sykes	Aldred	Downing	Hughes	Nichols 1(p)	Maund 3(1p)	L Smith	Jones	Bailey 1	Butler	
Walsall	0	Strong	Kelly	Male	Crutchley	Foulkes	Newman	Hancocks	Walton	Alsop	Talbot	Bulger	
South Liverpool	1	Roper	Bates	Halliwell	Beaumont	Healey	Monk	G Jones 1	Urmston	Riding	Salmon	Oxton	
Tranmere Rovers	1	Riley	Anderson	Hornby	Steele	Richards	S Williamson	Ashcroft	Lamb	Bridges	Rosenthal 1	Jones	
Southport	1	Smith	Preece	Gemmell	Warburton	Atherton	Howarth	Bond	McGough	Oakes 1	Banks	Jones	
Oldham Athletic	2	Radcliffe	Marlor	Shipman	Horton	Williamson	Lawton	Chapman 2	West	Ferrier	Brierley	Bowden	
Stockport County	1	Bowles	Topping	Redfern	Gleave	Lawrence	Burrows	Shaw 1	Hyde	Johnson	Clarke	Worrall	
Rochdale	2	Chesters	Pomphrey	Sneddon	Duff	Pearce	Partridge	Jones	Brindle 1	Hargreaves	Woods 1	Cunliffe	
Sutton United	1	Caffyn	Parrott	Ridgwell	Austin	Francis	Pettit	Young	Crisp	Vaughan 1	Scott	Hinshelwood	
Walthamstow Avenue	4	Gledhill	Lamprill	Childs	Swift	Oliver	Callegari	Green 3	Lewis	Groves 1	Insole	Palmer	
Swindon Town	1	Burton	Woodman	Kelso	Lloyd	Cousins	Lovesey	Denyer	Francis	Emery 1	Painter	Williams	
Bristol Rovers	0	Burgess	Topping	Watkins	McGahie	Warren	Whitfield	Butterworth	Long	Lamden	Mills	Clark	
Torquay United	0	Joslin	Keeton	Markham	McDonough	Hellier	Coley	Williams	Kernick	Tait	Cothiff	Lewis	
Newport County	1	Ferguson	Meade	Webb	Clarke	Low	Thomas	Wookey	Owen	Derrick 1	Wilkins	Carr	
Trowbridge Town	1	Vince	Bott	Blake 1	Travis	Atack	Hansford	Durham	Powell	Stratton	Coleman	Scullard	
Exeter City	3	Thomson	Murray	Roughton	Jordan	Blood	Lewis	Tickell	Bowden	Walker 1	Ebdon 1	Challis 1	
Watford	1	Bland	O'Brien	Harris	Gillespie	Shaw	Gray	Jones	Davies 1	Lewis	Beckett	Drinkwater	
Southend United	1	Conway	Jackson	Harvey	Leighton	Jones	Walton	Smirk 1	Thompson	Gardiner	Dudley	Peters	
Willington	0	Coe	Hutton	Sharpe	Craggs	Burdess	Graham	G Ross	G Thompson	Lawton	J Taylor	R Ross	
Bishop Auckland	5	Sedgwick	Humble	Hole	Longstaff	Hadfield	Fairs	Shergold	Clapham 1	Richardson 3	Tait	Anderson 1	
Wisbech Town	0	Simpson	Lake	Barr	J Fletcher	Nutt	Briscoe	Corey	Hanley	Pownall	Melton	Roberts	
Ipswich Town	3	Newman	Bell	Parry	Fox	O'Mahony	McLuckie	Edwards	Little 2	Price	Parker	Fletcher 1	
Yeovil & Petters United	2	Owen	Kingdon	Reed	Mann	Edwards	Heward	Hunt	Roy	Langley	Calverley	Hamilton 2	
Bristol City	2	Eddolls	Guy	Bailey	Morgan	Roberts	Thomas	Artus 1	Curran 1	Clark	Williams	Chilcott	
Yorkshire Amateur	1	Churchill	Roylance	Kitchen	Fox	Fairman	Metcalfe	Gage	Watt-Smith	Melling 1	Lyon	Saxton	
Lincoln City	0	Parkin	Cartwright	Bean	Wroe	Emery	Hardy	Wilkinson	Davies	Cheetham	Grummett	Smedley	

Games played 17 November 1945 except for Bromley v Slough United on 21 November. The clubs met on the 17th but the game was abandoned.

ROUND ONE, SECOND LEG

Team			Att	1	2	3	4	5	6	7	8	9	10	11	Notes
Accrington Stanley	2	3	6223	Hacking	Hutton	Malcolm	Lythgoe	Briggs	Wood	Conroy	Rothwell 1	Hudson 1	Keeley	Clark	
Chorley	0	2		Harper	Parr	Horrocks	A Hartley	T Hartley	Macaulay	Blackburn	Wilkinson	Harrison	Haworth	Cload	
Aldershot	7	8	6610	Reynolds	Horton 1	Sheppard	Ray	J White	Summerbee	Hobbs	Hold	Brooks 5	Fitzgerald 1	Sinclair	
Reading	3	6		Peters	Chitty	Glidden	Pattison	V Niblett	Layton	Fisher	Edelston	MacPhee 2	Summerfield 1	McCrohan	
Bishop Auckland	0	5	2551	Sedgwick	Humble	Hole	Longstaff	Hadfield	Fairs	Shergold	Clapham	Richardson	Tait	Anderson	
Willington	2	2		Coe	Hutton	Sharpe	Craggs	Burdess	Graham 1	G Ross	G Thompson	Lawton 1	J Taylor	R Ross	
Bournemouth & Bos. Ath.	3	4	8894	Bird	Marsden	Cooke	Burke	Troke	DJ Thomas	Mayes	Paton 1	JE Thomas 2	Gallacher	McDonald	
Lovells Athletic	2	6		Jennings	Slattery	Whitehouse	Prangley	H Clarke	Bye	Williams	Hardwicke	Holland 2	A Clarke	Morgan	
Bradford City	1	3	11000	Matier	Rozier	Jales	Joyce	Beardshaw	Cockroft	Schofield	Isaac	Hinsley	Hastie	Pickles 1	
Notts County	2	4		Kirkby	Southwell	Robinson	Harris	Corkhill	Peacock	Beresford	McPherson 1	Hubbard	Pye	Parker 1	
Bristol City	3	5	13469	Eddolls	Guy	Bailey	Morgan	Roberts	Thomas	Bentley	Curran 1	Clark	Williams	Chilcott 2	
Yeovil & Petters United	0	2		Harris	Kingdon	Reed	Mann	Edwards	Heward	Hunt	Roy	Langley	Calverley	Hamilton	
Bristol Rovers	4	4	11500	Burgess	Topping	Watkins	McGahie	Warren	Whitfield	Butterworth 2	Mills 2	Lamden	Gardiner	Clark	
Swindon Town	1	2		Wildman	Woodman	Kelso	Lloyd	Cousins	Lovesey	Denyer	Francis 1	Emery	Lucas	Williams	
Chelmsford City	0	1	6700	Willsher	Clapham	Potter	Eaton	Farley	Parry	R Marden	Burley	Foreman	Tunnicliffe	H Marden	
Northampton Town	5	10		Scott	Smalley	Barron	Lowery	Dennison	Yarker	Roberts 1	Smith 1	Morrall 2	Hughes	Fowler 1	
Cheltenham Town	0	2	3200	Francis	Stokes	Hawkins	Green	Whitney	Lisle	Edwards	Roberts	Goring	Holder	Hurst	
Bath City	2	5		Maggs	Owens	Johnson	Mitchell	Thompson	Caldwell	Farrington	Browne 1	McConnon 1	Wood	Simmons	
Exeter City	7	10	6971	Thomson	Murray	Roughton	Jordan	Blood	Lewis	Tickell 1	Walker 4	Ebdon	Bowden	Challis 1	Atack (og)
Trowbridge Town	2	3		Vince	Bott	Hansford	Travis	Atack	Coleman	Durham	Powell 1	Stratton 1	Blake	Scullard	
Gainsborough Trinity	4	4	3657	Wilkinson	Taylor	Walker	Mills	Bradley 1(p)	Clapham	Carr	Churms 1	Curtis 1	Thompson	Sampson 1	a.e.t
Mansfield Town	2	5		Oakley	Bramley	Chessell	Smith	Barke	Everett	Hewitt	Thorpe	Wombwell 1	Robertson	Poole 1	
Gateshead	6	8	6152	Wilson	Robinson	Bell	J Callender	Devlin	Atkinson	McCormack 3	Johnson	Cairns 2	Thompson	Howden 1	
Hartlepools United	2	3		Jarrie	Gorman	Porter	Brown	Troman	Woods	Morris	Holland 1	West	Robertson	McMahon 1	
Grantham	2	7	3200	Brannan	Gilbert	Cuthbert	Gregory	Taylor	Wood	Ranshaw 1	Searby	Russell 1	Ashton	Mitchell	
Kettering Town	2	3		Ward	Telar	Tite	Malloy 1	Linnell	Wragg	Dean	Brooks	A Smith 1	Brown	Newberry	
Ipswich Town	5	8	10598	Saphin	Bell	Parry	Wardlaw	O'Mahony	Fox	Edwards	Little	Price 2	Parker 3	Fletcher	
Wisbech Town	0	0		Simpson	Briscoe	Barr	J Fletcher	Nutt	Melton	Corey	Hanley	Pownall	Robinson	Roberts	
Lincoln City	5	5	6587	Parkin	Cartwright	Bean	Wroe 1	Emery	Hardy	Wilkinson	Stillyards	Cheetham 2	Grummett	Marlow 1	Farman (og)
Yorkshire Amateur	1	2		Churchill	Roylance	Kitchen	Kilkenny	Fairman	Metcalfe	Gage	Watt-Smith	Melling	Lyon 1	Saxton	
Netherfield (Kendal)	2	2	4629	Salisbury	Ellary	Biggs	Wilman	Baxter	Bell	Henderson	Richardson 1	Shakeskaft	Woods	Hickson 1	
Barrow	2	3		Phillipson	Collings	Fenny	Caine	Hall	Quigley	Clarkson	Hull 1	Clarke 1	Mullen	McIntosh	
Newport (IOW)	2	3	4300	Riddick	Phillips	Parkman	Lanham	Smith	Knight	Miles	Holmes	A Rose 1	Hall	Driscoll	Merritt (og)
Clapton Orient	0	2		Hall	Rumbold	Farley	Froom	Bartlett	Black	Gore	Parr	Lucas	Merritt	Liddell	
Newport County	1	2	7178	Ferguson	Roberts	Webb	Owen	Thomas	Brinton	Wookey	Clarke	Derrick 1	Wilkins	Carr	
Torquay United	1	1		Joslin	Head	Markham	Keeton	Vallance	McDonough	Williams	Kernick	Tait	Cothliff	Coley 1	
North Shields	2	3	3000	Johnson	Thompson	Hearne	Smith	Gledson	Dobson	Jamieson 1	Bohill	McLean 1	Ferguson	Rackham	
Carlisle United	3	8		Monk	Clark 1	Hindmarsh	Reay	Wollacott	Pond	Dellow	Hayton	Cape	Douglas 1	Hamilton 1	

Team	Leg	Agg	Att	1	2	3	4	5	6	7	8	9	10	11
Oldham Athletic	3	5	5000	Radcliffe	Marlor	Shipman	Horton	Williamson	Lawton 1	Chapman	West 1	Standring 1	Brierley	Tilling
Southport	1	2		Smith	Brown	Gemmell	McGough	Howarth	Banks	Bond	Hawkins	Oakes 1	Underhill	Jones
Queen's Park Rangers	2	8	11600	Allan AR	Rose	Jefferson	Daniels	Ridyard	Farrow	Neary 1	Mallett	Heathcote	Swinfen 1	Whitehead
Barnet	1	3		Powell	Bowker	Green	Weightman	Pullen	Pymm	Finch 1	Jordan	Hawkins	Chandler	Reilly
Rochdale	1	3	8158	Chesters	Pomphrey	Sneddon	Duff	Pearce	Partridge	Jones	Brindle	Hargreaves 1	Woods	Cunliffe
Stockport County	1	2		Bowles	Redfern	Rich	Gleave	Morris	Burrows	Shaw	Woodcock	Johnson	Hyde 1	Worrall
Romford	1	2	8000	Grover	Wallace	Dennis	McKenzie	Paviour	Fryatt	Brooks	Bolton 1	Harries	Clay	Denham
Brighton & Hove Albion	1	4		Baldwin	Risdon	Longdon	Darling	Trainor	Whent	Hindley	Wilson	Day	Moore	Stephens 1
Rotherham United	2	3	14362	Warnes	Courts	Harson	Mills	H Williams	D Williams	Nightingale 1	J Shaw	Ardron	Kearney 1	Dawson
Doncaster Rovers	1	1		Hardwicke	Stevenson	Wooldridge	Striland	Archer	Heydon	Tindill	Mitcheson	Jordan	Todd 1	Gregory
Slough United	1	2	4200	Wakefield	Elderfield	Potter	Williams	Brown 1	Clements	Angell	Clarke	Hewitt	McKenzie	Fox
Bromley	0	6		Barron	Mallett	Clark	Scott	Holder	Sheen	Coulson	Crowther	Ruddy	Viles	Reece
Southend United	0	1	7200	Conway	Humphreys	Harvey	Jackson	Jones	Leighton	Dudley	Hockey	Gardiner	Smirk	Walton
Watford	3	4		Mee	O'Brien	Jones	Gillespie	Shaw	Gray 1	Jezzard	Beckett	Lewis 2	Davies	Drinkwater
Stalybridge Celtic	3	3	2600	Dykes	Hartle	Egerton 1	Winterbottom	Macdonald	Carrick	Williams	Mills	Clarke	Webster 2	Pye
Marine	3	7		Foster	Hanson	Welsby	Edwards	Dachler	Joliffe 1	Craig	Jackson	Veacock	Fenton 1	Bretton 1
Stockton	1	1	3978	Armstrong	Hewitt	Turnbull	Stephens	Oliver	Thompson	Hale	Laidman	Butler	Middleton 1	Cowells
Darlington	4	6		Dunn	Kelly	Hutchinson	Parsley	Blythe	Towers 1	Simpson	Harrison 2	Sykes 1	Varty	Stubbs
Tranmere Rovers	6	7	9018	Lloyd	Anderson	Hornby	Steele	Richards	S Williamson 1	Ashcroft 2	Rosenthal 2	Atkinson 1	Bridges	Jones
South Liverpool	1	2		Roper	Bates	Halliwell	Urmston	Healey	Monk	Leadbitter	G Jones 1	Riding	Salmon	Oxton
Walsall	4	4	3500	Strong	Kelly	Shelton	Crutchley	Foulkes	Jarvis	Hancocks	Mullard 1	Bennett 1	Talbot 1	Alsop 1
Shrewsbury Town	1	6		Streten	Sykes	Aldred	Downing	Hughes	Nichols 1	Maund	L Smith	Jones	Bailey	Butler
Walthamstow Avenue	7	11	5000	Gledhill	Burchell	Childs	Lewis	Oliver	Callegari	Wright	Insole 1	Groves 4	Davis 2	Palmer
Sutton United	2	3		Caffyn	Parrott	Ridgwell	Austin	Francis	Pettit	Young	Crisp	Vaughan	Scott 1	Hinshelwood 1
Wellington Town	0	0	5056	E Bates	Lea	Gannoe	H Bates	Childs	Driscoll	Phillips	Saxon	Simms	Cross	Hopley
Port Vale	2	6		Jepson	Smith	Pursell	Felton	Griffiths	Cooper	Allen	McDowell 1	Pointon	Bellis 1	Shore
Wrexham	3	5	8551	Ashton	Cook	Tunney	Mortimer	Jackson	Bellis	Collins	Hayward 1	C Jones 1	Lloyd	Wainwright 1
Crewe Alexandra	0	4		Poskett	Bainbridge	Still	Hayward	Cope	Hill	E Kelly	Shaw	Boothway	Corkan	Roberts
York City	4	4	7573	Ferguson	Pinder	Poole	Gledhill 1(p)	Bentall	Rodgers	Reagan	Scott 2	Winters	Robbins	Lee 1
Halifax Town	2	3		Rayner	Allsop	Jackson	Green	Ruecroft	Wood	Doran	Gordon	Taylor	Barkas 2	Oliver

All games played 24 November 1945

ROUND TWO, FIRST LEG

Team	Score	Att	1	2	3	4	5	6	7	8	9	10	11
Aldershot	7	5268	Reynolds	Horton	Sheppard	Ray	J White	Summerbee	Sinclair	Hold 1	Brooks 5	Fitzgerald	Hobbs 1
Newport (IOW)	0		Ruddick	Phillips	Parkman	Lanham	Smith	Knight	Miles	Holmes	A Rose	Hall	Driscoll
Barrow	4	3700	Phillipson	Birch	Fenny	Caine	Hall	McGrath	Clarkson	Dunnigan 1	Clarke 3	Mullen	McIntosh
Carlisle United	2		Monk	Clark	Hindmarsh	Taylor	Wollacott	Pond	Dellow	Douglas	Cape 2	Kirkpatrick	Hamilton
Bishop Auckland	1	5647	Washington	Hole	Farrar	Longstaff	Hadfield	Stones	Humble	Fairs	Richardson	Tait 1	Anderson
York City	2		Ferguson	Pinder	Poole	Gledhill	Young	Rodgers	Reagan	Scott	Winters 1	Robbins	Maddison 1
Bristol City	4	19295	Eddolls	Guy	Bailey	Morgan 2	Roberts	Thomas	Collins	Bentley	Clark 1	Williams 1	Chilcott
Bristol Rovers	2		Burgess	Smith	Watkins	McGahie	Warren	Whitfield	Butterworth 2	Davis	Lamden	Gardiner	Clark
Bromley	1	5092	Barron	Mallett	Clark	Scott	Holder	Sheen	Coulson	Crowther	Ruddy 1	Viles	Reece
Watford	3		Mee	O'Brien	Jones	Gillespie	Shaw	Gray 1(p)	Jezzard 1	Beckett	Lewis	Davies	Drinkwater
Darlington	2	9765	Dunn	Kelly	Hutchinson	Parsley	Thyne	Towers 1	Simpson	Harrison	Clarke	Varty 1	Williams
Gateshead	4		Wilson	Devlin	Bell	J Callender 1	Dudgeon	T Callender	McCormack 1	Johnson	Cairns 1	Rutherford 1	Howden
Grantham	1	2854	Brannan	Glider	Cuthbert	Gregory	Taylor	Wood	Ranshaw	Searby 1	Russell	Ashton	Mitchell
Mansfield Town	2		Oakley	Chessell	Marsh	Smith	Barke	Everett	Akers	Thorpe 1	Wombwell 1	Hogg	Poole
Lovells Athletic	2	1000	Jennings	Whitehouse	Cross	Prangley	Slattery	Bye	Williams 1	Hardwicke	Wetter	A Clarke	Morgan 1
Bath City	1		Ellis	Owens	Johnson	Mitchell	Thompson	Caldwell	Farrington	Browne	McConnon	Woods 1	Simmons
Newport County	5	5606	Ferguson	Avery	Thomas	Owen	Low	Brinton 1	Wookey 1	Wilkins	Derrick 2	Boatwright	Car 1
Exeter City	1		Thomson	Murray	Roughton	Gallagher 1	Blood	Angus	Tickell	Wardle	Ebdon	Walker	Challis
Northampton Town	3	10000	Scott	Smalley	Barron	Lowery	Dennison	Sankey	Roberts	Blunt 1	Morrall 2	Hughes	Fowler
Notts County	1		Kirkby	Southwell	Ratcliffe	Harris	Corkhill	Peacock	Beresford	McPherson 1	Hubbard	Pye	Meredith
Oldham Athletic	2	6729	Radcliffe	Marlor	Shipman	Horton	Williamson	Lawton	Chapman	West 1	Standring 1	Brierley	Goodwin
Accrington Stanley	1		Hacking	Hutton	Webster	Lythgoe	Briggs	Malcolm	Conroy	Rothwell	Hudson 1	Keeley	Mauchline
Port Vale	3	5800	Jepson	Pursell	Felton	Smith	Griffiths	Cooper	Allen 2	McDowell	Gregory 1	Bellis	Shore
Marine	1		Foster	Jackson	Hanson	Edwards	Dachler	Birtles	Craig	King	Veacock 1	Fenton	Bretton
Queen's Park Rangers	4	12300	Allan AR	Rose	Jefferson	Daniels	Ridyard	Farrow	Neary 1	Mallett	Addinall 2	Stock 1	Whitehead
Ipswich Town	0		Saphin	Bell	Parry	Wardlaw	O'Mahony	McLuckie	Smyth	Little	Price	Parker	Fletcher
Rotherham United	2	8145	Warnes	Selkirk	Hanson	Mills	H Williams	D Williams	Nightingale 1	J Shaw 1	Ardron	Chafer	Kearney
Lincoln City	1		Parkin	Cartwright	Bean	Wroe	Emery	Hardy	Wilkinson	Stillyards	Cheetham	Grummett	Marlow 1
Shrewsbury Town	0	8000	Streten	Sykes	Aldred	Wheatley	Hughes	Nichols	Maund	L Smith	Richardson	Bailey	Butler
Wrexham	1		Ashton	Cook	Tunney	Mortimer	Jackson	Bellis	Collins	C Jones	Hewitt 1	Lloyd	Hayward
Tranmere Rovers	3	5700	Lloyd	Anderson	Hornby	Steele	Richards	S Williamson	Bell 1	Rosenthal 1	Atkinson 1	Bridges	Jones
Rochdale	1		Chesters	Pomphrey	Duff	McCormick	Pearce	Partridge	Makin	Brindle	Hargreaves	Wood 1	Cunliffe
Walthamstow Avenue	1	8338	Simmonds	Burchell	Childs	Lewis	Oliver	Callegari	Green	Insole	Groves 1	Davis	Wright
Brighton & Hove Albion	1		Baldwin	Risdon	Martin	Darling	Trainor	Watson	Longdon 1	Wilson	Moore	Whent	Stephens

Sheen (og)

All games played 8 December 1945

ROUND TWO, SECOND LEG

Team			Att											
Accrington Stanley	3	4	6308	Hacking	Hutton	Webster	Lythgoe	Briggs	Malcolm	Clark	Rothwell 1	Hudson 1	Keeley	Mauchline
Oldham Athletic	1	3		Radcliffe	Marlor	Shipman	Horton	Williamson	Lawton	Chapman	West	Ferrier 1	Brierley	Tilling
Bath City	2	3	3700	Maggs	Owens	Johnson	Mitchell	Sawyer	Caldwell	Farrington 2	Browne	McConnon	Woods	Simmons
Lovells Athletic	5	7		Jennings	Slattery	Whitehouse	Prangley	H Clarke	Bye	Williams 1	Hardwicke 2	Holland 1	A Clarke	Morgan 1
Brighton & Hove Albion	4	5	9453	Baldwin	Marriott	Watson	Darling	Trainor	Whent	Longdon 1	Wilson 1	Davie 1	Moore	Stephens 1
Walthamstow Avenue	2	3		Simmonds	Burchell	Childs	Lewis	Oliver	Callegari	Green	Insole	Groves	Wright	Davis 2
Bristol Rovers	0	2	21043	Burgess	Smith	Watkins	McGahie	Warren	Whitfield	Butterworth	Mills	Lamden	Gardiner	Clark
Bristol City	2	6		Eddolls	Guy	Bailey	Morgan	Roberts	Thomas 1	Chilcott	Bentley	Clark 1	Williams	Hargreaves
Carlisle United	3	5	6890	Monk	Clark 1(p)	Hindmarsh	Pond	Taylor	Ferguson	Dellow 1	Kirkpatrick	Cape	Adamson 1	Hamilton
Barrow	4	8		Phillipson	Birch	Fenny	Caine	Hall	McGrath	Conway	Dunnigan	Clarke 3	Mullen	McIntosh 1
Exeter City	1	2	7703	Thomson	Murray	Roughton	Jordan	Blood	Haddock	Challis	Wardle	Crawshaw 1	Walker	Ebdon
Newport County	3	8		Ferguson	Avery	Thomas	Owen	Low	Brinton	Wookey	Hydes 2	Derrick 1	Boatwright	Carr
Gateshead	1	5	8000	Wilson	Devlin	Robinson	J Callender	Dudgeon	T Callender	McCormack 1	Johnson	Cairns	Rutherford	Howden
Darlington	2	4		Dunn	Kelly	Hutchinson	Parsley	Thyne	Towers	Simpson	Harrison 2	Clarke	Varty	Williams
Ipswich Town	0	0	10571	Saphin	Bell	Parry	Smyth	Wardlaw	McLuckie	Edwards	Little	Price	Parker	Williams
Queen's Park Rangers	2	6		Allan AR	Rose	Jefferson	Ridyard	Daniels 1	Farrow	Blizzard	Mallett	Addinall 1	Stock	Whitehead
Lincoln City	1	2	8004	Parkin	Cartwright	Bean	Wroe	Emery	Hardy	Wilkinson	Stillyards	Cheetham	Grummett	Marlow 1
Rotherham United	1	3		Warnes	Selkirk	Hanson	Mills	H Williams	D Williams	Nightingale	Kearney	Ardron 1	Chafer	Hooper
Mansfield Town	2	4	8206	Oakley	Chessell	Marsh	Smith	Barke	Everett	Hewitt	Thorpe	Wombwell 1	Hogg 1	Poole
Grantham	1	2		Brannan	Glider	Cuthbert	Gregory	Taylor	Ashton	Ranshaw	Russell	Wallace	Searby 1	Mitchell
Marine	1	2	5000	Foster	Hanson 1	Welsby	Edwards	Dachler	Birtles	Craig	Jackson	Veacock	Fenton	Bretton
Port Vale	1	4		Jepson	Smith	Felton	McDowell	Griffiths	Cooper	Allen	Wootton	Gregory 1	Pointon	Bellis
Newport (IOW)	0	0	3000	Bluff	Phillips	Parkman	Hall	Smith	Knight	Miles	A Rose	B Rose	Holmes	Driscoll
Aldershot	5	12		Reynolds	Horton	Sheppard	Ray 1	J White	Summerbee 1	Hobbs	Bell	Brooks 1	Fitzgerald 2	A White
Notts County	1	2	17000	Kirkby	Southwell	Ratcliffe	Harris	Corkhill	Peacock	Beresford	Pye	Martin 1	Hubbard	Meredith
Northampton Town	0	3		Scott	Smalley	Welsh	Lowery	Dennison	Sankey	Roberts	Blunt	Morrall	Hughes	Fowler
Rochdale	3	4	6500	Chesters	Pomphrey	Sneddon	McCormick	Pearce	Partridge	Makin 1	Brindle	Hargreaves 2	Wood	Cunliffe
Tranmere Rovers	0	3		Lloyd	Anderson	Hornby	Bell	Richards	S Williamson	Philpotts	Rosenthal	Atkinson	Bridges	Jones
Watford	1	4	5481	Mee	O'Brien	Jones	Gillespie	Shaw	Gray 1(p)	Jezzard	Beckett	Lewis	Davies	Drinkwater
Bromley	1	2		Barron	Mallett	Clark	Scott	Holder	Stone	Coulson 1	Crowther	Ruddy	Viles	Reece
Wrexham	1	2	11566	Ashton	Cook	Tunney	Mortimer	Jackson	Bellis	Jones R	C Jones	Hewitt	Lloyd	Hayward 1
Shrewsbury Town	1	1		Streten	Sykes	Aldred	Wheatley	Hughes	Nichols	Jones 1	L Smith	Richardson	Bailey	Maund
York City	3	5	8651	Ferguson	Pinder	Poole	Gledhill	Young	Rodgers	Scott	Brenen 1	Winters 1	Robbins 1	Routledge
Bishop Auckland	0	1		Washington	Hole	Farrar	Longstaff	Hadfield	Stones	Humble	Fairs	Richardson	Tait	Anderson

Accrington Stanley also: Shipman (og)

All games played 15 December 1945

ROUND THREE, FIRST LEG

Team	Score	Att	1	2	3	4	5	6	7	8	9	10	11	Notes
Accrington Stanley	2	9968	Hacking	Cornwell	Webster	Lythgoe	Briggs	Malcolm	Clark	Rothwell	Conroy 1	Keeley 1	Mauchline	
Manchester United	2		Crompton	Whalley	Roach	Warner	Chilton	Cockburn	Hanlon	Carey	Smith 1	Rowley	Wrigglesworth 1	
Aldershot	2	4800	Reynolds	Horton	Sheppard	Palmer	Summerbee	J White	Brooks 1	Bell	Hold	Fitzgerald	Hobbs 1	Flewin (og)
Plymouth Argyle	0		Middleton	Rundle	Dyer	Adams	Dixon	Gorman	Hodge	Prescott	Smith	Thomas	Tinker	
Birmingham City	1	33845	Merrick	Duckhouse	Jennings	Harris	Turner	Mitchell	Mulraney	Dougal	Jones	Bodle	Edwards	
Portsmouth	0		Walker	Morgan	Crossley	Guthrie	Flewin	Bushby	Worrall	Anderson	Stott	Barlow	Harris	
Bolton Wanderers	1	26307	Hanson	Threlfall	Hubbick	Hurst	Hamlett	Murphy	Geldard	Hunt	Moir 1	Westwood	Woodward	
Blackburn Rovers	0		Patterson	Tomlinson	Green	Whiteside	Pryde	Wightman	Campbell	Baldwin	Wyles	Stephan	Glaister	
Bradford Park Avenue	2	14822	Farr	Hepworth	Farrell	McTaff	Greenwood	Hallard	Smith	Shackleton	Gibbons 1	Downie 1	Dix	
Port Vale	1		Jepson	Smith	Birchall	Oldfield	Griffiths	Cooper	Allen	Pointon	Davies	Bellis 1	Shore	
Bristol City	5	26551	Cousins	Guy	Bailey	Morgan	Roberts	Thomas	Chilcott 1	Bentley 1	Clark 3	Williams	Hargreaves	
Swansea Town	1		Roberts	Davies	Fisher	Weston	Briddon	Smeddon	Jones	Burns	Ford 1(p)	Payne	Scrine	
Bury	3	13248	Bradshaw	W Griffiths	G Griffiths	Jones	Hart	Halton 2	Moss	Berry	Herbert	Tompkin	Davies 1	
Rochdale	3		Chesters	Duff	Sneddon	McCormick	Neary	Partridge	Reynolds 1	Brindle	Hargreaves 1	Wood	Cunliffe 1	
Cardiff City	1	28928	McLoughlin	Sherwood	Raybould	Wright	Stansfield	Lester	Gibson	Hollyman	Allen 1	Wood	Clarke	
West Bromwich Albion	1		Sanders	C Shaw	Kinsell	Witcomb	Tranter	Millard	Elliott	Clarke	Newsome	Connelly 1	Saunders	
Charlton Athletic	3	35000	Bartram	Croker	Shreeve	HG Turner	Oakes	Johnson	Fell 1	Brown	Welsh 1	AA Turner	Duffy 1	
Fulham	1		Rickett	Bacuzzi	Lloyd	Freeman	Taylor	Wallbanks	Rampling 1	Woodward	Rooke	Beasley	Shepherd	
Chelsea	1	39678	Robertson	Winter	Tennant	Russell	Harris	Williams	Spence	Payne	Lawton 1	Goulden	Bain	
Leicester City	1		Calvert	Jones	Howe	Osborne	Sheard	Towers	Campbell	Smith	Mercer	Soo	Adam 1	
Chester	0	12200	Shortt	Stubbs	McNeil	Marsh	Lee	Cole	Turner	Burden	Yates	Astbury	Hamilton	
Liverpool	2		Nickson	Harley	Lambert	Finney	Hughes	Paisley	Liddell 1	Baron	Fagan 1	Nieuwenhuys	Priday	
Chesterfield	1	15287	Middleton	Pringle	Kidd	Hart	Whitaker	Hobson	Sinclair	Wilson	Goodfellow	Dooley	Roberts 1	
York City	1		Ferguson	Pinder	Rodgers	Brenen	Young	Gledhill	Scott	Robbins	Winters	Thompson	Mahon 1	
Coventry City	2	27197	Wood	Elliott	Metcalf	Snape	Mason	Crawley	Warner	Simpson 1	Barratt 1	Matthews	Aldecoa	
Aston Villa	1		Wakeman	Potts	Cummings	Parkes	Callaghan	Lowe	Kerr	Martin	Edwards	Iverson	Smith 1	
Grimsby Town	1	12050	Moulson	Mouncer	J Hodgson	Hall	S Hodgson	Jones	Chadwick	Moore	Johnson	Rodi 1	Wardle	
Sunderland	3		Mapson	Stelling	Jones	Willingham	Lockie	Housam 1	Whitelum	White	Brown 1	Hastings 1	Duns	
Huddersfield Town	1	21169	Clegg	Bailey	Simpson	Morton	Barker	Howe	Bateman	Glazzard	Price 1	Green	Poole	
Sheffield United	1		Smith	Furniss	Hooper	Jackson	Latham	Forbes	Jones 1	Nightingale	Thompson	Brook	Rickett	
Leeds United	4	18000	Hodgson	Duthoit	Gadsby	Butterworth	Holley	Coyne	Henry 1	Short 1	Ainsley 1	Hindle	Grainger	Hardwick (og)
Middlesbrough	4		Cumming	Laking	Robinson	Bell	Hardwick	Douglas	Spuhler	Murphy 1	Fenton 1	Dews 2	Chadwick	
Lovells Athletic	2	10000	Jennings	Slattery	Whitehouse	Prangley	H Clarke	Bye	Williams	Hardwicke 1	Phillips	A Clarke	Morgan 1	
Wolverhampton Wanderers	4		Williams	Morris	Ashton	Alderton	McLean	Crook 1	King	Dunn	Galley 1	Wright	Davies 2	
Luton Town	0	16792	Duke	Beech	Dunsmore	Goodyear	Vinall	Campbell	Daniel	Brice	Needham	Gardiner	Waugh	
Derby County	6		Boulton	Nicholas	Parr	Bullions	Leuty	Ward	Crooks 1	Carter 1	Stamps 4	Doherty	Morrison	
Manchester City	6	19589	Swift	Clark	Barkas	Robinson	Cardwell	Walsh	Pritchard	Herd 3	Constantine 3	Smith	Bootle	
Barrow	2		Phillipson	Birch	Fenny	Caine	Hall	McGrath	Clarkson	Dunnigan	Clarke 2	Mullen	McIntosh	

ROUND THREE, FIRST LEG (Continued)

Team	Score	Att	1	2	3	4	5	6	7	8	9	10	11	
Mansfield Town	0	13188	Cromack	Chessell	Marsh	Smith	Barke	Everett	Thorpe	Akers	Wombwell	Hogg	Poole	
Sheffield Wednesday	0		Goodfellow	Swift	Pickering	Cockroft	Stewart	Wands	Ward	Robinson	Aveyard	Froggatt	Tomlinson	
Newcastle United	4	60384	King	Cowell	Corbett	Harvey	Smith	Crowe	Milburn 2	Clifton	Stubbins 1	Wayman	Hair 1	Harvey (og)
Barnsley	2		Holdcroft	Cunningham	Pallister 1(p)	Mansley	Wilson	Logan	Smith	Cooling	Robledo	Baxter	Kelly	
Northampton Town	2	15100	Scott	Smalley	Barron	Lowery	Sankey	Yarker	Roberts	Blunt 1	Morrall	Hughes 1	Fowler	
Millwall	2		Dunkley	Dudley	Fisher	Ross	Brolly	Tyler	Richardson	Gordon	Ridley 1	Brown	Smith 1	
Norwich City	1	16188	Davis	Reid	Taylor	Flack	Robinson	Proctor	Plunkett	Furness	Johnson	Graham 1	Jones	
Brighton & Hove Albion	2		Baldwin	Marriott	Darling	Wilson	Risdon	Whent	Longdon	Chase	Davie	Moore 1	Stephens 1	
Nottingham Forest	1	15394	Savage	Thomas	McCall	Simpson	Blagg	Baxter	Mee	Allen 1	Barks	North	Johnston	Blagg (og)
Watford	1		Mee	O'Brien	Gallimore	Gillespie	Shaw	Gray	Davies	Weir	Lewis	Davies	Drinkwater	
Preston North End	2	22000	Fairbrother	Beattie	Scott	Shankly	Williams	Hamilton	Dougal	Mutch	Livesey 1	Wharton	McIntosh	Humphreys (og)
Everton	1		Burnett	Jackson	Greenhalgh	Bentham	Humphreys	Mercer	Rawlings	Elliott	Catterick 1	Fielding	Boyes	
Queen's Park Rangers	0	20080	Allan AR	Rose	Jefferson	Daniels	Ridyard	Heath	Neary	Mallett	Heathcote	Stock	Pattison	
Crystal Palace	0		Graham	Gregory	Dawes	J Lewis	Bassett	Hudgell	Gillespie	Reece	Kurz	G Lewis	Wilson	
Rotherham United	2	13728	Warnes	Selkirk	Hanson	Mills	H Williams	D Williams	Hooper	Kearney	Ardron	J Shaw 1	Dawson 1	
Gateshead	2		Wilson	Devlin	Robinson	J Callender	T Callender	Atkinson 1	Lancaster	Johnson	McCormack	Howden	Thompson 1	
Southampton	4	19465	Stansbridge	Emmanuel	Roles	Evans	Dodgin	Stroud	Bates 1	McGibbon 1	Roper 1	Veck	Bradley 1	
Newport County	3		Ferguson	Avery	Thomas	Owen	Low	Brinton	Wookey 1	Granville 1	Derrick 1	Batty	Carr	
Stoke City	3	21776	Herod	Brigham	McCue	F Mountford	Franklin	Cowden	Matthews	G Mountford	Steele 3	Antonio	Basnett	
Burnley	1		Foxcroft	Woodruff	Mather	Martindale	Johnson	Loughran	Hays	Morris 1	Jackson	Haigh	Kippax	
Tottenham Hotspur	2	30202	Hughes	Ward	Willis	White	Page	Burgess 1	Medley	Hall 1	Ludford	Dix	Lyman	
Brentford	2		Crozier	Gorman	Poyser	Scott	Brown	Whitaker	Hopkins	Townsend	Durrant 1	Jones	Thomas 1	
West Ham United	6	35000	Medhurst	Bicknell	Cater	Small	Walker	Fenton	Woodgate	Hall 2	Foreman 1	Wood 2	Bainbridge 1	
Arsenal	0		Swindin	Scott	Wade	Nelson	Joy	Collett	O'Flanagan	Henley	Lewis	Drury	Bastin	
Wrexham	1	14109	Ashton	Cook	Tunney	C Jones	Jackson	Bellis	Gardner	Rogers	Hewitt	Haycock 1	Speed	
Blackpool	4		Wallace	Burke	Lewis	Farrow	Suart	Todd	Buchan 1	Mortensen 1	Dodds 1	Blair 1	O'Donnell	

All games played 5 January 1946

ROUND THREE, SECOND LEG

Team			Att	1	2	3	4	5	6	7	8	9	10	11	Notes
Arsenal	1	1	21733	Swindin	Scott	Wade	Male	Joy	Waller	Nelson	Jones	O'Flanagan	Logie	Cumner 1	
West Ham United	0	6		Medhurst	Bicknell	Cater	Small	Walker	Fenton	Woodgate	Hall	Foreman	Wood	Bainbridge	
Aston Villa	2	3	30000	Wakeman	Potts	Cummings	Parkes	Callaghan	Lowe	Kerr	Goffin 1	Edwards	Iverson	Smith 1	
Coventry City	0	2		Wood	Elliott	Metcalf	Ward	Mason	Crawley	Warner	Simpson	Barratt	Aldecoa	Matthews	
Barnsley	3	5	26000	Holdcroft	Cunningham	Pallister	Mansley	Wilson 1	Logan	Smith 1	Cooling	Robledo	Baxter 1	Kelly	
Newcastle United	0	4		King	Cowell	Corbett	Harvey	Smith	Crowe	Milburn	Taylor	Stubbins	Clifton	Hair	
Barrow	2	4	7377	Phillipson	Fenny	Simpson	Caine	Hall	McGrath	Clarkson 1	Dunnigan	Clarke	Mullen	McIntosh 1	
Manchester City	2	8		Swift	Clark	Barkas	Walsh	Cardwell	McDowall	Dunkley 1	Hart 1	Constantine	Smith	Cunliffe	
Blackburn Rovers	1	1	16800	Patterson	Forbes	Green	Whiteside	Pryde	Wightman	Campbell	Baldwin	Wyles 1	Stephan	Glaister	
Bolton Wanderers	3	4		Hanson	Hamlet	Hubbick	Hurst	Atkinson	Murphy	Geldard	Hunt 1	Moir	Westwood 2	Woodward	
Blackpool	4	8	11200	Wallace	Burke	Lewis	Farrow	S Jones	Todd	Buchan	Mortensen	Dodds 3	Blair	O'Donnell 1	
Wrexham	1	2		Ashton	Cook	Tunney	C Jones	Jackson	Bellis	Gardner	McLarty 1	Hewitt	Haycock	Speed	
Brentford	2	4	21500	Crozier	Gorman	Brown	Scott	Smith	Whitaker	Hopkins 2	McAloon	Durrant	Jones	Thomas	
Tottenham Hotspur	0	2		Hughes	Ward	Willis	White	Buckingham	Burgess	Adams	Hall	Ludford	Dix	Lyman	
Brighton & Hove Albion	4	6	9349	Baldwin	Marriott	Darling	Wilson	Risdon	Whent	Longdon	Chase 1	Davie 2	Moore	Stephens 1	
Norwich City	1	2		Davis	Reid	Taylor	Flack	Robinson	Proctor	Johnson	Russell	Ware 1	Plunkett	Jones	
Burnley	2	3	18403	Breedon	Woodruff	Mather	Wilson	Johnson	Loughran	Hays	Morris	Jackson 1	Haigh	Kippax 1	
Stoke City	1	4		Herod	Brigham	McCue	F Mountford	Franklin	Kirton	Matthews	G Mountford	Steele	Antonio 1	Ormston	
Crystal Palace	0	0	16200	Graham	Gregory	Dawes	J Lewis	Bassett	Hudgell	Blackman	Smith	Kurz	G Lewis	Wilson	Aban. after 27 mins of e.t.
Queen's Park Rangers	0	0		Allan AR	Rose	Jefferson	Daniels	Ridyard	Heath	Whitehead	Mallett	Neary	Stock	Pattison	
Derby County	3	9	16629	Boulton	Nicholas	Parr	Bullions	Leuty	Eggleston	Crooks	Carter 2	Stamps	Doherty	Morrison 1	
Luton Town	0	0		Duke	Lake	Dunsmore	Goodyear	Gager	Campbell	Isaacs	Daniel	Needham	Vinall	Waugh	
Everton	2	3	35461	Burnett	Jackson	Greenhalgh	Bentham	Humphreys	Mercer 1	Rawlings	Elliott 1	Catterick	Fielding	Boyes	a.e.t.
Preston North End	2	4		Fairbrother	Beattie	Scott	Shankly 1(p)	Williams	Hamilton	Dougal	Mutch	Livesey	Wharton	McIntosh 1	
Fulham	2	3	20000	Rickett	Bacuzzi	Lloyd	Freeman	Taylor	Wallbanks	Rampling	Woodward	Rooke 2	Beasley	Shepherd	
Charlton Athletic	1	4		Bartram	Croker	Shreeve	HG Turner	Oakes	Johnson	Fell	Brown	Tadman 1	Welsh	Duffy	
Gateshead	0	2	10052	Wilson	Devlin	Bell	J Callender	T Callender	Atkinson	Howden	Johnson	McCormack	Cassidy	Thompson	
Rotherham United	2	4		Warnes	Selkirk	Hanson	Mills	H Williams	D Williams	Hooper	Kearney 1	Ardron 1	J Shaw	Dawson	
Leicester City	0	1	25368	Calvert	Frame	Howe	Osborne	Sheard	Towers	Adam	Smith	Mercer	Soo	Liddle	
Chelsea	2	3		Robertson	Winter	Tennant	Russell	Harris	Foss	Spence	Williams 1	Lawton	Goulden 1	Bain	
Liverpool	2	4	11207	Nickson	Harley	Lambert	Finney	Hughes	Paisley	Nieuwenhuys	Baron	Fagan 2	Taylor	Priday	
Chester	1	1		Shortt	Stubbs	McNeil	Marsh	Lee	Cole	Turner	Burden	Yates	Astbury 1	Hamilton	
Manchester United	5	7	15339	Crompton	Whalley	Roach	Warner	Carey	Cockburn	Hanlon	Rowley 2	Smith	Bainbridge 1	Wrigglesworth 1	Briggs (og)
Accrington Stanley	1	3		Hacking	Cornwell	Webster	Lythgoe	Briggs	Malcolm	Clark	Rothwell	Conroy	Keeley 1	Mauchline	
Middlesbrough	7	11	23878	Cumming	Brown	Robinson	Bell	Hardwick 1	Gordon 1	Spuhler 1	Murphy	Fenton 3	Dews	Douglas 1	
Leeds United	2	6		Hodgson	Duthoit	Gadsby	Coyne	Butterworth	Price	Henry	Short	Ainsley 1	Hindle	Grainger 1	
Millwall	3	5	15384	Dunkley	Fisher	Dudley	Ross	Brolly	Tyler	Richardson	Gordon	Phillips 1	Brown	Smith 1	Smalley (og)
Northampton Town	0	2		Scott	Barron	Smalley	Lowery	Sankey	Yarker	Roberts	Blunt	Morrall	Hughes	Fowler	

ROUND THREE, SECOND LEG (Continued)

Teams	2nd Leg	Agg	Att	1	2	3	4	5	6	7	8	9	10	11	Notes
Newport County	1	4	8509	Ferguson	Roberts	Avery	Owen 1	Low	Brinton	Wookey	Granville	Derrick	Batty	Carr	
Southampton	2	6		Stansbridge	Emmanuel	Roles	Evans	Dodgin	Stroud	Bates	McGibbon 1	Roper	Veck 1	Bradley	
Plymouth Argyle	0	0	5000	Middleton	Royston	Rundle	Adams	Dixon	Gorman	Hodge	Stephenson	Prescott	Came	Tinker	
Aldershot	1	3		Reynolds	Horton	Sheppard	Palmer	Summerbee	J White	Brooks	Bell	Hold 1	Fitzgerald	Hobbs	
Port Vale	1	2	11086	Jepson	Smith	Felton	Oldfield	Griffiths	Cooper	Allen	Pointon	Davies	Bellis 1	Shore	
Bradford Park Avenue	1	3		Farr	Hepworth	Farrell	McTaff	Greenwood	Hallard	Smith	Shackleton	Gibbons 1	Downie	Dix	
Portsmouth	0	0	23716	Walker	Morgan	Crossley	Guthrie	Flewin	Foxton	Worrall	Anderson	Froggatt	Barlow	Harris	
Birmingham City	0	1		Merrick	Duckhouse	Jennings	Harris	Turner	Mitchell	Mulraney	Dougal	Jones	Bodle	Edwards	
Rochdale	2	5	8712	Chesters	Duff	Sneddon	McCormick	Neary	Partridge	Reynolds	Brindle	Hargreaves 2	Wood	Cunliffe	
Bury	4	7		Bradshaw	G Griffiths	Lyons	W Griffiths	Hart	Halton	Davies 1	Herbert	Jones 1	Tompkin 1	Moss 1	
Sheffield United	2	3	31992	White	Furniss	Hooper	Jackson	Latham	Machent	Jones	Nightingale	Collindridge 1	Brook 1	Rickett	
Huddersfield Town	0	1		Clegg	Bailey	Simpson	Morton	Barker	Green	Bateman	Glazzard	Price	Carr	Metcalfe	
Sheffield Wednesday	5	5	22208	Goodfellow	Swift	Pickering	Cockroft	Stewart	Wands	Ward 1	Thompson 1	Aveyard 1	Froggatt 1	Tomlinson 1	
Mansfield Town	0	0		Cromack	Chessell	Marsh	Smith	Barke	Everett	Thorpe	Harkin	Wombwell	Hogg	Poole	
Sunderland	2	5	18000	Mapson	Stelling	Jones	Willingham	Lockie	Housam	Duns	Whitelum 1	Brown	Hastings 1	Burbanks	
Grimsby Town	1	2		Moulson	Vincent	J Hodgson	S Hodgson	Charlesworth	Blenkinsopp	Harvey	Rodi	Moore 1	Jones	Wardle	
Swansea Town	2	3	18400	Roberts	Davies	Fisher	Weston	Briddon	Phillips	Jones	Payne	Ford 2	Coleman	Comley	
Bristol City	2	7		Cousine	Guy	Bailey	Morgan	Roberts	Thomas	Chilcott 1	Curran	Clark	Williams 1	Hargreaves	
Watford	1	2	7008	Mee	O'Brien	Gallimore	Gillespie	Shaw	Gray	Davies	Beckett	Lewis 1	Curran	Drinkwater	aban. after 53 mins of e.t.
Nottingham Forest	1	2		Savage	Thomas	Baxter	Simpson	Blagg	Walker	Mee	Allen	Barks 1	North	Johnston	
West Bromwich Albion	4	5	18025	Twigg	C Shaw	Kinsell	Witcomb	Tranter	Millard	Elliott	Clarke 2	Newsome 2	Connelly	Hodgetts	
Cardiff City	0	1		McLoughlin	Sherwood	Raybould	Wright	Stansfield	Hollyman	Moore	Allen	Rees	Wood	Clarke	
Wolverhampton Wanderers	8	12	14885	Williams	Kelly	Ashton	Alderton	McLean	Crook	King 1	Dunn 1	Galley 3	Wright 2	Mullen 1	
Lovells Athletic	1	3		Jennings	Slattery	Whitehouse	Prangley 1	H Clarke	Bye	Williams	Fisher	A Clarke	Witcombe	Morgan	
York City	3	4	14207	Ferguson	Pinder	Rodgers	Brenen	Young	Gledhill	Scott	Robbins	Winters 2	Thompson	Mahon	Kidd (og)
Chesterfield	2	3		Middleton	Milburn G	Kidd	Hart	Whitaker	Hobson	Sinclair	Wilson	Goodfellow	Dooley 1	Roberts 1	a.e.t.

Games played 9 January 1946 except for those at Burnley, Fulham, Millwall, Port Vale and Sheffield United (7 January), Aston Villa and Rochdale (8 January) and Barrow, Brentford, Leicester, Newport, Sheffield Wednesday and Swansea Town (10 January).

THIRD ROUND REPLAYS

Teams	Score	Att	1	2	3	4	5	6	7	8	9	10	11	12	Notes
Nottingham Forest	0	6500	Savage	Baxter	McCall	Simpson	Blagg	Rawson	Mee	Allen	Mallett	Barks	Walker	Johnston	Blagg (og), a.e.t.
Watford	1		Mee	O'Brien	Gallimore	Gillespie	Shaw	Gray	Davies	Weir	Robson	Lewis	Curran	Drinkwater	
Queen's Park Rangers	1	24600	Brown, Harry	Rose	Jefferson	Daniels	Ridyard	Farrow	Blizzard	Mallett	Addinall 1	Stock	Pattison		
Crystal Palace	0		Graham	Gregory	Dawes	J Lewis	Bassett	Hudgell	Wilson	Robson	Kurz	Smith	G Lewis		

Both games played 16 January 1946. Forest/Watford at White Hart Lane, QPR/Crystal Palace at Craven Cottage

ROUND FOUR, FIRST LEG

Team	G	Att	1	2	3	4	5	6	7	8	9	10	11
Barnsley	3	37100	Holdcroft	Cunningham	Pallister	Mansley	Wilson	Logan	Smith 1	Cooling	Robledo 1	Baxter	Kelly 1
Rotherham United	0		Warnes	Courts	Hanson	Mills	H Williams	D Williams	Hooper	J Shaw	Ardron	Kearney	Dawson
Birmingham City	5	23973	Merrick	Duckhouse	Jennings	Harris	Turner	Mitchell	Mulraney 3	Dougal	Jones 1	Bodie 1	Edwards
Watford	0		Mee	O'Brien	Gallimore	Gillespie	Shaw	Gray	Davies	Weir	Lewis	Curran	Drinkwater
Blackpool	3	17150	Wallace	Burke	Lewis	Farrow	Suart	Todd	Buchan	Mortensen 2	Dodds 1	Blair	O'Donnell
Middlesbrough	2		Cumming	Stuart	Robinson	Bell	Hardwick	Gordon	Spuhler 1	Murphy	Fenton	Dews	Douglas
													Stuart (og)
Bolton Wanderers	5	39682	Hanson	Threlfall	Hubbick	Hurst	Hamlett	Murphy	Geldard	Howe	Lofthouse 2	Westwood 3	Woodward
Liverpool	0		Hobson	Harley	Lambert	Kaye	Hughes	Paisley	Liddell	Balmer	Fagan	Nieuwenhuys	Priday
Bradford Park Avenue	1	25014	Farr	Hepworth	James	Greenwood	Danskin	Britton	Downie	Shackleton	Knott	Gibbons 1	Walker
Manchester City	3		Swift	Clark	Barkas	Walsh	Cardwell	McDowall	Dunkley	Herd 1	Constantine	Smith 2	Pritchard
Brighton & Hove Albion	3	13321	Baldwin	Darling	Watson	Wilson	Risdon	Whent	Longdon	Moore	Davie 3	Willemse	Stephens
Aldershot	0		Reynolds	Horton	Sheppard	J White	Summerbee	Palmer	Brooks	Bell	Hold	Fitzgerald	Hobbs
Bristol City	2	35684	Cousine	Guy	Bailey	Morgan	Roberts	Thomas	Collins	Bentley	Clark	Williams 1	Hargreaves 1
Brentford	1		Crozier	Gorman	Poyser	Scott	Smith	Brown	Hopkins	McAloon	Townsend 1	Jones	Thomas
Charlton Athletic	5	44271	Bartram	Croker	Shreeve	Johnson	Oakes	Hobbis	Fell 1	Robinson 1	AA Turner 1	Brown	Duffy 2
Wolverhampton Wanderers	2		Williams	Morris	Ashton	Alderton	Cullis	Crook	King	Dunn	Chatham 2	Wright	Mullen
Chelsea	2	65726	Robertson	Winter	Tennant	Williams	Harris	Foss	Spence 1	Payne	Lawton	Machin 1	Bain
West Ham United	0		Medhurst	Bicknell	Cater	Macaulay	Walker	Fenton	Woodgate	Hall	Foreman	Small	Wood
Derby County	1	31795	Boulton	Nicholas	Parr	Bullions	Leuty	Musson	Harrison	Carter	Morrison	Doherty 1	Duncan
West Bromwich Albion	0		Sanders	C Shaw	Kinsell	Witcomb	Tranter	Millard	Elliott	Clarke	Newsome	Connelly	Butler
Manchester United	1	36237	Crompton	Whalley	Walton	Warner	Chilton	Cockburn	Hanlon	Smith	Rowley 1	Carey	Wrigglesworth
Preston North End	0		Fairbrother	Beattie	Scott	Shankly	Williams	Hamilton	Dougal	Mutch	Livesey	Wharton	McIntosh
Millwall	2	30000	Dunkley	Dudley	Fisher	Gordon	Ford	Brolly	Gregson	Fenton	Jinks 2	Brown	Smith
Aston Villa	4		Wakeman	Potts	Cummings	Parkes	Callaghan	Lowe	Goffin 1	Broome	Edwards 2	Iverson	Smith 1
Sheffield Wednesday	5	33363	Goodfellow	Swift	Pickering	Cockroft	Gale	Wands	Driver 2	Thompson 1	Aveyard 1	Froggatt 1	Tomlinson
York City	1		Ferguson	Pinder	Rodgers	Brenen	Young	Gledhill	Scott 1(p)	Robbins	Winters	Thompson	Mahon
Southampton	0	19000	Stansbridge	Ellerington	Roles	Evans	Dodgin	Stroud	Roper	Bates	McGibbon	Bradley	Veck
Queen's Park Rangers	1		Allan AR	Rose	Jefferson	Daniels	Ridyard	Farrow	Neary	Mallett	Addinall 1	Stock	Whitehead
Stoke City	2	33222	Herod	Brigham	McCue	F Mountford	Franklin	Kirton	Matthews	G Mountford 1	Steele 1	Antonio	Ormston
Sheffield United	0		Smith	Hooper	Shimwell	Machent	Latham	Forbes	Jones	Nightingale	Collindridge	Hutchinson	Rickett
Sunderland	3	29003	Mapson	Stelling	Jones	Willingham	Lockie	Housam	Duns 1	Whitelum	Brown 2	Hastings	Burbanks
Bury	1		Taylor	Hart	G Griffiths	Jones	Watson	W Griffiths	Moss	McGill 1	Davies	Halton	Tompkin

Games played 26 January 1946

ROUND FOUR, SECOND LEG

Team	Leg	Agg	Att	1	2	3	4	5	6	7	8	9	10	11	Notes
Aldershot	1	1	5226	Reynolds	Horton	Sheppard	Palmer	Wainwright	Summerbee	Bell	J White 1	Brooks	Fitzgerald	Hobbs	
Brighton & Hove Albion	4	7		Baldwin	Darling	Watson	Wilson	Risdon	Whent	Londgon	Chase 1	Davie 2	Willemse	Stephens 1	
Aston Villa	9	13	28000	Wakeman	Potts	Cummings	Parkes 1	Morby	Lowe	Goffin 2	Broome 3	Edwards 1	Iverson 1	Smith 1	Guy (og)
Millwall	1	3		Dunkley	Dudley	Tyler	Gordon	Ford	Brolly	Gregson	Fenton	Jinks	Brown	Smith 1	
Brentford	5	6	18000	Crozier	Gorman	Brown	Scott	Smith	Whitaker	Hopkins	McAloon 3	Durrant 1	Thomas	Gotts	
Bristol City	0	2		Fairhurst	Guy	Bailey	Morgan	Roberts	Thomas	Chilcott	Bentley	Clark	Williams	Hargreaves	
Bury	5	6	11236	Taylor	G Griffiths	Aston	W Griffiths	Hart	Halton	Roberts 3	Jones 1	Davies 1	Tompkin	Moss	a.e.t.
Sunderland	4	7		Mapson	Stelling	Jones	Willingham	Lockie	Housam	Whitelum 1	White	Brown 1	Walshaw 1	Burbanks 1	
Liverpool	2	2	35247	Nickson	Lambert	Ramsden	Paisley	Bush	Spicer	Nieuwenhuys 1	Baron	Fagan	Balmer 1	Priday	
Bolton Wanderers	0	5		Hanson	Threlfall	Hubbick	Hamlett	Atkinson	Murphy	Geldard	Howe	Lofthouse	Westwood	Woodward	
Manchester City	2	5	15026	Swift	Clark	Barkas	Walsh	Cardwell	McDowall	Dunkley	Herd	Constantine 1	Smith 1	Pritchard	
Bradford Park Avenue	8	9		Farr	Hepworth	Farrell 1	Greenwood	Danskin	Hallard	Knott	Shackleton	Gibbons 4	Downie 1	Dix 2	
Middlesbrough	3	5	46556	Cumming	Stuart	Robinson	Bell	Hardwick	Gordon	Spuhler 1	Murphy	Fenton 2	Dews	Stobbart	a.e.t.
Blackpool	2	5		Wallace	Burke	Lewis	Farrow	Suart	Todd	Buchan	Mortensen 1	Dodds	Blair	O'Donnell 1	
Preston North End	3	3	21000	Fairbrother	Beattie	Watson	Shankly 1(p)	Williams	Hamilton	Livesey 1	Mutch	Dougal	Wharton	McIntosh 1	a.e.t.
Manchester United	1	2		Crompton	Whalley	Walton	Warner	Chilton	Cockburn	Hanlon 1	Smith	Rowley	Carey	Wrigglesworth	
Queen's Park Rangers	4	5	16000	Allan AR	Rose	Jefferson	Daniels	Ridyard	Farrow	Neary	Mallett	Addinall 3	Stock 1	Pattison	
Southampton	3	3		Stansbridge	Ellerington 1	Roles	Evans	Dodgin	Stroud	Roper	Bates	McGibbon	Bradley 1	Bevis 1	
Rotherham United	2	2	19563	Warnes	Selkirk	Hanson	Hargreaves	H Williams	Nightingale	Shaw R 1	Ardron	J Shaw	Dawson		Wilson (og)
Barnsley	1	4		Holdcroft	Harston	Pallister 1	Mansley	Wilson	Logan	Smith	Cooling	Robledo	Baxter	Kelly	
Sheffield United	3	3	50859	Smith	Furniss	Shimwell	Machent	Latham	Forbes	Jones	Nightingale	Collindridge 3	Brook	Rickett	
Stoke City	2	4		Herod	Brigham	McCue	F Mountford	Franklin	Kirton	Matthews	G Mountford	Steele 1	Antonio 1	Ormston	
Watford	1	1	5277	Mee	O'Brien	Gallimore	Gillespie	Shaw	Jones	Davies	Weir	Gray 1(p)	Curran	Drinkwater	
Birmingham City	1	6		King	Duckhouse	Jennings	Harris	Turner	Mitchell	Mulraney	Dougal	Jones 1	Bodie	Edwards	
West Bromwich Albion	1	1	35882	Sanders	C Shaw	Kinsell	Witcomb	Tranter	Jones	Elliott	Clarke 1	Newsome	Connelly	Butler	
Derby County	3	4		Boulton	Nicholas	Parr	Bullions	Leuty	Musson	Harrison 1	Carter 1	Morrison	Stamps 1(p)	Duncan	
West Ham United	1	1	31000	Medhurst	Bicknell	Cater	Small	Walker	Fenton	Woodgate	Hall 1	Macaulay	Wood	Bainbridge	
Chelsea	0	2		Robertson	Winter	Tennant	Williams	Harris	Foss	Spence	Payne	Lawton	Goulden	Bain	
Wolverhampton Wanderers	1	3	27720	Williams	Morris	Ashton	Alderton	Bicknell	Crook	King	Dunn	Chatham	Wright 1	Davies	Morris (og)
Charlton Athletic	1	6		Bartram	Croker	Shreeve	Johnson	Oakes	Hobbis	Fell	Robinson	AA Turner	Brown	Duffy	
York City	1	2	10447	Ferguson	Pinder	Rodgers	Brenen	Bentall	Gledhill	Scott	Robbins	Allen 1	Thompson 1	Porritt	
Sheffield Wednesday	6	11		Goodfellow	Swift	Pickering	Cockroft	Gale	Wands	Driver 1	Thompson 3	Aveyard	Froggatt 1	Tomlinson 1	

Games played 30 January 1946 except at Aston Villa and Sheffield United (28 January), Bury (29 January) and Brentford and Rotherham (31 January)

ROUND FOUR REPLAY

Team	Score	Att	1	2	3	4	5	6	7	8	9	10	11	Notes
Blackpool	0	30000	Wallace	Burke	Lewis	Farrow	Suart	Kelly	Buchan	Mortensen	Dodds	Blair	O'Donnell	At Elland Road
Middlesbrough	1		Cumming	Laking	Robinson	Bell	Hardwick 1(p)	Gordon	Spuhler	Murphy	Fenton	Dews	Stobbart	51 mins of e.t.

Played 4 February 1946

ROUND FIVE, FIRST LEG

Team	Gls	Att	1	2	3	4	5	6	7	8	9	10	11
Barnsley	0	37770	Holdcroft	Cunningham	Ferrier	Mansley	Wilson	Logan	Smith	Robledo	Fisher	Baxter	Kelly
Bradford Park Avenue	1		Farr	Hepworth	Farrell	Greenwood	Danskin	Hallard	Knott	Shackleton 1	Gibbons	Downie	Dix
Bolton Wanderers	1	43453	Hanson	Threlfall	Hubbick	Hurst	Hamlett	Murphy	Geldard	Howe	Lofthouse	Westwood 1	Woodward
Middlesbrough	0		Cumming	Laking	Robinson	Bell	Hardwick	Gordon	Spuhler	Murphy	Fenton	Dews	Maddison
Brighton & Hove Albion	1	23456	Baldwin	Marriott	Watson	Wilson	Risdon	Whent	London	Moore	Davie	Willemse 1	Stephens
Derby County	4		Boulton	Nicholas	Parr	Bullions	Leuty	Musson	Harrison	Carter 2	Morrison	Doherty 2 (1p)	Duncan
Chelsea	0	65307	Robertson	Winter	Tennant	Williams	Harris	Foss	Spence	Payne	Lawton	Machin	Bain
Aston Villa	1		Wakeman	Potts	Cummings	Parkes	Morby	Lowe	Goffin	Broome 1	Edwards	Iverson	Smith
Preston North End	1	39303	Fairbrother	Beattie	Summerbee	Shankly	Williams	Hamilton	Livesey	Mutch	Dougal	Wharton 1	McIntosh
Charlton Athletic	1		Bartram	Croker	Shreeve	HG Turner	Phipps	Johnson	Fell	Brown	AA Turner 1	Welsh	Duffy
Queen's Park Rangers	1	19885	Allan AR	Rose	Jefferson	Daniels	Ridyard	Farrow	Swinfen	Mallett	Addinall	Stock	Pattison 1
Brentford	3		Crozier	Gorman	Brown	Scott	Smith	Whitaker	Hopkins 1	McAloon 1	Durrant 1	Thomas	Gotts
Stoke City	2	40452	Herod	Brigham	McCue	F Mountford	Franklin	Kirton	Matthews	G Mountford	Steele 2	Antonio	Ormston
Sheffield Wednesday	0		Goodfellow	Swift	Pickering	Cockroft	Gale	Wands	Driver	Thompson	Aveyard	Froggatt	Tomlinson
Sunderland	1	44820	Mapson	Stelling	Jones	Willingham	Lockie	Housam	Duns 1	Whitelum	Brown	Hastings	Burbanks
Birmingham City	0		Merrick	Duckhouse	Jennings	Harris	Turner	Mitchell	Mulraney	Dougal	Jones	Bodie	Edwards

Games played 9 February 1946

ROUND FIVE, SECOND LEG

Team	Gls	Agg	Att	1	2	3	4	5	6	7	8	9	10	11
Aston Villa	1	2	56000	Wakeman	Potts	Cummings	Parkes	Morby	Lowe	Goffin 1	Broome	Smith	Iverson	Smith
Chelsea	0	0		Robertson	Winter	Tennant	Williams	Harris	Foss	Spence	Payne	Knott	Machin	Dolding
Birmingham City	3	3	40000	King	Duckhouse	Jennings	Harris	Turner	Mitchell	Muraney 1	Dougal	Jones 2	Bodle	Edwards
Sunderland	1	2		Mapson	Stelling	Jones	Willingham	Lockie	Housam	Whitelum	White	Brown 1	Walshaw	Burbanks
Bradford Park Avenue	1	2	29341	Farr	Hepworth	Farrell	Greenwood	Danskin	Hallard	Flatley	Shackleton	Gibbons 1	Downie	Dix
Barnsley	1	1		Holdcroft	Harston	Cunningham	Mansley	Wilson	Logan	Smith	Robledo 1	Asquith	Baxter	Kelly
Brentford	0	3	20000	Crozier	Gorman	Poyser	Scott	Smith	Brown	Hopkins	Jones	Durrant	McAloon	Thomas
Queen's Park Rangers	0	1		Allan AR	Reay	Jefferson	Daniels	Ridyard	Farrow	Swinfen	Mallett	Addinall	Heath	Pattison
Charlton Athletic	6	7	50000	Bartram	Croker	Shreeve	HG Turner	Oakes	Johnson	Fell	Brown	AA Turner 2	Welsh	Duffy 3
Preston North End	0	1		Fairbrother	Beattie	Watson	Shankly	Williams	Hamilton	Anders	Mutch	Dougal	Wharton	McIntosh
Derby County	6	10	32000	Boulton	Nicholas	Parr	Bullions	Leuty	Musson	Crooks 1	Carter 3	Morrison	Doherty 2	Duncan
Brighton & Hove Albion	0	1		Baldwin	Marriott	Watson	Wilson	Risdon	Whent	Hindley	Moore	Davie	Willemse	Stephens
Middlesbrough	1	1	49329	Cumming	Laking	Robinson	Bell	Hardwick	Gordon	Spuhler	Murphy	Fenton 1	Dews	Maddison
Bolton Wanderers	1	2		Hanson	Threlfall	Hubbick	Hurst	Hamlett	Murphy	Geldard	Howe	Hunt 1	Westwood	Moir
Sheffield Wednesday	0	0	62728	Goodfellow	Swift	Pickering	Cockroft	Gale	Wands	Driver	Robinson	Aveyard	Froggatt	Tomlinson
Stoke City	0	2		Herod	Brigham	McCue	F Mountford	Franklin	Kirton	Matthews	Peppitt	Steele	Antonio	Baker

Games played 13 February 1946 except at Sheffield Wednesday (11 February), Aston Villa (12 January) and Brentford, Charlton and Derby (14 February)

ROUND SIX, FIRST LEG

Team	Score	Att	1	2	3	4	5	6	7	8	9	10	11
Aston Villa	3	76588	Wakeman	Potts	Cummings	Moss	Parkes	Lowe	Goffin	Broome 1	Edwards 1	Iverson 1	Smith
Derby County	4		Townsend	Nicholas	Parr	Bullions	Leuty	Musson	Crooks 1	Carter 1	Stamps	Doherty 2	Duncan
Bradford Park Avenue	2	19732	Farr	Hepworth	Farrell	Greenwood	Danskin	Hallard 1	Dix 1	Shackleton	Gibbons	Downie	Walker
Birmingham City	2		Merrick	Duckhouse	Jennings	Harris	Turner	Mitchell	Mulraney	Dougal 1	Jones 1	Bodle	Edwards
Charlton Athletic	6	44060	Bartram	Croker	Shreeve	HG Turner	Oakes	Johnson	Fell	Brown 1	AA Turner 2	Welsh 2	Duffy 1
Brentford	3		Crozier	Gorman	Oliver	Scott	Smith	Brown	Hopkins	McAloon 2	Durrant 1	Thomas	Bamford
Stoke City	0	50735	Herod	Brigham	McCue	F Mountford	Franklin	Kirton	Matthews	G Mountford	Steele	Antonio	Basnett
Bolton Wanderers	2		Hanson	Threlfall	Hubbick	Hurst	Hamlett	Murphy	Woodward	Howe	Lofthouse	Westwood 2	Moir

Games played 2 March 1946

ROUND SIX, SECOND LEG

Team	Score	Att	1	2	3	4	5	6	7	8	9	10	11
Birmingham City	6 8	49858	Merrick	Duckhouse	Jennings	Harris	Turner	Mitchell	Mulraney 2	Dougal 2	Jones	Bodle 2	Edwards
Bradford Park Avenue	0 2		Farr	Hepworth	Leonard	Greenwood	Danskin	Hallard	Dix	Shackleton	Knott	Gibbons	Walker
Bolton Wanderers	0 2	65419	Hanson	Threlfall	Hubbick	Hurst	Hamlett	Murphy	Geldard	Howe	Lofthouse	Westwood	Woodward
Stoke City	0 0		Herod	Brigham	McCue	F Mountford	Franklin	Kirton	Matthews	Peppitt	Steele	Sale	Baker
Brentford	1 4	36000	Crozier	Gorman	Oliver	Scott 1	Smith	Brown	Hopkins	McAloon	Townsend	Thomas	Bamford
Charlton Athletic	3 9		Bartram	Croker	Shreeve	HG Turner	Oakes	Johnson	Fell	Brown	AA Turner 1	Welsh 1	Duffy 1
Derby County	1 5	32000	Townsend	Nicholas	Parr	Bullions	Leuty	Musson	Crooks	Carter 1	Stamps	Doherty	Duncan
Aston Villa	1 4		Wakeman	Potts	Cummings	Parkes	Callaghan	Lowe	Goffin	Broome 1	Edwards	Iverson	Smith

Games played 6 March 1946 except at Birmingham (9 March)

SEMI-FINALS

Team	Score	Att	1	2	3	4	5	6	7	8	9	10	11	Venue
Charlton Athletic	2	70819	Bartram	Croker	Shreeve	HG Turner	Oakes	Johnson	Fell	Brown	AA Turner	Welsh	Duffy 2	Villa Park
Bolton Wanderers	0		Hanson	Threlfall	Hubbick	Hurst	Hamlett	Murphy	Geldard	Howe	Lofthouse	Westwood	Woodward	
Derby County	1	65013	Woodley	Nicholas	Parr	Bullions	Leuty	Musson	Fell	Carter 1	Stamps	Doherty	Duncan	Hillsborough
Birmingham City	1		Merrick	Duckhouse	Jennings	Harris	Turner	Mitchell	Harrison	Dougal	Jones	Bodle	Edwards	

Games played 23 March 1946

SEMI-FINAL REPLAY

Team	Score	Att	1	2	3	4	5	6	7	8	9	10	11	
Derby County	4	80483	Woodley	Nicholas	Parr	Bullions	Leuty	Musson	Harrison	Carter	Stamps 2	Doherty 2	Duncan	a.e.t.
Birmingham City	0		Merrick	Duckhouse	Jennings	Harris	Mitchell	Mulraney	Dougal	Jones	Bodle	Edwards		

Played 27 March 1946 at Maine Road, Manchester

FINAL

Team	Score	Att	1	2	3	4	5	6	7	8	9	10	11	
Derby County	4	98215	Woodley	Nicholas	Howe	Bullions	Leuty	Musson	Harrison	Carter	Stamps 2	Doherty 1	Duncan	HG Turner (og)
Charlton Athletic	1		Bartram	Phipps	Shreeve	HG Turner 1	Oakes	Johnson	Fell	Brown	AA Turner	Welsh	Duffy	a.e.t.

Played 27 April 1946 at Wembley Stadium

PLAYER DETAILS

The following pages list every player that appeared in the rounds proper of the 1945-46 FA Cup. Their date and place of birth are given when known, with thanks to Michael Joyce for the use of his player database. Further career details for most of these men will be found in the two volumes of "Football League Players' Records". The period 1888 to 1939 (by Michael Joyce) is a SoccerData publication from Tony Brown. The period 1946 to 2005 (by Barry Hugman, with Michael Joyce) is published by Queen Anne Press and available from Soccer Books, 01472 696226.

Other player details include the year of death, the club played for in 1945-46, FA Cup appearances and goals, and a marker to indicate that they won one or more full international caps at some stage in their career (i.e. they may have been capped after 1946). Some of the men listed here won amateur international caps, but these are not shown. Countries for which they were capped are e (England), s (Scotland), w (Wales), i (Northern Ireland), r (Republic of Ireland), ch (Chile) and sp (Spain).

Dick Spence, Chelsea

The oldest known players appearing in the 1945-46 FA Cup were:

Mark Hooper (Rotherham) b. July 14 1901
Alex Ferguson (Newport County) b Aug 5 1903
Stan Wood (Halifax Town) b July 1 1905

and the youngest:

Wally Hinshelwood (Sutton United) b. Oct 29 1929
Ronnie Allen (Port Vale) b. Jan 15 1929
Bobby Cunliffe (Manchester City) b. Dec 27 1928
Ray Daniel (Swansea Town) b. Nov 2 1928)

Personal details of some players are unknown. If any readers can fill in some of the gaps they should please write or email the publisher.

Player photographs are not always from the 1945-46 season.

Name		D.o.B	Place of Birth	Died	Club	Ap.	Gl.	Int
Adam C	Charlie	22/03/1919	Glasgow	1996	Leicester City	2	1	
Adams WH	Billy	08/01/1919	Arlecdon	1989	Tottenham Hotspur	1		
Adams WV	Bill	10/05/1921	Plymouth	1997	Plymouth Argyle	2		
Adamson RMcC	Bert	21/05/1914	Balbeggie	1995	Carlisle United	2	2	
Addinall AW	Bert	30/01/1921	Paddington		Queen's Park Rgs.	7	8	
Ainsley GE	George	15/04/1915	South Shields	1985	Leeds United	2	2	
Akers WWG	Wally	29/07/1917	West Auckland	1975	Mansfield Town	2		
Aldecoa EG	Emilio	30/11/1922	Bilbao, Spain	1999	Coventry City	2		sp
Alderton JH	Jim	06/12/1924	Wingate	1998	Wolverhampton Wan.	4		
Aldred					Shrewsbury Town	4		
Allen AR	Reg	03/05/1919	Marylebone	1976	Queen's Park Rgs.	10		
Allen BW	Bryn	23/03/1921	Gilfach Goch	2005	Cardiff City	2	1	w
Allen HA	Anthony	27/10/1924	Beeston		Nottingham Forest	3	1	
Allen R	Ronnie	15/01/1929	Fenton	2001	Port Vale	6	2	e
Allen W	Bill	22/10/1917	Newburn	1981	York City	1	1	
Allsop WH	Bill	29/01/1922	Ripley	1997	Halifax Town	2		
Alsop GA	Gilbert	10/09/1908	Frampton Cotterell	1992	Walsall	2	1	
Anders H	Harry	28/11/1926	St Helens	1994	Preston North End	1		
Anderson EW	Ted	17/07/1911	Dudley, Northumberland	1979	Tranmere Rovers	4		
Anderson JC	Jock	08/05/1915	Dundee	1987	Portsmouth	2		
Anderson R					Bishop Auckland	4	1	
Angell					Slough United	2		
Angus J	Jack	12/03/1909	Amble	1965	Exeter City	1		
Antonio GR	George	20/10/1914	Whitchurch	1997	Stoke City	7	2	
Archer WH	Bill	05/02/1914	Scunthorpe	1992	Doncaster Rovers	2		
Ardron W	Wally	19/09/1918	Swinton-on-Dearne	1978	Rotherham United	8	2	
Armstrong					Stockton	2		
Artus KG	Kenneth				Bristol City	1	1	
Ash JW	Jack	31/12/1911	Hebburn	2003	Accrington Stanley	1		
Ashcroft LL	Llew	10/07/1921	Flint		Tranmere Rovers	2	2	
Ashton DO	Derrick	04/07/1922	Worksop	1997	Wolverhampton Wan.	4		
Ashton E	Teddy	19/01/1906	Kilnhurst	1978	Grantham	4	1	
Ashton RW	Roger	16/08/1921	Llanidloes	1985	Wrexham	5		
Asquith B	Beaumont	16/09/1910	Painthorpe	1977	Barnsley	1		
Astbury TA	Tommy	09/02/1920	Buckley	1993	Chester	2	1	
Aston WV	Viv	16/10/1918	Coseley	1999	Bury	1		
Atack S	Sidney	10/05/1918	Methley	1983	Trowbridge Town	2		
Atherton JA	Alec	08/12/1914	Cheetham	1985	Southport	1		
Atkinson FJ	Fred	24/08/1919	Newcastle	1991	Gateshead	4	1	
Atkinson H	Harold	28/07/1925	Liverpool	2003	Tranmere Rovers	3	2	
Atkinson JE	Jack	20/12/1913	New Washington	1977	Bolton Wanderers	2		
Austin					Sutton United	2		
Avery R	Ralph				Newport County	4		
Aveyard W	Walter	11/06/1918	Thurnscoe	1985	Sheffield Wed.	6	2	
Bacuzzi GLD	Joe	25/09/1916	Holborn	1995	Fulham	2		
Bailey A	Arthur	11/01/1914	Beswick	2006	Shrewsbury Town	4	1	
Bailey EJ	Jack	17/06/1921	Bristol	1986	Bristol City	8		
Bailey TG	Graham	22/03/1920	Dawley		Huddersfield Town	2		
Bain JA	Jimmy	14/12/1919	Blairgowrie		Chelsea	5		
Bainbridge A	Arthur				Crewe Alexandra	2		
Bainbridge KV	Ken	15/01/1921	Barking		West Ham United	3	1	
Bainbridge WV	Bill	09/03/1922	Gateshead		Manchester United	1	1	
Baker F	Frank	22/10/1918	Stoke-on-Trent	1989	Stoke City	2		
Baldwin HJA	Harry	17/07/1920	Saltley		Brighton & Hove A.	10		
Baldwin JJ	Jimmy	12/01/1922	Blackburn	1985	Blackburn Rovers	2		
Balmer J	Jack	06/02/1916	Liverpool	1984	Liverpool	2	1	
Bamford HFE	Harry	08/04/1914	Kingston	1949	Brentford	2		
Banks K	Kenny	19/10/1923	Wigan	1994	Southport	2		
Barkas S	Sam	29/12/1909	Wardley Colliery	1989	Manchester City	4		e
Barkas T	Tommy	27/03/1912	Gateshead	1991	Halifax Town	2	2	
Barke JL	Lloyd	16/12/1912	Nuncargate	1976	Mansfield Town	6		
Barker J	Jeff	16/10/1915	Scunthorpe	1985	Huddersfield Town	2		
Barks E	Eddie	01/09/1921	Ilkeston	1989	Nottingham Forest	3	1	
Barlow H	Bert	22/07/1916	Kilnhurst	2004	Portsmouth	2		
Baron KMP	Kevin	19/07/1926	Preston	1971	Liverpool	3		
Barr					Wisbech Town	2		
Barratt H	Harry	25/12/1918	Headington	1989	Coventry City	2	1	

Wally Ardron

Sam Barkas

Name		D.o.B	Place of Birth	Died	Club	Ap.	Gl.	Int
Barron G	George				Bromley	4		
Barron W	Bill	26/10/1917	Houghton-le-Spring	2006	Northampton Town	5		
Bartlett FL	Fred	05/03/1913	Reading	1968	Clapton Orient	2		
Bartram S	Sam	22/01/1914	Simonside	1981	Charlton Athletic	10		
Basnett AE	Fred	1924	Stoke-on-Trent		Stoke City	2		
Bassett WEG	Billy	08/06/1912	Brithdir	1977	Crystal Palace	3		
Bastin CS	Cliff	14/03/1912	Exeter	1991	Arsenal	1		e
Bateman A	Albert	13/06/1924	Stocksbridge		Huddersfield Town	2		
Bates					South Liverpool	2		
Bates E					Wellington Town	2		
Bates ET	Ted	03/05/1918	Thetford	2003	Southampton	4	1	
Bates H					Wellington Town	2		
Batty SG	Stan	14/02/1913	Tottenham	1998	Newport County	2		
Baxter					Netherfield (Kendal)	2		
Baxter JC	Jimmy	08/11/1925	Dunfermline	1994	Barnsley	6	1	
Baxter WA	Bill	06/09/1917	Nottingham	1992	Nottingham Forest	3		
Beach DF	Doug	02/02/1920	Watford		Luton Town	1		
Bean AS	Alf 'Billy'	25/08/1915	Lincoln	1993	Lincoln City	4		
Beardshaw EC	Colin	26/11/1912	Crawcrook	1977	Bradford City	1		
Beasley AE	Pat	27/07/1913	Stourbridge	1986	Fulham	2		e
Beattie A	Andy	11/08/1913	Kintore	1983	Preston North End	6		s
Beaumont A	Alan	09/01/1927	Liverpool	1999	South Liverpool	1		
Beckett W	Billy	04/07/1915	Kirkdale	1999	Watford	5		
Bell					Netherfield (Kendal)	2		
Bell D	Dave	24/12/1909	Gorebridge	1986	Ipswich Town	4		
Bell E	Ernie	22/07/1918	Hull	1968	Aldershot	6		
Bell H	Harold	22/11/1924	Liverpool	1994	Tranmere Rovers	2	1	
Bell HD	Harry	14/10/1924	Sunderland		Middlesbrough	7		
Bell JH	John	29/08/1919	Morpeth	1994	Gateshead	4		
Bellis A	Alf	08/10/1920	Ellesmere Port		Port Vale	6	3	
Bellis TG	Gib	21/04/1919	Mold	2000	Wrexham	6		
Bennett S	Stanley				Walsall	1	1	
Bentall CE	Edward	28/01/1922	Helmsley	1947	York City	3		
Bentham SJ	Stan	17/03/1915	Leigh	2002	Everton	2		
Bentley TFR	Roy	17/05/1924	Shirehampton		Bristol City	6	1	e
Beresford RJ	Reg	29/06/1924	Lower Pilsley		Notts County	4		
Berry N	Norman	15/08/1922	Bury	2002	Bury	1		
Bevis WE	Billy	29/09/1918	Warsash	1994	Southampton	1	1	
Bicknell C	Charlie	06/11/1905	Pye Bridge	1994	West Ham United	4		
Bicknell R	Roy	19/02/1926	Doncaster	2005	Wolverhampton Wan.	1		
Biggs					Netherfield (Kendal)	2		
Birch HK	Harry	11/01/1914	Crieff	1985	Barrow	3		
Birchall EW	Ellis				Port Vale	1		
Bird KB	Ken	25/09/1918	Norwich	1987	Bournemouth	2		
Birtles					Marine	3		
Black RW	Bobby	17/07/1915	Washington	1979	Clapton Orient	2		
Blackburn					Chorley	1		
Blackman JJ	Jack	25/11/1911	Bermondsey	1987	Crystal Palace	1		
Blagg EA	Ted	09/02/1918	Shireoaks	1976	Nottingham Forest	3		
Blair JA	Jimmy	06/01/1918	Whiteinch	1983	Blackpool	5	1	s
Blake HCE	Bert	16/03/1908	Bristol	1986	Trowbridge Town	2	1	
Bland GP	Pat	24/02/1915	Tutbury	1970	Watford	1		
Blenkinsopp TW	Tommy	13/05/1920	Witton Park	2004	Grimsby Town	1		
Blizzard LWB	Les	13/03/1923	Acton	1996	Queen's Park Rgs.	3		
Blood JF	Jack	02/10/1914	Nottingham	1992	Exeter City	4		
Bluff					Newport (IOW)	1		
Blunt E	Eddie	21/05/1918	Tunstall	1993	Northampton Town	4	2	
Blythe JA	John	31/01/1924	Darlington		Darlington	2		
Boatwright F	Fred				Newport County	2		
Bodle H	Harold	04/10/1920	Adwick-le-Street	2005	Birmingham City	10	3	
Bohill					North Shields	2		
Bolton					Romford	2		
Bond A	Tony	27/12/1913	Preston	1991	Southport	2		
Boothway J	Jack	04/02/1919	Manchester	1979	Crewe Alexandra	2	2	
Bootle W	William	09/01/1926	Ashton-under-Lyne		Manchester City	1		
Bott					Trowbridge Town	2		
Boulton FP	Frank	12/08/1917	Chipping Sodbury	1987	Derby County	6		

Andy Beattie

Roy Bentley

Name		D.o.B	Place of Birth	Died	Club	Ap.	Gl.	Int
Bowden AJ	Albert		Exeter		Exeter City	2		
Bowden J	Jack	25/08/1921	Manchester	1981	Oldham Athletic	1		
Bowker					Barnet	1		
Bowles JC	Jack	04/08/1914	Cheltenham	1987	Stockport County	2		
Boyes WE	Wally	05/01/1913	Killamarsh	1960	Everton	2		e
Bradley J	Jack	27/11/1916	Hemsworth	2002	Southampton	4	2	
Bradshaw GF	George	10/03/1913	Southport	1989	Bury	2		
Bramley E	Ernest	29/08/1920	Mansfield	1993	Mansfield Town	2		
Brannan MH	Mike	1911	Wath-on-Dearne		Grantham	4		
Bratley					Gainsborough Trinity	2	1	
Breedon J	Jack				Burnley	1		
Brenen A	Bert	05/10/1915	South Shields	1995	York City	5	1	
Bretton					Marine	4		
Brice GHJ	Gordon	04/05/1924	Bedford	2003	Luton Town	1		
Briddon S	Sam	26/07/1915	Alfreton	1975	Swansea Town	2		
Bridges H	Harold	30/06/1915	Burton-on-Trent	1989	Tranmere Rovers	4		
Brierley K	Ken	03/04/1926	Ashton-under-Lyne	2004	Oldham Athletic	4		
Briggs JC	Cyril	24/11/1918	Lower Broughton	1998	Accrington Stanley	6		
Brigham H	Harry	19/11/1914	Selby	1978	Stoke City	8		
Brindle JJ	Jack	12/07/1917	Blackburn	1975	Rochdale	6	1	
Brinton EJ	Ernie	26/05/1908	Bristol	1981	Newport County	5	1	
Briscoe					Wisbech Town	2		
Britton J	Jimmy	27/05/1920	Salford		Bradford Park Ave.	1		
Brolly TH	Tom	01/06/1912	Belfast	1986	Millwall	4		i
Brook H	Harold	15/10/1921	Sheffield	1998	Sheffield United	3	1	
Brooks					Kettering Town	1		
Brooks H	Harry	02/06/1915	Tibshelf	1994	Aldershot	8	13	
Brooks H					Romford	2		
Broome FH	Frank	11/06/1915	Berkhamsted	1994	Aston Villa	6	6	e
Broughton E	Ted	09/02/1925	Bradford		Bradford City	1		
Brown					Slough United	2		
Brown C	Cyril	25/05/1918	Ashington	1990	Sunderland	6	5	
Brown CM	Charlie	1915	Tinsley		Hartlepool United	1		
Brown G	George		Maghull		Southport	1		
Brown HT	Harry	09/04/1924	Kingsbury	1982	Queen's Park Rgs.	1		
Brown RAJ	Robert 'Sailor'	07/11/1915	Great Yarmouth		Charlton Athletic	10	1	
Brown S					Kettering Town	2		
Brown TL	Tommy	17/04/1921	Glenbuck	1966	Millwall	4		
Brown WH	Billy	11/03/1909	Choppington	1996	Middlesbrough	1		
Brown WI	Billy 'Buster'	06/09/1910	Silvertown	1993	Brentford	8		
Browne					Bath City	4	1	
Buchan WRM	Willie	17/10/1914	Grangemouth	2003	Blackpool	5	1	
Buckingham VF	Vic	23/10/1915	Greenwich	1995	Tottenham Hotspur	1		
Bulger CG	Charlie	19/01/1915	Manchester	1976	Walsall	1		
Bullions JL	Jimmy	12/03/1924	Dennyloanhead		Derby County	11		
Burbanks WE	Eddie	01/04/1913	Campsall	1983	Sunderland	5	1	
Burchell GS	George				Walthamstow Avenue	3		
Burden TD	Tommy	21/02/1924	Andover	2001	Chester	2		
Burdess					Willington	2		
Burgess RJ	Ronald		Bristol		Bristol Rovers	4		
Burgess WAR	Ron	09/04/1917	Cwm	2005	Tottenham Hotspur	2	1	w
Burke C	Charlie	13/09/1921	Arran	1995	Bournemouth	2		
Burke RJ	Dick	28/10/1920	Ashton-under-Lyne	2004	Blackpool	5		
Burley B	Ben	02/11/1912	Sheffield		Chelmsford City	2		
Burnett GG	George	11/02/1920	Liverpool	1985	Everton	2		
Burns FJ	Frankie	11/11/1924	Workington	1987	Swansea Town	1		
Burrows A	Arthur	04/12/1919	Stockport	2005	Stockport County	2		
Burton S	Sam	10/11/1926	Swindon		Swindon Town	1		
Bush WT	Tom	22/02/1914	Hodnet	1969	Liverpool	1		
Bushby TW	Billy	21/08/1913	Shildon	1997	Portsmouth	1		
Butler E	Ernie	28/08/1924	Middlesbrough		Stockton	2		
Butler J	Jackie				Shrewsbury Town	3		
Butler S	Stan	07/01/1919	Stillington	1979	West Bromwich Alb.	2		
Butterworth A	Albert	20/03/1912	Ashton-under-Lyne	1991	Bristol Rovers	4	4	
Butterworth FC	Frank		Barking		Leeds United	2		
Bye L	Leslie	30/06/1913	Bedwellty	1970	Lovells Athletic	6		
Caffyn					Sutton United	2		

Harry Brooks

Eddie Burbanks

Billy Cairns

Name		D.o.B	Place of Birth	Died	Club	Ap.	Gl.	Int
Caine WG	Billy	01/07/1927	Barrow		Barrow	6		
Cairns WH	Billy	07/10/1914	Newcastle	1988	Gateshead	4	5	
Caldwell					Bath City	4		
Callaghan E	Ernie 'Mush'	21/01/1910	Birmingham	1972	Aston Villa	4		
Callegari					Walthamstow Avenue	4		
Callender JW	Jack	02/04/1923	West Wylam	2001	Gateshead	6	1	
Callender TS	Tom	20/09/1920	Bywell	2002	Gateshead	4		
Calverley A	Alf	24/11/1917	Huddersfield	1991	Yeovil & Petters U	1		
Calvert JWH	Joe	03/02/1907	Beighton	1999	Leicester City	2		
Came A	Ambrose				Plymouth Argyle	1		
Campbell J	Jim	25/11/1918	Glasgow		Leicester City	1		
Campbell JJ	John	17/03/1922	Liverpool		Blackburn Rovers	2		
Campbell R	Robson		Pegswood		Luton Town	2		
Cape JP	Jackie	16/11/1911	Carlisle	1994	Carlisle United	4	3	
Cardwell L	Louis	20/08/1912	Blackpool	1986	Manchester City	4		
Carey JJ	Johnny	23/02/1919	Dublin	1995	Manchester United	4		r
Carr					Gainsborough Trinity	2		
Carr EM	Eddie	03/10/1917	Wheatley Hill	1998	Huddersfield Town	1		
Carr LL	Lance	18/02/1910	Johannesburg, South Af.	1983	Newport County	6	1	
Carrick					Stalybridge Celtic	2		
Carswell					Netherfield (Kendal)	1		
Carter HS	Raich	21/12/1913	Sunderland	1994	Derby County	11	12	e
Cartwright GL	George				Lincoln City	4		
Cassidy W	Bill	30/06/1917	Gateshead		Gateshead	1		
Cater R	Ron	02/02/1922	Fulham		West Ham United	4		
Catterick H	Harry	26/11/1919	Darlington	1985	Everton	2	1	
Chadwick C	Cliff	26/01/1914	Bolton		Middlesbrough	1		
Chadwick H	Harold	25/01/1919	Oldham	1987	Grimsby Town	1		
Chafer J	Jack				Rotherham United	2		
Challis SM	Stan	22/04/1918	Lympstone		Exeter City	4	2	
Chandler					Barnet	2		
Chandler FEJ	Fred	02/08/1912	Hythe, Hampshire	2005	Crewe Alexandra	1		
Chapman E	Eddie	02/05/1919	Blackburn	1976	Oldham Athletic	4	2	
Charlesworth S	Stan	08/03/1920	Conisbrough	2003	Grimsby Town	1		
Chase CT	Charlie	31/01/1924	Steyning		Brighton & Hove A.	4	2	
Chatham RH	Ray	20/07/1924	Wolverhampton	1999	Wolverhampton Wan.	2	2	
Cheetham TM	Tommy	11/10/1910	Byker	1993	Lincoln City	4	2	
Chessell S	Sammy	09/07/1921	Shirebrook	1996	Mansfield Town	6		
Chesters A	Arthur	14/02/1910	Salford		Rochdale	6		
Chilcott K	Ken	17/03/1920	Rhondda	2001	Bristol City	7	4	
Childs E	Eric				Walthamstow Avenue	4		
Childs					Wellington Town	2		
Chilton AC	Allenby	16/09/1918	South Hylton	1996	Manchester United	3		e
Chitty WS	Wilf	10/07/1912	Walton-on-Thames	1997	Reading	2		
Churchill					Yorkshire Amateur	2		
Churms					Gainsborough Trinity	2	1	
Clapham					Bishop Auckland	2	1	
Clapham					Chelmsford City	1		
Clapham					Gainsborough Trinity	2		
Clark FD	Don	25/10/1917	Bristol		Bristol City	8	5	
Clark GH	'Nobby'				Bromley	4		
Clark GV	Gordon	15/06/1913	Gainsborough	1997	Manchester City	4		
Clark H	Harry	30/03/1913	Cloughdene		Accrington Stanley	4		
Clark R	Bert 'Nobby'		Bristol		Bristol Rovers	4		
Clark T	Tom				Carlisle United	4	3	
Clarke					Chelmsford City	1		
Clarke					Slough United	2		
Clarke					Stalybridge Celtic	2		
Clarke AW	Alfie	1914	Newport	1953	Lovells Athletic	6	2	
Clarke HA	Harry	23/02/1923	Woodford	2000	Lovells Athletic	5		
Clarke I	Ike	09/01/1915	Tipton	2002	West Bromwich Alb.	4	3	
Clarke JH	Harry	27/03/1921	Darlington		Darlington	3	2	
Clarke KJ	Kevin	29/04/1921	Drogheda	2004	Barrow	6	9	
Clarke RJ	Roy	01/06/1925	Newport	2006	Cardiff City	2		w
Clarke W	William				Stockport County	1		
Clarke WV	Billy	17/01/1911	Newport	1970	Newport County	2		
Clarkson CS	Cliff	21/01/1917	Barrow	1986	Barrow	4	1	

Jack Callender

Tom Callender

Raich Carter

Name		D.o.B	Place of Birth	Died	Club	Ap.	Gl.	Int
Clay					Romford	2		
Clegg D	Don	02/06/1921	Huddersfield		Huddersfield Town	2		
Clements					Slough United	2		
Cliff J	John				Hartlepool United	1		
Clifton H	Harry	28/05/1914	Marley Hill	1998	Newcastle United	2		
Cload					Chorley	2		
Cockburn H	Henry	14/09/1921	Ashton-under-Lyne	2004	Manchester United	4		e
Cockroft H	Hubert	21/11/1918	Barnsley	1979	Bradford City	2		
Cockroft J	Joe	20/06/1911	Barnsley	1994	Sheffield Wed.	6		
Coe					Willington	2		
Cole GD	Doug	02/07/1916	Heswall	1959	Chester	2		
Coleman D	Dennis				Swansea Town	1		
Coleman					Trowbridge Town	2		
Coley WE	Bill	17/09/1916	Wolverhampton	1974	Torquay United	2	1	
Collett E	Ernie	17/11/1914	Sheffield	1980	Arsenal	1		
Collindridge C	Colin	15/11/1920	Barnsley		Sheffield United	3	4	
Collings W	William				Barrow	2		
Collins AJ	Anthony				Wrexham	3		
Collins RD	Ron 'Sammy'	13/01/1923	Bristol	1998	Bristol City	2		
Comley LG	Len	25/01/1922	Swansea		Swansea Town	1		
Connelly EJ	Eddie	09/12/1916	Dumbarton	1990	West Bromwich Alb.	4	1	
Conroy RM	Maurice	26/04/1919	Bradford		Accrington Stanley	5	1	
Constantine JJ	Jimmy	16/02/1920	Ashton-under-Lyne	1998	Manchester City	4	4	
Conway E	Edward				Barrow	1		
Conway H	Herman	11/10/1908	Gainsborough	1983	Southend United	2		
Cook W	Billy	20/01/1909	Coleraine	1993	Wrexham	6		i
Cooke WH	Harry	07/03/1919	Oswestry	1992	Bournemouth	2		
Cooling R	Roy	09/12/1921	Barnsley	2003	Barnsley	4		
Cooper A	Arthur	16/03/1921	Etruria		Port Vale	6		
Cope G	George	26/01/1915	Crewe	1988	Crewe Alexandra	2		
Corbett R	Bobby	16/03/1922	Throckley	1988	Newcastle United	2		
Corey					Wisbech Town	2		
Corkan L	Leslie				Crewe Alexandra	1		
Corkhill WG	Bill	23/04/1910	Belfast	1978	Notts County	4		
Cornwell E	Ellis	14/11/1913	Coppull	1986	Accrington Stanley	2		
Cothliff HT	Harold	24/03/1916	Liverpool	1976	Torquay United	2		
Coulson B					Bromley	4		
Courts F	Frank	1914	Rotherham		Rotherham United	3		
Cousins H	Harry	25/09/1907	Pilsley	1981	Swindon Town	2		
Cousins KF	Ken	06/08/1922	Bristol		Bristol City	3		
Cowden S	Stuart	1921	Alsager		Stoke City	1		
Cowell GR	Bobby	05/12/1922	Trimdon	1996	Newcastle United	2		
Cowells					Stockton	1		
Coyne C	Cyril	21/05/1924	Barnsley	1981	Leeds United	2		
Craggs W					Willington	2		
Craig WD	David	27/12/1921	Liverpool	1994	Marine	4		
Crawley T	Tommy	10/11/1911	Hamilton	1976	Coventry City	2		
Crawshaw C	Cyril	02/03/1916	Barton-on-Irwell	2003	Exeter City	1	1	
Crisp					Sutton United	2		
Croker PHL	Peter	21/12/1921	Kingston		Charlton Athletic	9		
Cromack V	Vic	17/03/1920	Mansfield	1984	Mansfield Town	2		
Crompton J	Jack	18/12/1921	Chorlton		Manchester United	4		
Crook WC	Billy	07/06/1926	Cannock		Wolverhampton Wan.	4	1	
Crooks SD	Sammy	16/01/1908	Bearpark	1981	Derby County	5	3	e
Cross					Lovells Athletic	1		
Cross					Wellington Town	2		
Crossley J	James	29/07/1922	Belfast	2001	Portsmouth	2		
Crowe CA	Charlie	30/10/1924	Walker		Newcastle United	2		
Crowther SG					Bromley	4		
Crozier J	Joe	02/12/1914	Coatbridge	1985	Brentford	8		
Crutchley WR	Ron	20/06/1922	Walsall	1987	Walsall	2		
Cullis S	Stan	25/10/1915	Ellesmere Port	2001	Wolverhampton Wan.	1		e
Cumming DS	Dave	06/05/1910	Aberdeen	1993	Middlesbrough	7		s
Cummings GW	George	05/06/1913	Thornbridge	1987	Aston Villa	8		s
Cumner RH	Horace	31/03/1918	Cwmaman	1999	Arsenal	1	1	w
Cunliffe A	Arthur	05/02/1909	Blackrod	1986	Rochdale	6	1	e
Cunliffe RA	Bobby	27/12/1928	Garswood	2000	Manchester City	1		

George Cummings

Stan Cullis

Name		D.o.B	Place of Birth	Died	Club	Ap.	Gl.	Int
Cunningham L	Laurie	20/10/1921	Consett		Barnsley	5		
Curran F	Frank	31/05/1917	Ryton-on-Tyne	1998	Bristol City	3	2	
Curran PJ	Pat	13/11/1917	Sunderland	2003	Watford	4		
Curry R	Bob	02/11/1918	Gateshead	2001	Gainsborough Trinity	2		
Curtis WN	Norman	10/09/1924	Dinnington		Gainsborough Trinity	2	1	
Cuthbert W	Wes	1913	Morpeth		Grantham	4		
Dachler					Marine	4		
Daniel MVRJ	Mel	26/01/1916	Llanelli	1997	Luton Town	2		
Daniel WR	Ray	02/11/1928	Swansea	1997	Swansea Town	2		w
Daniels HAG	Harry	25/06/1920	Kensington	2002	Queen's Park Rgs.	11	1	
Daniels JF	Jack	06/10/1913	Prestwich	1970	Bradford City	1		
Danskin R	Bob	28/05/1908	Scotswood	1985	Bradford Park Ave.	6		
Darling HL	Len	09/08/1911	Gillingham	1958	Brighton & Hove A.	8		
Davie J	Jock	19/02/1913	Dunfermline	1994	Brighton & Hove A.	8	10	
Davies AMcL	Alec	21/05/1920	Dundonald	1964	Lincoln City	1		
Davies E	Eddie	03/05/1923	Burslem	1995	Port Vale	2		
Davies G	George	04/04/1916	Earlestown	1980	Bury	4	2	
Davies K	Ken	20/09/1923	Doncaster		Wolverhampton Wan.	2	2	
Davies W	William 'Taffy'	22/06/1910	Troedyrhiw	1995	Watford	10	1	
Davis DEC	Derek	19/06/1922	Colwyn Bay	1985	Norwich City	2		
Davis FA	Freddie	1913	Hackney		Walthamstow Avenue	3	4	
Davis R	Ronald				Bristol Rovers	1		
Dawes FW	Fred	02/05/1911	Frimley Green	1989	Crystal Palace	3		
Dawson JR	Reg	04/10/1914	Sheffield	1973	Rotherham United	6	1	
Day A	Albert	07/03/1918	Camberwell	1983	Brighton & Hove A.	1		
Dean S					Kettering Town	2		
Dellow RW	Ron	13/07/1914	Crosby		Carlisle United	4	1	
Denham					Romford	2		
Dennis					Romford	2		
Dennison RS	Bob	06/03/1912	Amble	1996	Northampton Town	3		
Denyer ATF	Bertie	06/12/1924	Swindon		Swindon Town	2		
Derrick AE	Albert	08/09/1908	Newport	1975	Newport County	6	6	
Devlin E	Joe	06/03/1920	Gateshead	1976	Gateshead	6		
Dews G	George	05/06/1921	Ossett	2003	Middlesbrough	7	2	
Dickson					Bath City	1		
Dix R	Richard	17/01/1924	South Shields	1990	Bradford Park Ave.	7	3	
Dix RW	Ronnie	05/09/1912	Bristol	1998	Tottenham Hotspur	2		e
Dixon					Stalybridge Celtic	1		
Dixon S	Stan	28/08/1920	Burnley	1996	Plymouth Argyle	2		
Dobson					North Shields	2		
Dodds E	Jock	07/09/1915	Grangemouth	2007	Blackpool	5	5	
Dodgin W	Bill	17/04/1909	Gateshead	1999	Southampton	4		
Doherty PD	Peter	05/06/1913	Magherafelt	1990	Derby County	10	10	i
Dolding DL	Len	13/12/1922	Nundydroog, India	1954	Chelsea	1		
Dooley GW	George	29/12/1922	Chesterfield	2004	Chesterfield	2	1	
Doran S	Sam	22/12/1912	Bradford		Halifax Town	2		
Dougal C	Neil	07/11/1921	Falkirk		Birmingham City	10	3	s
Dougal J	Jimmy	03/10/1913	Denny	1999	Preston North End	6		s
Douglas D	David				Carlisle United	2	1	
Douglas JS	John	01/12/1917	West Hartlepool	2001	Middlesbrough	3	1	
Downie JD	Johnny	19/07/1925	Lanark		Bradford Park Ave.	7	2	
Downing					Shrewsbury Town	2		
Drinkwater CJ	Charlie	25/06/1914	Willesden	1998	Watford	9		
Driscoll					Newport (IOW)	4		
Driscoll JH	Jack	27/07/1909	Grays	1997	Wellington Town	2		
Driver A	Allenby	29/09/1918	Blackwell, Derbyshire	1997	Sheffield Wed.	4	3	
Drury GB	George	22/01/1914	Hucknall	1972	Arsenal	1		
Duckhouse E	Ted	09/04/1918	Walsall	1978	Birmingham City	10		
Dudgeon A	Andrew	23/12/1913	Newcastle	1993	Gateshead	2		
Dudley FE	Frank	09/05/1925	Southend-on-Sea		Southend United	2		
Dudley RA	Reg	03/02/1915	Hemel Hempstead	1994	Millwall	4		
Duff JH	Joe	01/05/1913	Ashington	1985	Rochdale	5		
Duffy C	Chris	21/10/1918	Methil	1978	Charlton Athletic	10	10	
Duke GE	George	06/09/1920	West Hampnett	1988	Luton Town	2		
Duncan D	Dally	14/10/1909	Aberdeen	1990	Derby County	9		s
Dunkley GA	George	19/07/1924	Ipswich	2006	Millwall	4		
Dunkley MEF	Maurice	19/02/1914	Kettering	1989	Manchester City	3	1	
Dunn J	Jimmy	25/11/1923	Edinburgh		Wolverhampton Wan.	4	1	

Jock Dodds

Peter Doherty

Johnny Downie

Chris Duffy

66

Name		D.o.B	Place of Birth	Died	Club	Ap.	Gl.	Int
Dunn WC	Billy	25/03/1920	Hebburn	1982	Darlington	4		
Dunnigan JY	John	30/11/1920	Dalmuir		Barrow	5	1	
Duns L	Len	28/09/1916	Newcastle	1989	Sunderland	4	2	
Dunsmore TH	Tom		Motherwell		Luton Town	2		
Durham					Trowbridge Town	2		
Durrant FH	Fred	19/06/1921	Dover		Brentford	6	4	
Duthoit J	Jack	04/11/1918	Leeds	2001	Leeds United	2		
Dyer JA	Alec	13/04/1913	Crewe	1984	Plymouth Argyle	1		
Dykes					Stalybridge Celtic	1		
Eades C	Colin				Doncaster Rovers	1		
Eardley					Bath City	1		
Eaton					Chelmsford City	2		
Ebdon RG	Dick 'Digger'	03/05/1913	Ottery St Mary	1987	Exeter City	4	1	
Eddolls JD	John	19/08/1919	Bristol	1994	Bristol City	4		
Edelston M	Maurice	27/04/1918	Hull	1976	Reading	2	1	
Edwards					Cheltenham Town	2	1	
Edwards					Marine	4		
Edwards DS	Dai	11/09/1916	Bargoed	1990	Ipswich Town	3		
Edwards G	George	02/12/1920	Treherbert		Birmingham City	10		w
Edwards GR	George	01/04/1918	Great Yarmouth	1993	Aston Villa	8	4	
Edwards W	Wyndham				Yeovil & Petters U	2		
Egerton					Stalybridge Celtic	2		
Eggleston T	Tommy	21/02/1920	Consett	2004	Derby County	1		
Elderfield					Slough United	2		
Ellary					Netherfield (Kendal)	2		
Ellerington W	Bill	30/06/1923	Southampton		Southampton	2	1	e
Elliott CS	Charlie	24/04/1912	Bolsover	2004	Coventry City	2		
Elliott T	Thomas				Everton	2	1	
Elliott WB	Billy	06/08/1919	Harrington	1966	West Bromwich Alb.	4		
Ellis					Bath City	1		
Emery AJ	Tony	04/11/1927	Lincoln	2005	Lincoln City	4		
Emery DKJ	Don	11/06/1920	Cardiff	1993	Swindon Town	2	1	
Emmanuel TD	Tom	01/08/1915	Treboeth	1997	Southampton	2		
Evans HA	Harry	17/04/1919	Lambeth	1962	Southampton	4		
Everett HP	Harold	09/06/1922	Worksop	2000	Mansfield Town	6		
Fagan	Willie	20/02/1917	Inveresk	1992	Liverpool	4	3	
Fairbrother J	Jack	16/08/1917	Burton-on-Trent	1999	Preston North End	6		
Fairhurst WG	Bill	23/05/1910	St Helens	1984	Bristol City	1		
Fairman					Yorkshire Amateur	2		
Fairs JD					Bishop Auckland	4		
Farley AJ	Alec	11/05/1925	Finchley		Clapton Orient	2		
Farley HB	Brian	01/01/1927	Craven Arms		Chelmsford City	2		
Farr TF	Chick	19/02/1914	Bathgate	1980	Bradford Park Ave.	8		
Farrar LT					Bishop Auckland	2		
Farrell A	Arthur	01/11/1920	Huddersfield	2000	Bradford Park Ave.	6	1	
Farrington					Bath City	4	3	
Farrow DA	Des	11/02/1926	Peterborough		Queen's Park Rgs.	9		
Farrow GH	George	04/10/1913	Whitburn	1980	Blackpool	5		
Fell LJ	Les	16/12/1920	Leyton		Charlton Athletic	10	3	
Felton RFF	Robert	12/08/1918	Gateshead	1982	Port Vale	5		
Fenney S	Stan	21/06/1923	Barry	2003	Barrow	6		
Fenton					Marine	4		
Fenton BRV	Benny	28/10/1918	West Ham	2000	Millwall	2		
Fenton EBA	Ted	07/11/1914	Forest Gate	1992	West Ham United	4		
Fenton M	Micky	30/10/1913	Stockton	2003	Middlesbrough	7	7	e
Ferguson					Carlisle United	1		
Ferguson ASB	Alex	05/08/1903	Lochore	1974	Newport County	6		
Ferguson C	Charlie	22/11/1910	Dunfermline	1995	North Shields	2		
Ferguson R	Bob	25/07/1917	Grangetown	2006	York City	8		
Ferrier HR	Harry	20/05/1920	Ratho	2002	Barnsley	1		
Ferrier RJ	Ron	26/04/1914	Cleethorpes	1991	Oldham Athletic	2	1	
Fielding AW	Wally	26/11/1919	Edmonton		Everton	2		
Finch LC	Lester	26/08/1909	Hadley		Barnet	2	1	
Finney F	Fred	10/03/1924	Prescot		Liverpool	2		
Fisher C					Lovells Athletic	1		
Fisher CK	Charlie	04/01/1915	Pontypridd	1986	Swansea Town	2		
Fisher F	Freddie	28/11/1924	Hetton-le-Hole	2004	Reading	2		
Fisher GS	George	19/06/1925	Bermondsey		Millwall	3		

Micky Fenton

Neil Franklin

Name		D.o.B	Place of Birth	Died	Club	Ap.	Gl.	Int
Fisher S	Stan	29/09/1924	Barnsley	2003	Barnsley	1		
Fitzgerald AM	Alf	25/01/1911	Conisbrough	1981	Aldershot	8	3	
Flack WLW	Len	01/06/1916	Cambridge	1995	Norwich City	2		
Flatley AA	Albert	05/09/1919	Bradford	1987	Bradford Park Ave.	1		
Fletcher CA	Charlie	28/10/1905	Homerton	1980	Ipswich Town	3	1	
Fletcher J					Wisbech Town	2		
Flewin R	Reg	28/11/1920	Portsmouth		Portsmouth	2		
Flower T	Tom	1915	Liverpool	1962	Notts County	1		
Forbes AR	Alex	21/01/1925	Dundee		Sheffield United	3		s
Forbes GP	George	21/07/1914	Dukinfield	1964	Blackburn Rovers	1		
Ford FGL	Fred	10/02/1916	Dartford	1981	Millwall	2		
Ford T	Trevor	01/10/1923	Swansea	2003	Swansea Town	2	3	
Foreman AG	George	01/03/1914	Walthamstow	1969	West Ham United	3	1	
Foreman D	Denny				Chelmsford City	2	1	
Foss SLR	Dick	28/11/1912	Barking	1995	Chelsea	5		
Foster					Marine	4		
Foulkes RE	Reg	23/02/1923	Shrewsbury		Walsall	2		
Fowler T	Tommy	16/12/1924	Prescot		Northampton Town	6	1	
Fox					Slough United	2		
Fox					Yorkshire Amateur	1		
Fox GR	Geoff	19/01/1925	Bristol	1994	Ipswich Town	2		
Foxcroft G	George				Burnley	1		
Foxton JD	Jack	17/06/1921	Salford		Portsmouth	1		
Frame WL	Billy	07/05/1912	Carluke	1992	Leicester City	1		
Francis					Sutton United	2		
Francis CT	Cliff	28/12/1915	Merthyr Tydfil	1961	Swindon Town	2	1	
Francis TG	Tom	30/10/1920	Bermondsey	1996	Cheltenham Town	2		
Franklin C	Neil	24/01/1922	Stoke-on-Trent	1996	Stoke City	8		e
Freeman HG	Harry	04/11/1918	Worcester	1997	Fulham	2		
Froggatt J	Jack	17/11/1922	Sheffield	1993	Portsmouth	1		e
Froggatt R	Redfern	23/08/1924	Sheffield	2003	Sheffield Wed.	6	3	e
Froom R	Ray		London		Clapton Orient	2		
Fryatt FE					Romford	2		
Furness WI	Billy	08/06/1909	New Washington	1980	Norwich City	1		e
Furniss F	Fred	10/07/1922	Sheffield		Sheffield United	3		
Gadsby KJ	Ken	03/07/1916	Chesterfield	2003	Leeds United	2		
Gage					Yorkshire Amateur	2		
Gager HE	Horace	25/01/1917	West Ham	1984	Luton Town	1		
Gale T	Tommy	04/11/1920	Washington	1975	Sheffield Wed.	4		
Gallacher P	Pat	09/01/1913	Glasgow	1983	Bournemouth	1		
Gallagher J	Jimmy	02/09/1911	Bury	1972	Exeter City	1	1	
Galley T	Tom	04/08/1915	Hednesford	1999	Wolverhampton Wan.	2	4	e
Gallimore L	Len	14/09/1912	Northwich	1978	Watford	5		
Gannoe					Wellington Town	2		
Gardiner D	Doug	29/03/1917	Douglas		Luton Town	1		
Gardiner J	John	05/11/1914	Chester-le-Street	1997	Southend United	2		
Gardiner R	Bobby	1913	Dundee	1993	Bristol Rovers	3		
Gardner T	Tommy	28/05/1910	Huyton	1970	Wrexham	2		e
Geldard A	Albert	11/04/1914	Bradford	1989	Bolton Wanderers	8		e
Gemmell J	Jimmy	17/11/1911	Sunderland	1992	Southport	2		
Gibbons AH	Jackie	10/04/1914	Fulham		Bradford Park Ave.	8	8	
Gibson CH	Colin	16/09/1923	Normanby	1992	Cardiff City	1		
Gilbert					Grantham	2		
Gilder R					Grantham	2		
Gillespie IC	Ian	06/05/1913	Plymouth	1988	Crystal Palace	1		
Gillespie P	Pat	22/09/1922	Bellshill		Watford	9		
Glaister G	George	18/05/1918	Bywell		Blackburn Rovers	2		
Glazzard J	Jimmy	23/04/1923	Normanton	1996	Huddersfield Town	2		
Gleave C	Colin	06/04/1919	Stockport	2004	Stockport County	2		
Gledhill					Walthamstow Avenue	2		
Gledhill S	Sammy	07/07/1913	Castleford	1994	York City	8	1	
Gledson					North Shields	2		
Glidden GS	Gilbert	15/12/1915	Sunderland	1988	Reading	2		
Goffin WC	Billy	12/02/1920	Tamworth	1987	Aston Villa	7	5	
Goodfellow DO	Derwick	26/06/1914	Shilbottle	2001	Sheffield Wed.	6		
Goodfellow S	Syd	06/07/1915	Wolstanton		Chesterfield	2		
Goodwin L	Leslie				Oldham Athletic	1		
Goodyear GW	George	05/07/1916	Luton	2001	Luton Town	2		

Redfern Froggatt

Len Goulden

Name		D.o.B	Place of Birth	Died	Club	Ap.	Gl	Int
Gordon J	Jimmy	23/10/1915	Fauldhouse	1996	Middlesbrough	6	1	
Gordon L	Lewis				Halifax Town	2	1	
Gordon RB	Robert	05/09/1923	Ormiston	2001	Millwall	4		
Gore FL	Les	21/01/1914	Coventry	1991	Clapton Orient	2	1	
Goring H	Peter	02/01/1927	Bishop's Cleeve	1994	Cheltenham Town	2	1	
Gorman AM	Archie	10/04/1909	Lochore	1992	Plymouth Argyle	2		
Gorman JJ	Jimmy	03/03/1910	Liverpool	1991	Hartlepool United	2		
Gorman WC	Bill	13/07/1911	Sligo	1978	Brentford	8		r
Gotts JA	Jim	17/01/1917	Seaton Delaval	1998	Brentford	2		
Goulden LA	Len	09/07/1912	Hackney	1995	Chelsea	3	1	e
Graham					Willington	2		
Graham DR	Dick	06/05/1922	Corby		Crystal Palace	3		
Graham W	Billy	03/10/1914	Hetton-le-Hole	1996	Norwich City	1	1	
Grainger D	Dennis	05/03/1920	Royston, West Yorks	1986	Leeds United	2	1	
Granville NT	Trevor	25/11/1919	Newport	1992	Newport County	2	1	
Gray R	Ron	25/06/1920	North Shields	2002	Watford	9	4	
Green A					Barnet	2		
Green					Walthamstow Avenue	3	3	
Green RE	Bob		Tewkesbury		Cheltenham Town	2		
Green A	Alan				Blackburn Rovers	2		
Green GF	George	21/12/1914	Northowram	1995	Huddersfield Town	2		
Green H	Horace	23/04/1918	Barnsley	2000	Halifax Town	2		
Green S	Stan		Newcastle		York City	1		
Greenhalgh N	Norman	10/08/1916	Bolton	1995	Everton	2		
Greenwood R	Ron	11/11/1921	Worsthorne	2006	Bradford Park Ave.	8		
Gregory					Grantham	4		
Gregory CF	Fred	24/10/1911	Doncaster	1985	Crystal Palace	3		
Gregory F	Fred				Doncaster Rovers	2		
Gregory RJ	Ralph				Port Vale	2	2	
Gregson A	Arthur				Millwall	2		
Griffiths G	George	23/06/1924	Earlestown	2004	Bury	4		
Griffiths HS	Harry	17/11/1912	Liverpool	1981	Port Vale	6		
Griffiths W	Bill	13/01/1921	Earlestown	1964	Bury	4		
Grover					Romford	2		
Groves RD	Bunny				Walthamstow Avenue	4	6	
Grummett J	Jimmy	03/07/1918	Birdwell	1996	Lincoln City	4		
Guthrie JE	Jimmy	13/06/1913	Luncarty	1981	Portsmouth	2		
Guy I	Ivor	27/02/1926	Chipping Sodbury	1986	Bristol City	8		
Hacking J	Jack	24/08/1925	Blackpool		Accrington Stanley	6		
Haddock H	Harry	26/07/1925	Glasgow	1998	Exeter City	1		s
Hadfield AT					Bishop Auckland	4		
Haigh G	Gordon	18/08/1921	Barnsley		Burnley	2		
Hair G	George	28/04/1925	Ryton-on-Tyne	1994	Newcastle United	2	1	
Hale					Stockton	2		
Hall					Newport (IOW)	4		
Hall AEB	Albert	03/09/1918	Cadoxton	1998	Tottenham Hotspur	2	1	
Hall AF	Alec	17/09/1909	Grimsby	1992	Grimsby Town	1		
Hall AG	Almer	12/11/1912	Hove	1994	West Ham United	4	3	
Hall L	Lance	23/01/1915	Darlington	1985	Barrow	6		
Hall SA	Stan	18/02/1917	Southgate	1999	Clapton Orient	2		
Hallard W	Billy	28/08/1913	St Helens	1980	Bradford Park Ave.	7	1	
Halliwell					South Liverpool	2		
Halton RL	Reg	11/07/1916	Leek	1988	Bury	4		
Hamilton R					Yeovil & Petters U	2	2	
Hamilton RM	Bobby	25/04/1924	Edinburgh	1999	Chester	2		
Hamilton S	Sydney	01/04/1912	Penrith		Carlisle United	4	3	
Hamilton W	Willie	01/09/1918	Hamilton		Preston North End	6		
Hamlett TL	Lol	24/01/1917	Stoke-on-Trent	1986	Bolton Wanderers	9		
Hancocks J	Johnny	30/04/1919	Oakengates	1994	Walsall	2		e
Hanley					Wisbech Town	2		
Hanlon JJ	Johnny	12/10/1917	Manchester	2002	Manchester United	4	1	
Hansford					Trowbridge Town	2		
Hanson					Marine	4		
Hanson F	Fred	23/05/1915	Sheffield	1967	Rotherham United	8		
Hanson S	Stan	27/12/1915	Bootle	1987	Bolton Wanderers	9		
Hardwick GFM	George	02/02/1920	Saltburn	2004	Middlesbrough	7	2	e
Hardwick K	Ken	27/01/1924	West Auckland	1983	Doncaster Rovers	2		
Hardwicke					Lovells Athletic	5	3	

Ron Greeenwood

Stan Hanson

George Hardwick

Name		D.o.B	Place of Birth	Died	Club	Ap.	Gl.	Int
Hardy JH	Jack	15/06/1910	Chesterfield	1978	Lincoln City	4		
Hargreaves J	Jackie	01/05/1915	Rotherham	1978	Bristol City	5	1	
Hargreaves JA	Joe	30/10/1915	Accrington	1992	Rochdale	6	6	
Hargreaves WO	Wilf	15/12/1921	Rawmarsh	1993	Rotherham United	1		
Harkin J	Jim	08/08/1913	Brinsworth	1988	Mansfield Town	3	1	
Harley J	Jim	02/02/1917	Methil	1989	Liverpool	3		
Harper					Chorley	2		
Harries					Romford	2		
Harris					Yeovil & Petters U	1		
Harris F	Fred	02/07/1912	Sparkbrook	1998	Birmingham City	10		
Harris J	John	30/06/1917	Glasgow	1988	Chelsea	6		
Harris PP	Peter	19/12/1925	Portsmouth	2003	Portsmouth	2		e
Harris TK	Kevin	20/02/1918	Dublin	1984	Notts County	4		
Harris WT	Tommy	30/06/1913	Aberbargoed	1997	Watford	1		
Harrison					Chorley	2		
Harrison R	Ron	15/05/1923	Hebburn	2004	Darlington	4	4	
Harrison RF	Reg	22/05/1923	Derby		Derby County	6	1	
Harston JC	Jack	07/10/1920	Barnsley		Barnsley	2		
Hart JL	Les	28/02/1917	Ashton-in-Makerfield	1996	Bury	4		
Hart JP	Johnny	08/06/1928	Golborne		Manchester City	1	1	
Hart WR	Bill	01/04/1923	North Shields	1990	Chesterfield	2		
Hartle					Stalybridge Celtic	2		
Hartley A					Chorley	2		
Hartley T					Chorley	2		
Harvey J	Joe				Southend United	2		
Harvey J	Joe	11/06/1918	Edlington	1989	Newcastle United	2		
Harvey W	Bill	08/10/1920	Grimsby	2002	Grimsby Town	1		
Hastie					Chorley	1		
Hastie A	Archibald		Shotts		Bradford City	2		
Hastings AC	Alex	17/03/1912	Falkirk	1988	Sunderland	4	2	s
Hawkins					Cheltenham Town	2		
Hawkins EW					Barnet	2	1	
Hawkins GH	Harry	24/11/1915	Middlesbrough	1992	Southport	1		
Haworth					Chorley	2		
Haycock FJ	Freddie	19/04/1912	Liverpool	1989	Wrexham	2	1	
Hays CJ	Jack	12/12/1918	Ashington	1983	Burnley	2		
Hayton E	Eric	14/01/1922	Carlisle		Carlisle United	1		
Hayward A	Aubrey				Wrexham	4	2	
Hayward EJ	Eric				Crewe Alexandra	2	1	
Head BJ	Bert	08/06/1916	Midsomer Norton	2002	Torquay United	1		
Healey					South Liverpool	2		
Hearne					North Shields	2		
Heaselgrave SE	Sammy	01/10/1916	Smethwick	1975	Northampton Town	1		
Heath WJ	Bill	26/06/1920	Stepney	1994	Queen's Park Rgs.	3		
Heathcote W	Wilf	29/06/1911	Hemsworth	1991	Queen's Park Rgs.	3	1	
Hellier WJ	Bill		Tonypandy		Torquay United	1		
Henderson					Netherfield (Kendal)	2		
Henley LD	Les	26/09/1922	Lambeth	1996	Arsenal	1		
Henry GR	Gerry	05/10/1920	Hemsworth	1979	Leeds United	2	1	
Hepworth R	Ronnie	25/01/1919	Barnsley	2006	Bradford Park Ave.	8		
Herbert F	Frank	29/06/1916	Stocksbridge	1972	Bury	2		
Herd A	Alex	08/11/1911	Bowhill	1982	Manchester City	3	4	
Herod DJ	Dennis	27/10/1923	Stoke-on-Trent		Stoke City	8		
Heward H	Harold				Yeovil & Petters U	2		
Hewitt					Slough United	2		
Hewitt					Stockton	2		
Hewitt H	Harold	24/06/1919	Chesterfield		Mansfield Town	3		
Hewitt L	Len	20/03/1920	Wrexham	1979	Wrexham	4	1	
Heydon C	Cecil	24/05/1919	Birkenhead		Doncaster Rovers	2		
Hickson					Netherfield (Kendal)	2		
Hill FR	Frank	21/05/1906	Forfar	1993	Crewe Alexandra	2		s
Hindle T	Tom	22/02/1921	Keighley		Leeds United	2		
Hindley FC	Frank	02/11/1915	Worksop	2003	Brighton & Hove A.	3	1	
Hindmarsh E	Eddie	07/09/1922	Sunderland	1997	Carlisle United	4		
Hinshelwood WAA	Wally	29/10/1929	Battersea		Sutton United	2	1	
Hinsley G	George	19/07/1914	Sheffield	1989	Bradford City	2		
Hobbis HHF	Harold	09/03/1913	Dartford	1991	Charlton Athletic	2		e
Hobbs RG	Ronnie	23/08/1921	Aldershot	2006	Aldershot	8	2	

Fred Harris

Wally Hinshelwood

Name		D.o.B	Place of Birth	Died	Club	Ap.	Gl.	Int
Hobson A	Alf	09/09/1913	Leamside	2004	Liverpool	1		
Hobson L	Leonard				Chesterfield	2		
Hockey E	Edward				Southend United	1		
Hodge J	Jack		Plymouth		Plymouth Argyle	2		
Hodgetts F	Frank	30/09/1924	Dudley		West Bromwich Alb.	1		
Hodgson JP	John	10/05/1922	Dawdon	1973	Leeds United	2		
Hodgson JV	Jack	30/09/1913	Seaham Harbour	1970	Grimsby Town	2		
Hodgson S	Sam	21/01/1919	Seaham Harbour	2000	Grimsby Town	2		
Hogg FW	Fred	24/04/1918	Bishop Auckland		Mansfield Town	4	1	
Hold O	Oscar	19/10/1918	Carlton, West Yorks	2005	Aldershot	6	2	
Holdcroft GH	Harry	23/01/1909	Burslem	1983	Barnsley	6		e
Holder					Cheltenham Town	2		
Holder R	Bob				Bromley	4		
Hole N					Bishop Auckland	4		
Holland					Lovells Athletic	3	3	
Holland J	John				Hartlepool United	1	1	
Holley T	Tom	15/11/1913	Sunderland	1992	Leeds United	1		
Hollyman KC	Ken	18/11/1922	Cardiff		Cardiff City	2		
Holmes					Newport (IOW)	4		
Hooper HR	Harry	16/12/1910	Burnley	1970	Sheffield United	3		
Hooper M	Mark	14/07/1901	Darlington	1974	Rotherham United	4		
Hopkins IM	Dai	11/10/1910	Merthyr Tydfil	1994	Brentford	8	3	w
Hopley D	Dennard				Wellington Town	2		
Hornby EV	Eric	31/03/1923	Birkenhead		Tranmere Rovers	4		
Horrocks					Chorley	2		
Horton JC	Jimmy	1909	Rotherham		Aldershot	8	1	
Horton L	Les	12/07/1921	Salford		Oldham Athletic	4		
Houldsworth FC	Freddie	29/05/1911	Henley-on-Thames	1994	Reading	1		
Housam A	Arthur	01/10/1917	Sunderland	1975	Sunderland	6	1	
Howarth H	Harold	25/11/1908	Little Hulton	1973	Southport	2		
Howdon S	Steve	01/02/1922	Prudhoe	1998	Gateshead	5	1	
Howe D	Don	26/11/1917	Outwood	1978	Bolton Wanderers	7		
Howe G	George	10/01/1924	Wakefield	1971	Huddersfield Town	1		
Howe HA	Bert	01/04/1916	Rugby	1972	Leicester City	2		
Howe JR	Jack	07/10/1915	West Hartlepool	1987	Derby County	2		e
Hubbard J	Jack	24/03/1925	Wath-on-Dearne	2002	Notts County	4	1	
Hubbick HE	Harry	12/11/1910	Jarrow	1992	Bolton Wanderers	9		
Hudgell AJ	Arthur	28/12/1920	Hackney	2000	Crystal Palace	3		
Hudson CA	Charlie	03/04/1920	Bytham		Accrington Stanley	4	3	
Hughes L	Laurie	02/03/1924	Waterloo, Lancashire		Liverpool	3		e
Hughes S	Steve	1913	Aigburth		Shrewsbury Town	4		
Hughes TG	Gwyn	07/05/1922	Blaenau Ffestiniog	1999	Northampton Town	6	3	
Hughes WA	Archie	02/02/1919	Colwyn Bay	1992	Tottenham Hotspur	2		w
Hull WJ	William				Barrow	1	1	
Humble D	Dougie	16/2/1920	Wolsingham	1989	Bishop Auckland	4		
Humphreys JV	John	13/01/1920	Llandudno	1954	Everton	2		w
Humphreys RH	Ron	04/04/1925	Tonypandy		Southend United	1		
Hunt					Yeovil & Petters U	2		
Hunt GS	George	22/02/1910	Barnsley	1996	Bolton Wanderers	3	2	e
Hurst					Cheltenham Town	2		
Hurst GJ	Jack	27/10/1914	Lever Bridge	2002	Bolton Wanderers	8		
Hutchinson JA	Jimmy	28/12/1915	Sheffield	1997	Sheffield United	1		
Hutchinson KG	Keith	07/09/1920	South Shields	1986	Darlington	4		
Hutton					Willington	2		
Hutton TO	Tom	10/09/1922	Gateshead	2004	Accrington Stanley	4		
Hyde EW	Eric				Stockport County	2	1	
Hydes A	Arthur	24/11/1910	Barnsley	1990	Newport County	1	2	
Insole DJ	Doug	18/04/1926	Clapton		Walthamstow Avenue	4	1	
Isaac J	Jimmy	23/10/1916	Cramlington	1993	Bradford City	2		
Isaacs FC	Frederick				Luton Town	1		
Isherwood D	Dennis	09/01/1924	Northwich	1974	Wrexham	1		
Iverson RTJ	Bob	17/10/1910	Folkestone	1953	Aston Villa	8	2	
Jackson					Marine	4		
Jackson E	Ernest	11/06/1914	Sheffield	1996	Sheffield United	2		
Jackson G	George	14/01/1911	Liverpool	2002	Everton	2		
Jackson H	Harry	30/12/1918	Blackburn	1984	Burnley	2	1	
Jackson H	Harold	20/07/1917	Halifax	1996	Halifax Town	2		
Jackson R	Ron	15/10/1919	Crook	1980	Wrexham	6		

Frank Hodgetts

Tom Holley

Name		D.o.B	Place of Birth	Died	Club	Ap.	Gl.	Int
Jackson RG	Bob	12/05/1915	Cornsay	1991	Southend United	2		
Jales RA	Dick	03/04/1922	Chiswick		Bradford City	1		
James JS	Stan	12/09/1923	South Shields	2003	Bradford Park Ave.	1		
					North Shields	2		
Jamieson					Hartlepool United	2		
Jarrie F	Fred	02/08/1922	Hartlepool	2004	Walsall	1		
Jarvis L	Leonard				Queen's Park Rgs.	10		
Jefferson A	Arthur	14/12/1916	Goldthorpe	1997	Lovells Athletic	6		
Jennings					Birmingham City	10		
Jennings DB	Dennis	20/07/1910	Habberley	1996	Port Vale	6		
Jepson A	Arthur	12/07/1915	Selston	1997	Watford	3	1	e
Jezzard BAG	Bedford	19/10/1927	Clerkenwell	2005	Millwall	2	2	
Jinks JT	Jimmy	19/08/1916	Camberwell	1981	Bath City	3		
Johnson					North Shields	2		
Johnson					Grimsby Town	1		
Johnson J	Jim	26/03/1923	Stockton	1987	Stockport County	2		
Johnson J	Johnny	11/12/1921	Hazel Grove	2003	Burnley	2		
Johnson REO	Bob	25/10/1911	Fencehouses	1982	Gateshead	6		
Johnson T	Tom 'Tucker'	21/09/1921	Gateshead	1999	Norwich City	2		
Johnson VR	Ralph	15/04/1922	Hethersett		Charlton Athletic	10		
Johnson WH	Bert	04/06/1916	Stockton		Nottingham Forest	3		
Johnston TD	Tom	30/12/1918	Coldstream	1994	Marine	1		
Joliffe					Shrewsbury Town	3	1	
Jones					Rochdale	2		
Jones A	Arthur	23/04/1920	Harpurhey	2001	Southend United	2		
Jones C	Charlie	20/11/1911	Penmaen		Wrexham	6	1	
Jones C	Cyril	17/07/1920	Ponciau	1995	Birmingham City	10	5	w
Jones CW	Charlie	29/04/1914	Pentre Broughton	1986	Bury	4	2	
Jones D	David	09/04/1914	Hodthorpe	1998	Leicester City	1		w
Jones DO	Dai	28/10/1910	Cardiff	1971	Brentford	4		
Jones EN	Eric	05/02/1915	Stirchley	1985	Norwich City	2		
Jones ES	Sid	10/10/1921	Wrexham	1981	South Liverpool	2		
Jones G					Sheffield United	4	1	
Jones GH	George	27/11/1918	Sheffield	1995	Southport	2		
Jones J	Jimmy	29/02/1920	Orrell Park		Sunderland	6		
Jones JE	Jack	03/07/1913	Bromborough	1995	Arsenal	1		w
Jones LJ	Les	01/07/1911	Aberdare	1981	Wrexham	1		
Jones R	Ronnie	1914	Mold		Blackpool	1		i
Jones S	Sammy	11/06/1911	Lurgan	1993	Tranmere Rovers	4		
Jones TB	Benny	23/03/1920	Frodsham	1972	Watford	5		w
Jones TJ	Tommy	06/12/1909	Tonypandy		Grimsby Town	2		
Jones TW	Tommy	23/03/1907	Oakengates	1980	Swansea Town	2		
Jones WEA	Ernie	12/11/1920	Swansea	2002	Barnet	2		
Jordan AJ					Doncaster Rovers	2		
Jordan C	Clarrie	20/06/1922	South Kirkby	1992	Exeter City	3		
Jordan W	William		Southport		Torquay United	2		
Joslin PJ	Phil	01/09/1916	Kingsteignton	1981	Arsenal	2		e
Joy B	Bernard	29/10/1911	Fulham	1984	Bradford City	2		
Joyce E	Eric	03/07/1924	Durham	1977	Liverpool	1		
Kaye GH	Harry	19/04/1919	Liverpool	1992	Rotherham United	7	2	
Kearney P	Patrick				Accrington Stanley	6	3	
Keeley W	Walter	01/04/1921	Manchester	1995	Torquay United	2		
Keeton A	Bob	15/01/1918	Chesterfield	1996	Hartlepool United	1		
Keeys F	Fred				Walsall	2		
Kelly FC	Fred	11/02/1921	Wednesbury	2006	Blackpool	1		s
Kelly HT	Hugh	23/07/1923	Valleyfield		Barnsley	6	1	s
Kelly JC	Johnny	21/02/1921	Paisley	2001	Wolverhampton Wan.	1		
Kelly LJ	Laurie	28/04/1925	Wolverhampton	1972	Crewe Alexandra	2		
Kelly MJ	Mike				Darlington	4		
Kelly TW	Tom	22/11/1919	Darlington	1970	Swindon Town	2		
Kelso J	Jimmy	08/12/1910	Cardross	1987	Torquay United	2		
Kernick DHJ	Dudley	29/08/1921	Camelford		Aston Villa	2		
Kerr AW	Albert	11/08/1917	Lanchester	1979	Chesterfield	2		
Kidd WE	Billy	31/01/1907	Pegswood	1978	Yorkshire Amateur	1		
Kilkenny JC					Marine	1		
King					Wolverhampton Wan.	4	1	
King FAR	Bobby	19/09/1919	Northampton	2003	Newcastle United	2		
King R	Ray	15/08/1924	Amble		Birmingham City	2		
King SH	Syd	1914	Bordesley Green					

Arthur Jefferson

Charlie Wilson Jones

Tom Johnston

Name		D.o.B	Place of Birth	Died	Club	Ap.	Gl.	Int
Kingdon WIG	Billy	25/06/1905	Worcester	1977	Yeovil & Petters U	2		
Kinsell TH	Harry	31/05/1921	Cannock	2000	West Bromwich Alb.	4		
Kippax FP	Peter	17/07/1922	Burnley	1987	Burnley	2	1	
Kirby A	Alan	19/12/1926	Barrow	2003	Notts County	3		
Kirkpatrick J	John	03/03/1919	Annan		Carlisle United	3		
Kirton J	Jock	04/03/1916	Aberdeen	1996	Stoke City	7		
Kitchen					Yorkshire Amateur	2		
Knight					Newport (IOW)	4		
Knott H	Bert	05/12/1914	Goole	1986	Bradford Park Ave.	4		
Kurz FJ	Fred	03/09/1918	Grimsby	1978	Crystal Palace	3		
Laidman F	Fred	20/06/1913	Durham	1987	Stockton	2		
Lake					Wisbech Town	1		
Lake LE	Les	29/01/1923	Luton	1976	Luton Town	1		
Laking GE	George	17/03/1913	Harthill, Yorkshire	1997	Middlesbrough	4		
Lamb HE	Harry	03/06/1925	Bebington	1982	Tranmere Rovers	1		
Lambden VD	Vic	24/10/1925	Bristol	1996	Bristol Rovers	4		
Lambert R	Ray	18/07/1922	Bagillt		Liverpool	4		w
Lamprill					Walthamstow Avenue	1		
Lancaster W	William				Gateshead	1		
Langley WE	Bill		Wolverhampton		Yeovil & Petters U	2		
Lanham					Newport (IOW)	2		
Latham H	Harry	09/01/1921	Sheffield	1983	Sheffield United	4		
Laurence O	Oswald				Stockport County	1		
Lawton					Willington	2		
Lawton T	Tommy	06/10/1919	Bolton	1996	Chelsea	6	1	e
Lawton W	Bill	04/06/1920	Ashton-under-Lyne		Oldham Athletic	4	1	
Layton WH	Bill	13/01/1915	Shirley	1984	Reading	2	1	
Lea					Wellington Town	1		
Leadbitter					South Liverpool	1		
Lee EG	Eric	18/10/1922	Chester		Chester	2		
Lee GT	George	04/06/1919	York	1991	York City	1	1	
Leighton WA	Billy	08/12/1914	Walker	1981	Southend United	2		
Leonard H	Harry	19/05/1924	Jarrow	2006	Bradford Park Ave.	1		
Lester LJ	Danny	17/11/1923	Cardiff	1991	Cardiff City	1		
Leuty LH	Leon	23/10/1920	Meole Brace	1955	Derby County	10		
Lewis DG	Dennis	21/04/1925	Treherbert	1996	Torquay United	1		
Lewis G	Geoffrey		Abertillery		Exeter City	2		
Lewis G	Glyn	03/07/1921	Abertillery	1992	Crystal Palace	3		
Lewis J	Jack	26/08/1919	Walsall	2002	Crystal Palace	3		
Lewis JW	Jim	21/12/1905	Hackney		Walthamstow Avenue	4		
Lewis L					Hartlepool United	1		
Lewis RJ	Reg	07/03/1920	Bilston	1997	Arsenal	1		
Lewis TG	George	20/10/1913	Troedyrhiwfuwch	1981	Watford	8	3	
Lewis WA	Bill	23/11/1921	Silvertown	1998	Blackpool	5		
Liddell JGH	John	17/04/1915	Edinburgh	1986	Clapton Orient	2		
Liddell WB	Billy	10/01/1922	Townhill	2001	Liverpool	2	1	s
Liddle DHS	Danny	19/02/1912	Bo'ness	1982	Leicester City	1		s
Linnell					Kettering Town	2		
Lisle					Cheltenham Town	2		
Little JA	Jackie	17/05/1912	Gateshead		Ipswich Town	4	2	
Livesey J	Jack	08/03/1924	Preston	1988	Preston North End	5	2	
Lloyd C	Cliff	27/12/1913	Brymbo	1973	Wrexham	4	2	
Lloyd C	Cliff	14/11/1916	Frodsham	2000	Fulham	2		
Lloyd HD	Harold	12/03/1920	Flint	1984	Tranmere Rovers	3		
Lloyd WL	Billy	22/05/1915	Rhondda	1978	Swindon Town	2		
Lockie AJ	Alex	11/04/1911	South Shields		Sunderland	6		
Lofthouse N	Nat	27/08/1925	Bolton		Bolton Wanderers	6	2	e
Logan JW	John	16/08/1912	Horden	1980	Barnsley	6		
Logie JT	Jimmy	23/11/1919	Edinburgh	1984	Arsenal	1		s
Long C	Clifford				Bristol Rovers	1		
Longdon CW	Charlie	06/05/1917	Mansfield	1986	Brighton & Hove A.	9	2	
Longstaff JW					Bishop Auckland	4		
Loughran JL	Joe	12/08/1915	Consett	1994	Burnley	2		
Lovesey WS	William	08/12/1922	Marylebone	1994	Swindon Town	2		
Low NH	Norman	23/03/1914	Aberdeen	1994	Newport County	5		
Lowe E	Eddie	11/07/1925	Halesowen		Aston Villa	8		e
Lowery H	Harry	26/02/1918	Moor Row	2004	Northampton Town	6		
Lucas GR	Dickie		London		Clapton Orient	1		

Tommy Lawton

Leon Leuty

Billy Liddell

Name		D.o.B	Place of Birth	Died	Club	Ap.	Gl.	Int
Lucas WH	Billy	15/01/1918	Newport	1998	Swindon Town	1		w
Ludford GA	George	22/03/1915	Barnet	2001	Tottenham Hotspur	2		
Lyman CC	Colin	09/03/1914	Northampton	1986	Tottenham Hotspur	2		
Lyon					Yorkshire Amateur	2	1	
Lyons AE	Eddie	20/05/1920	Rochdale	1996	Bury	1		
Lythgoe AP	Arnold	07/03/1922	Bolton		Accrington Stanley	6		
McAloon GP	Gerry	13/09/1916	Gorbals	1987	Brentford	7	6	
McCall RH	Bob	29/12/1915	Worksop	1992	Nottingham Forest	2		
McCarthy					Barnet	1		
Macaulay					Chorley	2		
Macaulay AR	Archie	30/07/1915	Falkirk	1993	West Ham United	2		s
McConnon					Bath City	3	1	
McCormack JC	Cec	15/02/1922	Chester-le-Street	1995	Gateshead	6	5	
McCormick JM	Joe	15/07/1916	Holywell		Rochdale	4		
McCrohan AFT	Alan				Reading	2		
McCue JW	John	22/08/1922	Stoke-on-Trent	1999	Stoke City	8		
McDermott J	Joe		Fencehouses		Gateshead	1		
Macdonald					Stalybridge Celtic	2		
McDonald JC	Jack	27/08/1921	Maltby		Bournemouth	2		
McDonough FR	Frank	27/02/1915	Ponteland	1976	Torquay United	2		
McDowall LJ	Les	25/10/1912	Gunga Pur, India	1991	Manchester City	3		
McDowell I	Isaac				Port Vale	4	3	
McGahie J	John				Bristol Rovers	4		
McGibbon D	Doug	24/02/1919	Netley	2002	Southampton	4	2	
McGill J	Jimmy	10/03/1926	Kilsyth		Bury	1		
McGough J	Joe	27/10/1909	Tow Law		Southport	2		
McGrath JA	James	15/11/1921	Belfast	2000	Barrow	4		
McIntosh JMcL	Jimmy	05/04/1918	Dumfries	2000	Preston North End	6	2	
McIntosh RJ	Richard	21/12/1916	Kingston	1971	Barrow	6	3	
Mackenzie WF					Romford	2		
McKenzie					Slough United	2		
McLarty JJ	Jesse	03/03/1920	Ayr	2001	Wrexham	1	1	
McLaughlin KJ	Kevin				Cardiff City	2		
McLean					North Shields	2		
McLean A	Gus	20/09/1925	Queensferry	1979	Wolverhampton Wan.	2		
McLuckie JS	Jimmy	02/04/1908	Stonehouse, Lanarks	1986	Ipswich Town	3		s
McMahon HJ	Hughie	24/09/1909	Grangetown	1986	Hartlepool United	2	2	
McNeil D	Dave	14/05/1921	Chester	1993	Chester	2		
MacPhee MG	Tony	30/04/1914	Edinburgh	1960	Reading	2	2	
McPherson IB	Ian	26/07/1920	Glasgow	1983	Notts County	3	3	
McTaff S	Steve	11/03/1922	Tanfield	1983	Bradford Park Ave.	2		
Machent SC	Stan	23/03/1921	Chesterfield		Sheffield United	3		
Machin AH	Alec	06/07/1920	Hampstead	2005	Chelsea	3	1	
Maddison JP	Jimmy	09/11/1924	South Shields	1992	Middlesbrough	2		
Maddison R	Ralph	28/08/1918	Bentley, South Yorks	1994	York City	1	1	
Maggs					Bath City	3		
Mahon J	Jack	08/12/1911	Gillingham		York City	3	1	
Makin SH	Sammy	14/11/1925	Radcliffe	1981	Rochdale	2	1	
Malcolm JM	John	20/05/1917	Clackmannan		Accrington Stanley	6		
Male CG	George	08/05/1910	Plaistow	1998	Arsenal	1		e
Male NA	Norman	27/05/1917	West Bromwich	1992	Walsall	1		
Mallett FJ	Fred				Bromley	4		
Mallett J	Joe	08/01/1916	Gateshead	2004	Queen's Park Rgs.	11	2	
Mann T					Yeovil & Petters U	2		
Mansley VC	Cliff	05/04/1921	Skipton		Barnsley	6		
Mapson J	Johnny	02/05/1917	Birkenhead	1999	Sunderland	6		
Marden H					Chelmsford City	2		
Marden RJ	Ben	10/02/1927	Fulham		Chelmsford City	1		
Markham C	Colin	02/03/1916	Clowne	1967	Torquay United	2		
Marlor A	Alan				Oldham Athletic	4		
Marlow GA	Geoff	13/12/1912	Worksop	1978	Lincoln City	3	3	
Marriott E	Ernie	25/01/1913	Sutton-in-Ashfield	1989	Brighton & Hove A.	5		
Marsden F	Fred	06/09/1911	Blackburn	1989	Bournemouth	2		
Marsh FK	Frank	07/06/1916	Bolton	1978	Chester	2		
Marsh W	Walter				Mansfield Town	4		
Martin DK	Davy 'Boy'	01/02/1914	Belfast	1991	Notts County	1	1	i
Martin E	Ted	15/05/1910	Greasley	1990	Brighton & Hove A.	1		
Martin JR	Jackie	05/08/1914	Hamstead	1996	Aston Villa	1		

George Male

Johnny Mapson

74

Name		D.o.B	Place of Birth	Died	Club	Ap.	Gl.	Int
Martindale L	Len	30/06/1920	Bolton	1971	Burnley	1		
Mason GW	George	05/09/1913	Birmingham	1993	Coventry City	2		
Mather H	Harry	24/01/1921	Bolton	1999	Burnley	2		
Matier G	Gerry	01/12/1912	Lisburn	1984	Bradford City	1		
Matthews H	Horace	1913			Coventry City	2		
Matthews S	Stanley	01/02/1915	Hanley	2000	Stoke City	8		e
Mauchline RD	Bob		Falkirk		Accrington Stanley	4		
Maund JH	Jack	05/01/1916	Hednesford	1994	Shrewsbury Town	4	3	
Mawson R	Ron	16/09/1914	Bishop Auckland	1981	Crewe Alexandra	1		
Mayes TB	Thomas				Bournemouth	2		
Meade T	Trevor				Newport County	1		
Medhurst HEP	Harry	05/02/1916	Byfleet	1984	West Ham United	4		
Medley LD	Les	03/09/1920	Edmonton	2001	Tottenham Hotspur	1		e
Mee G	Gordon	13/05/1913	Belper	1975	Watford	8		
Mee GE	George	20/05/1923	Blackpool	1974	Nottingham Forest	3		
Melling F	Frank				Yorkshire Amateur	2	1	
Melton					Wisbech Town	2		
Mercer J	Joe	09/08/1914	Ellesmere Port	1990	Everton	2	1	e
Mercer S	Stan	11/09/1919	Birkenhead	2003	Leicester City	2		
Meredith RG	Robert	03/09/1917	Swansea	1994	Notts County	2		
Merrick GH	Gil	26/01/1922	Birmingham		Birmingham City	8		e
Merrington					Wellington Town	1		
Merritt HG	Harold	22/09/1920	Ormskirk	2004	Clapton Orient	2		
Metcalf WF	Walter	15/12/1910	Scarborough	1981	Coventry City	2		
Metcalfe					Yorkshire Amateur	2		
Metcalfe V	Vic	03/02/1922	Barrow	2003	Huddersfield Town	1		e
Middleton					Stockton	2		
Middleton MY	Matt	24/10/1907	Boldon Colliery	1979	Plymouth Argyle	2		
Middleton R	Ray	06/09/1919	Boldon	1977	Chesterfield	2		
Milburn GW	George	24/06/1910	Ashington	1980	Chesterfield	2		
Milburn JET	Jackie	11/05/1924	Ashington	1988	Newcastle United	2	2	e
Miles					Newport (IOW)	4		
Millard L	Len	07/03/1919	Coseley	1997	West Bromwich Alb.	4		
Mills					Stalybridge Celtic	1		
Mills					Gainsborough Trinity	2		
Mills J	Jimmy	30/09/1915	Dalton Brook	1994	Rotherham United	7		
Mills TJ	Tommy	28/12/1911	Ton Pentre	1979	Bristol Rovers	3	2	w
Mitchell FR	Frank	03/06/1922	Goulburn, Australia	1984	Birmingham City	10		
Mitchell K					Grantham	4		
Mitchell W	Billy	22/11/1910	Lurgan		Bath City	4		
Mitcheson FJ	Frank	10/03/1924	Stalybridge	1981	Doncaster Rovers	2		
Moir W	Willie	19/04/1922	Bucksburn	1988	Bolton Wanderers	4	1	s
Molloy P	Peter	20/04/1909	Rossendale	1993	Kettering Town	2		
Monk	Wilf	22/04/1910	Burscough	1988	South Liverpool	2		
Monk T	Tommy				Carlisle United	4		
Moore BJ	Bernard	18/12/1923	Brighton		Brighton & Hove A.	9	1	
Moore JFB	Beriah	25/12/1919	Cardiff		Cardiff City	1		
Moore NW	Norman	15/10/1919	Grimsby		Grimsby Town	2	1	
Morby JH	Jack	1920	Wednesfield		Aston Villa	3		
Morgan					Lovells Athletic	6	3	
Morgan Cl	Cliff	26/09/1913	Bristol	1975	Bristol City	8	2	
Morgan L	Lew	30/04/1911	Cowdenbeath	1988	Portsmouth	2		
Morrall AD	Alf	01/07/1916	Duddeston	1998	Northampton Town	6	6	
Morris A	Austin	10/02/1913	Thurcroft	1991	Gainsborough Trinity	1		
Morris D	Doug	29/07/1925	Durham		Hartlepool United	2		
Morris JH	James	16/11/1915	St Helens		Stockport County	1		
Morris W	Billy	30/07/1918	Llanddulas	2002	Burnley	2	1	w
Morris WW	Billy	26/03/1913	Handsworth	1995	Wolverhampton Wan.	3		e
Morrison AC	Angus	26/04/1924	Dingwall	2002	Derby County	6	1	
Mortensen SH	Stan	26/05/1921	South Shields	1991	Blackpool	5	4	e
Mortimer JMcC	Johnny	05/12/1923	Birkenhead		Wrexham	3		
Morton A	Arthur		Thurcroft		Huddersfield Town	2		
Moss F	Frank	16/09/1917	Aston	1997	Aston Villa	1		
Moss J	Jackie	01/09/1923	Blackrod	1975	Bury	4	1	
Moulson GB	George	06/08/1914	Clogheen	1994	Grimsby Town	2		r
Mouncer FE	Frank	22/11/1920	Grimsby	1977	Grimsby Town	1		
Mountford F	Frank	30/03/1923	Campsall	2006	Stoke City	8		
Mountford GF	George	30/03/1921	Stoke-on-Trent	1973	Stoke City	6	1	

Jackie Milburn

Lew Morgan

Name		D.o.B	Place of Birth	Died	Club	Ap.	Gl.	Int
Mullard AT	Albert	22/11/1920	Walsall	1984	Walsall	1	1	
Mullen J	Jimmy	06/01/1923	Newcastle	1987	Wolverhampton Wan.	2	1	e
Mullen JW	James	10/01/1921	Larne	2002	Barrow	5		
Mulraney AA	Jock	18/05/1916	Wishaw	2001	Birmingham City	10	7	
Murphy D	Danny	10/05/1922	Burtonwood	2001	Bolton Wanderers	9		
Murphy G	George	22/07/1915	Cwmfelinfach	1983	Bradford City	1	2	
Murphy TE	Eddie	25/03/1921	South Bank	2003	Middlesbrough	7	1	
Murray J	James	13/07/1922	Motherwell	1998	Exeter City	4		
Musson WU	Walter 'Chick'	08/10/1920	Kilburn, Derbyshire	1955	Derby County	9		
Mutch G	George	21/09/1912	Ferryhill, Aberdeens	2001	Preston North End	6		s
Neary HF	Frank	06/03/1921	Aldershot	2003	Queen's Park Rgs.	7	5	
Neary J	John	1916	Chorlton		Rochdale	2		
Needham D	Dennis				Luton Town	2		
Nelson D	Dave	03/02/1918	Douglas Water	1988	Arsenal	2		
Newberry					Kettering Town	2		
Newman AD	Albert	01/03/1915	Lichfield	1981	Walsall	1		
Newman EIA	Eric	24/11/1924	Romford	1971	Ipswich Town	1		
Newsome R	Robin	25/09/1919	Hebden Bridge	1999	West Bromwich Alb.	4	2	
Niblett V	Vic	09/12/1924	Frimley	2004	Reading	1		
Nicholas JT	Jack	26/11/1910	Derby	1977	Derby County	11		
Nichols H	Harry	1914	Hednesford		Shrewsbury Town	4	2	
Nickson HW	Harry	1919	Liverpool		Liverpool	3		
Nieuwenhuys B	Berry	05/11/1911	Boksburg, South Af.	1984	Liverpool	4	1	
Nightingale AJ	Albert	10/11/1923	Thrybergh	2006	Sheffield United	4		
Nightingale K	Ken				Rotherham United	5	2	
Noble N	Norman	08/08/1923	Barnsley	1973	Bradford City	1		
North TW	Tom	31/10/1919	Barrow-on-Soar	1996	Nottingham Forest	2		
Nuth					Bath City	1		
Nutt					Wisbech Town	2		
Oakes G	George	18/10/1918	Orrell	1990	Southport	2	2	
Oakes J	Jack	13/09/1905	Winsford	1992	Charlton Athletic	9		
Oakley JC	Jack				Mansfield Town	4		
O'Brien RV	Vic	01/05/1909	Coventry	1997	Watford	9		
O'Donnell H	Hugh	15/02/1913	Buckhaven	1965	Blackpool	5	2	
O'Flanagan KP	Kevin	10/06/1919	Dublin	2006	Arsenal	2		r
Oldfield JE	John	13/07/1918	Helsby		Port Vale	2		
Oliver					Stockton	2		
Oliver G	George	22/01/1919	Houghton-le-Spring	1981	Halifax Town	2		
Oliver H	Bert				Walthamstow Avenue	4		
Oliver HS	Harry	16/02/1921	Sunderland	1994	Brentford	2		
O'Mahony MA	Matt	19/01/1913	Mullinavat	1992	Ipswich Town	3		r
Ormston A	Alec	10/02/1919	Stoke-on-Trent	1975	Stoke City	4		
Osborne J	Johnny	14/10/1919	Renfrew	1981	Leicester City	2		
Owen					Yeovil & Petters U	2		
Owen J	Jonny				Clapton Orient	1		
Owen W	Billy	30/06/1914	Llanfairfechan	1976	Newport County	6	1	
Owens E	Tussy	07/11/1913	Trimdon Grange		Bath City	4		
Owens TL	Les	17/10/1919	Monkwearmouth	1974	Doncaster Rovers	1		
Oxton					South Liverpool	2		
Page AE	Albert	18/03/1916	Walthamstow	1995	Tottenham Hotspur	1		
Painter EG	Eddie	23/06/1921	Swindon	2001	Swindon Town	1		
Paisley R	Bob	23/01/1919	Hetton-le-Hole	1996	Liverpool	4		
Pallister G	Gordon	02/04/1917	Howden-le-Wear	1999	Barnsley	4	2	
Palmer A					Walthamstow Avenue	2		
Palmer RW	Ron 'Ginger'	1915	London		Aldershot	4		
Parker A	Albert				Notts County	1	1	
Parker TR	Tommy	13/02/1924	Hartlepool	1996	Ipswich Town	4	3	
Parkes HA	Harry	04/01/1920	Birmingham		Aston Villa	8	1	
Parkin FW	Fred				Lincoln City	4		
Parkman					Newport (IOW)	4		
Parr					Chorley	2		
Parr HE	Harry	23/10/1915	Newark	2004	Clapton Orient	2	1	
Parr J	Jackie	21/11/1920	Derby	1985	Derby County	10		
Parrott					Sutton United	2		
Parry O	Ossie	16/08/1908	Dowlais	1991	Ipswich Town	4		
Parry W	Bill	1917	Denaby		Chelmsford City	2		
Parsley WN	Norman	28/11/1923	Shildon	1993	Darlington	4		
Partridge D	Don	22/10/1925	Bolton	2003	Rochdale	6		

Stan Mortensen

Albert Nightingale

Bob Paisley

Name		D.o.B	Place of Birth	Died	Club	Ap.	Gl.	Int
Pass					Stockton	1		
Paton TG	Tommy	22/12/1918	Saltcoats	1991	Bournemouth	2	1	
Patterson JG	Jack	06/07/1922	Cramlington	2002	Blackburn Rovers	2		
Pattison JM	Johnny	19/12/1918	Glasgow		Queen's Park Rgs.	6	1	
Pattison JWP	John	23/02/1925	Portsmouth	1993	Reading	2		
Paviour JS					Romford	2		
Payne IEH	Joe	29/06/1921	Briton Ferry	2001	Swansea Town	2		
Payne J	Joe	17/01/1914	Brinnington Common	1975	Chelsea	5		e
Peacock EG	Ernie	11/12/1924	Bristol	1966	Notts County	4		
Pearce JG	Jim		Chirk		Rochdale	4		
Peppitt S	Syd	08/09/1919	Stoke-on-Trent	1992	Stoke City	2		
Peters PM	Peter				Reading	1		
Peters TJ	Tom	22/12/1920	Droylsden		Southend United	1		
Pettit					Sutton United	2		
Phillips					Lovells Athletic	1		
Phillips					Newport (IOW)	4		
Phillips PH	Philip				Swansea Town	1		
Phillips					Wellington Town	2		
Phillips RGT	Russell	22/06/1916	Exeter	2000	Millwall	1	1	
Phillipson WE	Bill	04/04/1917	Barrow	1974	Barrow	6		
Philpotts J	John				Tranmere Rovers	1		
Phipps HJ	Harold	15/01/1916	Dartford	2000	Charlton Athletic	2		
Phythian					Stalybridge Celtic	1		
Pickering WH	Bill	10/12/1919	Sheffield	1983	Sheffield Wed.	6		
Pickles F	Fred				Bradford City	1	1	
Pinder JJ	Jack	01/12/1912	Acomb	2004	York City	8		
Pitt L	Leslie				Barrow	1		
Plunkett SE	Sid	02/10/1920	Norwich	1986	Norwich City	2		
Pointon WJ	Bill	25/11/1920	Hanley		Port Vale	5	1	
Pomphrey EA	Syd	31/05/1916	Stretford	1987	Rochdale	4		
Pond H	Harold	19/04/1917	Kilnhurst		Carlisle United	4		
Poole B	Benjamin				York City	4		
Poole G	George				Mansfield Town	6	1	
Poole J	Joseph	25/05/1923	Huddersfield		Huddersfield Town	1		
Porritt WM	Walter	19/07/1914	Heckmondwike	1993	York City	1		
Porter W	Bill	23/11/1923	Durham	1975	Hartlepool United	2		
Poskett TW	Tom	26/12/1909	Esh Winning	1972	Crewe Alexandra	1		
Potter					Chelmsford City	1		
Potter					Slough United	2		
Potts VE	Vic	20/08/1915	Birmingham	1996	Aston Villa	8		
Powell					Trowbridge Town	2		
Powell HC					Barnet	2		
Pownall					Wisbech Town	2		
Poyser GH	George	06/02/1910	Stanton Hill	1995	Brentford	3		
Prangley S	Sam	30/09/1924	Newport		Lovells Athletic	6	1	
Preece JC	Jack	30/04/1914	Wolverhampton	2003	Southport	1		
Prescott JR	James		Waterloo, Lancashire		Plymouth Argyle	2		
Price A	Arthur	12/01/1921	Rowlands Gill	1995	Leeds United	1		
Price AJW	Billy	10/04/1917	Hadley	1995	Huddersfield Town	2	1	
Price GB	George				Ipswich Town	4	2	
Priday RH	Bob	29/03/1925	Cape Town, South Af.	1998	Liverpool	4		
Pringle A	Allen	26/03/1914	Craghead	1990	Chesterfield	1		
Pritchard HJ	Jack	30/01/1913	Meriden	2000	Manchester City	3		
Proctor MH	Harry	10/07/1912	Ushaw Moor	1984	Norwich City	2		
Pryde RI	Bob	25/04/1913	Methil	1998	Blackburn Rovers	2		
Pullen L					Barnet	2		
Pursell RW	Robert	28/09/1919	Glasgow	2006	Port Vale	3		
Pye F	Fred	11/03/1928	Stockport		Stalybridge Celtic	2		
Pye J	Jesse	22/12/1919	Treeton	1984	Notts County	4		e
Pymm F					Barnet	2		
Quigley G	Gilbert	17/02/1921	Ulverston		Barrow	2		
Rackham					North Shields	2		
Radcliffe M	Mark	26/10/1919	Hyde		Oldham Athletic	4		
Rampling DW	Dennis	25/11/1923	Gainsborough		Fulham	2	1	
Ramsden B	Barney	08/11/1917	Sheffield	1976	Liverpool	1		
Ranshaw J	Jack	19/12/1916	Nettleham	2003	Grantham	4		
Ratcliffe PC	Paddy	31/12/1919	Dublin		Notts County	2		
Rawlings JSD	Syd	05/05/1913	Wombwell	1956	Everton	2		

Joe Payne

Bob Pryde

Name		D.o.B	Place of Birth	Died	Club	Ap.	Gl.	Int
Rawson C	Colin	12/11/1926	Shirebrook		Nottingham Forest	1		
Ray CH	Cecil	25/10/1911	West Grinstead	1995	Aldershot	4	1	
Raybould ME	Marshall				Cardiff City	2		
Rayner E	Ted	28/09/1916	Hemsworth	1988	Halifax Town	2		
Reagan CM	Martin	12/05/1924	Scotswood		York City	2		
Reay EP	Ted	05/08/1914	Tynemouth		Queen's Park Rgs.	1		
Reay L	Les				Carlisle United	2		
Redfern F	Fred	28/09/1914	Hyde	1989	Stockport County	2		
Reece S	Stan				Bromley	4		
Reece TS	Tom	17/05/1919	Wolverhampton	1990	Crystal Palace	1		
Reed					Yeovil & Petters U	2		
Rees W	Billy	10/03/1924	Blaengarw	1996	Cardiff City	1		w
Reid EJ	Ernie	25/03/1914	Pentrebach		Norwich City	2		
Reilly P					Barnet	2	1	
Reynolds RSM	Ron	02/06/1928	Haslemere	1999	Aldershot	8		
Reynolds W	Wally	24/11/1906	Ecclesall		Rochdale	2	1	
Rich LT	Len	03/11/1912	Camelford		Stockport County	1		
Richards E	Ernest				Tranmere Rovers	4		
Richardson					Netherfield (Kendal)	2		
Richardson F	Fred	18/08/1925	Spennymoor		Bishop Auckland	4	3	
Richardson JR	Jimmy	08/02/1911	Ashington	1964	Millwall	2		e
Richardson W	Billy 'Ginger'	29/05/1909	Framwellgate Moor	1959	Shrewsbury Town	2		
Rickett HFJ	Horace	03/01/1912	Orsett	1989	Fulham	2		
Rickett W	Walter	20/03/1917	Sheffield	1991	Sheffield United	4		
Riddick					Newport (IOW)	2		
Ridgwell					Sutton United	2		
Riding					South Liverpool	2		
Ridley DGH	Dave	16/12/1916	Pontypridd	1998	Millwall	1	1	
Ridyard A	Alf	05/03/1908	Cudworth	1981	Queen's Park Rgs.	11		
Riley A	Alan				Tranmere Rovers	1		
Risdon SW	Stan	13/08/1913	Exeter	1979	Brighton & Hove A.	9		
Roach JE	John				Manchester United	2		
Robbins P	Paddy	18/11/1913	Birr	1986	York City	8	1	
Roberts					Cheltenham Town	2		
Roberts					Wisbech Town	2		
Roberts D	Dennis	05/02/1918	Monk Bretton	2001	Bristol City	8		
Roberts DG	Gordon	30/05/1925	Foleshill	1991	Northampton Town	6	2	
Roberts F	Fred	07/05/1916	Rhyl	1985	Bury	1	3	
Roberts H	Harold	12/01/1920	Liverpool		Chesterfield	2	2	
Roberts OJ	Owen	16/02/1919	Maerdy	2000	Swansea Town	2		
Roberts R	Richard				Crewe Alexandra	2		
Roberts WS	Bill	12/07/1908	Bargoed	1976	Newport County	2		
Robertson LV	Len	01/03/1916	Middlesbrough	1979	Hartlepool United	2		
Robertson WH	Bill	25/03/1923	Crowthorne	2003	Chelsea	6		
Robinson					Wisbech Town	1		
Robinson BC	Bernard	05/12/1911	Cambridge	2004	Norwich City	2		
Robinson E	Edward	15/01/1922	Bywell	1987	Gateshead	4		
Robinson GF	George	17/06/1925	Melton Mowbray	2000	Notts County	2		
Robinson GH	George	11/01/1908	Marlpool	1963	Charlton Athletic	2		
Robinson JA	Jackie	10/08/1917	Shiremoor	1972	Sheffield Wed.	2		e
Robinson P	Peter	29/01/1922	Manchester	2000	Manchester City	1		
Robinson R	Dicky	19/01/1927	Whitburn		Middlesbrough	7		
Robledo GO	George	14/04/1926	Iquique, Chile	1989	Barnsley	6	2	ch
Robson AP	Bert	14/11/1916	Crook	1990	Crystal Palace	1		
Rodgers CF	Cliff	03/10/1921	Rotherham	1990	York City	8		
Rodi J	Joe	23/07/1913	Glasgow	1965	Grimsby Town	2	1	
Rogers E	Tim	15/10/1909	Chirk	1996	Wrexham	1		
Roles AG	Albie	29/09/1921	Southampton		Southampton	4		
Rooke RL	Ronnie	07/12/1911	Guildford	1985	Fulham	2	2	
Roper DGB	Don	14/12/1922	Botley	2001	Southampton	4	1	
Roper WH	William	1914	Birkenhead		South Liverpool	2		
Rose A					Newport (IOW)	4		
Rose B					Newport (IOW)	2		
Rose J	Jack	26/10/1921	Sheffield		Queen's Park Rgs.	10		
Rosenthal AW	Abe	12/10/1921	Liverpool	1986	Tranmere Rovers	4	4	
Ross G					Willington	2		
Ross GA	George	01/11/1920	Deptford		Millwall	2		
Ross R					Willington	2		

Ronnie Rooke

Jack Rowley

Name		D.o.B	Place of Birth	Died	Club	Ap.	Gl.	Int
Rotherham E	Edward				Accrington Stanley	1		
Rothwell G	George	22/11/1923	Bolton	2004	Accrington Stanley	6	2	
Roughton WG	George	11/05/1909	Manchester	1989	Exeter City	4		
Routledge A					York City	2		
Rowley JF	Jack	07/10/1918	Wolverhampton	1998	Manchester United	4	3	e
Roy JR	Jack	22/03/1914	Woolston	1980	Yeovil & Petters U	2		
Roylance					Yorkshire Amateur	2		
Royston R	Bob 'Roy'	01/12/1915	Gallowgate	1996	Plymouth Argyle	1		
Rozier AT	Alfred				Bradford City	2		
Ruddick					Newport (IOW)	1		
Ruddy M					Bromley	4		
Ruecroft J	Jake	01/05/1915	Lanchester		Halifax Town	2		
Rumbold GA	George	10/07/1911	Alton	1995	Clapton Orient	2		
Rundle S	Sid				Plymouth Argyle	2		
Russell G					Grantham	4		
Russell JW	Jim	14/09/1916	Edinburgh	1994	Norwich City	1		
Russell RI	Bobby	27/12/1919	Aberdour	2004	Chelsea	2		
Rutherford R	Bobby	20/04/1922	South Shields	2004	Gateshead	2	1	
Sale T	Tommy	30/04/1910	Stoke-on-Trent	1990	Stoke City	1		
Salisbury					Netherfield (Kendal)	2		
Salmon LA	Len	24/06/1912	West Kirby	1995	South Liverpool	2		
Sampson					Gainsborough Trinity	2	1	
Sanders JA	Jim	05/07/1920	Holborn	2003	West Bromwich Alb.	3		
Sankey J	Jack	19/03/1912	Winsford	1985	Northampton Town	5		
Saphin RFE	Reg	08/08/1916	Kilburn		Ipswich Town	3		
Saunders DG	Douglas	1927	Birmingham		West Bromwich Alb.	1		
Savage R	Reg	05/07/1912	Eccles	1997	Nottingham Forest	3		
Sawyer					Bath City	1		
Saxon					Wellington Town	2		
Saxton					Yorkshire Amateur	2		
Schofield E	Ernie	29/03/1921	Sheffield		Bradford City	2		
Scott					Bromley	4		
Scott					Sutton United	2	1	
Scott DP	David	06/06/1918	Belfast	1977	Northampton Town	6		
Scott FH	Freddie	06/10/1916	Fatfield	1995	York City	8	3	
Scott L	Laurie	23/04/1917	Sheffield	1999	Arsenal	2		e
Scott WJ	Bill	14/06/1921	Preston	2002	Preston North End	3		
Scott WR	Billy	06/12/1907	Willington Quay	1969	Brentford	8	1	e
Scrine FH	Frankie	09/01/1925	Swansea	2001	Swansea Town	1		
Scullard					Trowbridge Town	2		
Searby					Grantham	4		
Sedgwick					Bishop Auckland	2		
Selkirk J	Jack	20/01/1923	Doncaster	1993	Rotherham United	5		
Shackleton LF	Len	03/05/1922	Bradford	2000	Bradford Park Ave.	8	1	e
Shakeskaft					Netherfield (Kendal)	1		
Shankly W	Bill	02/09/1913	Glenbuck	1981	Preston North End	6	2	s
Sharpe					Willington	2		
Shaw A	Alex				Crewe Alexandra	2	1	
Shaw CE	Cecil	22/06/1911	Mansfield	1977	West Bromwich Alb.	4		
Shaw J	John	02/10/1916	Oldham	1973	Watford	9		
Shaw JS	Jack	10/04/1924	Doncaster		Rotherham United	7	2	
Shaw K	Ken	15/12/1920	Dukinfield	2004	Stockport County	2	1	
Shaw R	Raymond				Rotherham United	1	1	
Sheard F	Frank	29/01/1922	Spilsby	1990	Leicester City	2		
Sheen R					Bromley	3		
Shelton JBT	Jack	09/11/1912	Wollaston	1992	Walsall	1		
Shepherd E	Ernie	14/08/1919	Wombwell	2001	Fulham	2		
Sheppard HH	Hedley	26/11/1909	West Ham	2006	Aldershot	8		
Shergold WR	Billy	22/01/1923	Newport	1968	Bishop Auckland	2		
Sherwood AT	Alf	13/11/1924	Aberaman	1990	Cardiff City	2		w
Shimwell E	Eddie	27/02/1920	Birchover	1988	Sheffield United	2		e
Shipman TER	Tom	04/08/1910	Langwith	1972	Oldham Athletic	4		
Shore EG	Ted	18/10/1927	Nuneaton	1976	Port Vale	5		
Short JD	John	25/01/1921	Gateshead	1986	Leeds United	2	1	
Shortt WW	Bill	13/10/1920	Wrexham	2004	Chester	2		w
Shreeve JTT	Jack	18/08/1917	Boldon	1966	Charlton Athletic	10		
Simmonds					Walthamstow Avenue	2		
Simmons					Bath City	4	1	

Len Shackleton

Bill Shankley

Jack Shaw

Alf Sherwood

Name		D.o.B	Place of Birth	Died	Club	Ap.	Gl.	Int
Simms HA	Hedley	04/06/1913	Jacksdale	1993	Wellington Town	2		
Simpson					Wisbech Town	2		
Simpson DE	Dennis	01/11/1919	Coventry	2002	Coventry City	2	1	
Simpson J	John	27/10/1918	Hedon	2000	Huddersfield Town	2		
Simpson NH	Noel	23/12/1922	Mansfield	1987	Nottingham Forest	3		
Simpson R	Bobby	15/09/1915	Bishop Auckland	1994	Darlington	4		
Simpson S	Sam	1915	Lanarkshire		Barrow	1		
Sinclair RD	Robert	29/06/1915	Winchburgh	1993	Chesterfield	2		
Sinclair T	Tommy	13/10/1921	Ince		Aldershot	3		
Slattery					Lovells Athletic	6		
Small SJ	Sam	15/05/1912	Birmingham	1993	West Ham United	4		
Smalley T	Tom	13/01/1912	Kinsley	1984	Northampton Town	6		e
Smart L	Leonard				Bournemouth	1		
Smedley L	Laurie	07/05/1922	Sheffield		Lincoln City	1		
Smirk AH	Alf	14/03/1917	Pershore	1996	Southend United	2	1	
Smith					Newport (IOW)	4		
Smith					North Shields	1		
Smith A					Kettering Town	2		
Smith D	Dave	12/10/1915	South Shields	1997	Northampton Town	1	1	
Smith DJ	Dennis				Southport	2		
Smith G	Gavin	25/09/1917	Cambuslang	1992	Barnsley	6	2	
Smith GB	George	07/02/1921	Fleetwood		Manchester City	4	3	
Smith GC	George	23/04/1919	Bromley-by-Bow	1983	Brentford	7		
Smith HS	Harry	11/10/1908	Throckley	1993	Bristol Rovers	2		
Smith J	Jackie		Littletown		Plymouth Argyle	1		
Smith J	Jack	17/02/1915	Batley	1975	Manchester United	4	1	
Smith JC	Jack	15/09/1910	Stocksbridge	1986	Sheffield United	3		
Smith JT	Trevor	08/09/1910	Stanley	1997	Crystal Palace	2		
Smith JW	Jackie	27/05/1920	St Pancras	1991	Bradford Park Ave.	2		
Smith L	Les 'Snowy'	16/11/1921	Tamworth	1993	Mansfield Town	6		
Smith L					Shrewsbury Town	4		
Smith LGF	Leslie	13/05/1918	Ealing	1995	Aston Villa	8	4	e
Smith SC	Sep	15/03/1912	Whitburn	2006	Leicester City	2		e
Smith 'Schmidt' JCR	Reg	20/01/1912	Battersea	2004	Millwall	4	3	e
Smith T	Tot	02/02/1923	Horden	1993	Newcastle United	2		
Smith T					Kettering Town	1		
Smith W	Wilfred	18/04/1917	Stoke-on-Trent	1995	Port Vale	6		
Smyth HR	Bob	28/02/1921	Manchester		Ipswich Town	2		
Snape J	Jack	02/07/1917	Birmingham	2000	Coventry City	1		
Sneddon T	Tom	22/08/1912	Livingston	1983	Rochdale	5		
Sneddon WC	Billy	01/04/1914	Wishaw	1995	Swansea Town	1		
Soo HY	Frank	12/03/1914	Buxton	1991	Leicester City	2		
Southwell AA	Aubrey	21/08/1921	Grantham	2005	Notts County	4		
Speed L	Les	03/10/1923	Caergwrle		Wrexham	2		
Spence R	Dickie	18/07/1908	Platts Common	1983	Chelsea	6	1	e
Spicer EW	Eddie	20/09/1922	Liverpool	2004	Liverpool	1		
Spuhler JO	Johnny	18/09/1917	Sunderland		Middlesbrough	7	3	
Stamps JD	Jackie	02/12/1918	Thrybergh	1991	Derby County	8	9	
Stancer LB	Les	1925	Grantham		Notts County	1		
Standring N	Norman				Oldham Athletic	2	2	
Stansbridge LEC	Len	19/02/1919	Southampton	1986	Southampton	4		
Stansfield F	Fred	12/12/1917	Cardiff		Cardiff City	2		w
Starsmore					Kettering Town	1		
Steele FC	Freddie	06/05/1916	Hanley	1976	Stoke City	8	7	e
Steele PE	Percy	26/12/1923	Liverpool		Tranmere Rovers	3		
Stelling JGS	Jack	23/05/1924	Washington	1993	Sunderland	6		
Stephan HW	Harry	24/02/1924	Farnworth		Blackburn Rovers	2		
Stephens					Stockton	2		
Stephens HJ	Bert	13/05/1909	Chatham	1987	Brighton & Hove A.	10	5	
Stephenson K	Kenneth				Plymouth Argyle	1		
Stevenson A	Arthur	02/03/1924	Lanchester	1989	Doncaster Rovers	2		
Stewart RP	Reg	30/10/1925	Sheffield		Sheffield Wed.	2		
Still RA	Bob	15/12/1912	Brinscall	1983	Crewe Alexandra	2		
Stillyards GEW	George	29/12/1918	Whisby		Lincoln City	3		
Stirland JC	Cec	15/07/1921	Adwick-le-Street	2004	Doncaster Rovers	1		
Stobbart GC	George	09/01/1921	Pegswood	1995	Middlesbrough	2		
Stock AWA	Alec	30/03/1917	Peasedown St John	2001	Queen's Park Rgs.	8	2	
Stokes					Cheltenham Town	2		

Leslie Smith

Sep Smith

Freddie Steele

Name		D.o.B	Place of Birth	Died	Club	Ap.	Gl.	Int
Stone S					Bromley	1		
Stones					Bishop Auckland	2		
Stott AG	Alex			1998	Portsmouth	1		
Stratton					Trowbridge Town	2		
Streten B	Bernard				Shrewsbury Town	4		
Strong GJ	Jimmy	07/06/1916	Morpeth	1989	Walsall	2		
Stroud WJA	Billy	07/07/1919	Hammersmith		Southampton	4		
Stuart RW	Bobby	09/10/1913	Middlesbrough	1987	Middlesbrough	2		
Stubbins A	Albert	13/07/1919	Wallsend	2002	Newcastle United	2	1	
Stubbs CF	Charlie	22/01/1920	West Ham	1984	Darlington	2		
Stubbs PEG	Eric	10/09/1912	Chester		Chester	2		
Suart R	Ron	18/11/1920	Kendal		Blackpool	4		
Summerbee GCS	Gordon	08/02/1913	Winchester	1983	Aldershot	7		
Summerbee GM	George	22/10/1914	Winchester	1955	Preston North End	1		
Summerfield AS	Archie				Reading	2	2	
Swift FV	Frank	26/12/1913	Blackpool	1958	Manchester City	4		e
Swift HM	Hugh	22/01/1921	Sheffield	1979	Sheffield Wed.	6		
Swift W	Bill				Walthamstow Avenue	1		
Swindells					Stalybridge Celtic	1		
Swindin GH	George	04/12/1914	Campsall	2005	Arsenal	2		
Swinfen R	Reg	04/05/1915	Battersea	1996	Queen's Park Rgs.	3	1	
Swinton					Queen's Park Rgs.	1		
Sykes K	Ken	29/01/1926	Darlington		Darlington	1	1	
Sykes W					Shrewsbury Town	4		
Tadman MR	Maurice	28/06/1921	Rainham, Kent	1994	Charlton Athletic	1	1	
Tagg E	Ernie	15/09/1917	Crewe		Bournemouth	1		
Tait J					Bishop Auckland	4	1	
Tait T	Tommy	20/11/1908	Hetton-le-Hole	1976	Torquay United	2		
Talbot FL	Les	03/08/1910	Hednesford		Walsall	2	1	
Taylor					Grantham	4		
Taylor A	Alex	25/12/1916	Menstrie	1982	Carlisle United	2		
Taylor AH	Bert	02/05/1924	Worksop		Bury	2		
Taylor C	Charles				Halifax Town	1		
Taylor E	Ernie	02/09/1925	Sunderland	1985	Newcastle United	1		e
Taylor G	George	21/03/1920	Wigan	1983	Gainsborough Trinity	1		
Taylor J	Jack	15/02/1914	Barnsley	1978	Norwich City	2		
Taylor J					Willington	2		
Taylor JG	Jim	05/11/1917	Cowley, Middlesex	2001	Fulham	2		e
Taylor PH	Phil	18/09/1917	Bristol		Liverpool	1		e
Telar					Kettering Town	1		
Tennant AE	Albert	29/10/1917	Ilkeston	1986	Chelsea	6		
Thomas					Chelmsford City	1		
Thomas DJ					Bournemouth	1		
Thomas DWJ	Dave	06/07/1917	Stepney	1991	Plymouth Argyle	1		
Thomas GS	Geoff	21/02/1926	Derby	2006	Nottingham Forest	2		
Thomas GW	Gwilym				Newport County	5		
Thomas JE	John	15/07/1922	Walsall	1999	Bournemouth	2	3	
Thomas RA	Bob	02/08/1919	Stepney	1990	Brentford	8	1	
Thomas WG	Bill	18/11/1918	Derby	2001	Bristol City	8	1	
Thompson					Bath City	3		
Thompson					North Shields	2		
Thompson					Stockton	2		
Thompson CA	Cyril	18/12/1918	Southend-on-Sea	1972	Southend United	1		
Thompson CM	Charlie	19/07/1920	Chesterfield	1997	Sheffield United	1		
Thompson G					Willington	2		
Thompson H	Harry	29/04/1915	Mansfield		York City	4		
Thompson J	Jack	21/03/1915	Cramlington	1996	Sheffield Wed.	4	5	
Thompson W	William	23/12/1921	Ashington	1986	Gateshead	4	1	
Thomson CM	Charlie	25/10/1905	Perth		Exeter City	4		
Thorpe L	Len	07/06/1924	Warsop		Mansfield Town	6	1	
Threlfall JR	Dick	05/03/1916	Ashton-under-Lyne	1994	Bolton Wanderers	8		
Thyne RB	Bob	09/01/1920	Glasgow	1986	Darlington	2		
Tickell ER	Roy	25/04/1924	Bootle	2006	Exeter City	3	1	
Tilling HK	Harry	06/01/1918	Warrington	1998	Oldham Athletic	2		
Tindill H	Bert	31/12/1926	South Hiendley	1973	Doncaster Rovers	1		
Tinkler L	Lou	04/12/1923	Chester-le-Street	1995	Plymouth Argyle	2		
Tite					Kettering Town	2		
Todd J	Jim	19/03/1921	Belfast		Blackpool	4		

Albert Stubbins

Frank Swift

George Swindon

Name		D.o.B	Place of Birth	Died	Club	Ap.	Gl.	Int
Todd PR	Paul	08/05/1920	Middlesbrough	2000	Doncaster Rovers	2	1	
Tomlinson CC	Charlie	02/12/1919	Sheffield	1971	Sheffield Wed.	6	2	
Tomlinson RW	Bob	04/06/1924	Blackburn	1996	Blackburn Rovers	1		
Tompkin M	Maurice	17/02/1919	Countesthorpe	1956	Bury	4	1	
Topping H	Harry	21/09/1913	Kearsley	2001	Bristol Rovers	2		
Topping HW	Harry	26/10/1915	Prescot		Stockport County	1		
Towers J	John	21/12/1913	Willington	1979	Darlington	4	2	
Towers WH	Bill	13/07/1920	Leicester	2000	Leicester City	2		
Townsend LF	Len	31/08/1917	Brentford	1997	Brentford	3	1	
Townsend W	Billy	27/12/1922	Bedworth	1988	Derby County	2		
Trainor P	Peter	02/03/1915	Cockermouth	1979	Brighton & Hove A.	4		
Tranter GH	George	11/09/1915	Birmingham	1998	West Bromwich Alb.	4		
Travis					Trowbridge Town	2		
Troke FJ	Frank				Bournemouth	2		
Troman JV	James				Hartlepool United	2		
Tunney EL	Eddie	23/09/1915	Liverpool		Wrexham	6		
Tunnicliffe					Chelmsford City	2		
Turnbull					Stockton	2		
Turner AA	Arthur	22/01/1922	Poplar		Charlton Athletic	9	7	
Turner AO	Arthur	01/04/1909	Chesterton	1994	Birmingham City	10		
Turner HG	Bert	19/06/1909	Rhymney	1981	Charlton Athletic	8	1	w
Turner PS	Phil	20/02/1927	Frodsham		Chester	2		
Twigg WL	William	1921	Buxton		West Bromwich Alb.	1		
Tyler LDV	Len	07/01/1919	Rotherhithe	1988	Millwall	3		
Underhill CE	Charlie				Southport	1		
Urmston					South Liverpool	2		
Urmston JR	James				Barrow	1		
Vallance THW	Tom	28/03/1924	Stoke-on-Trent	1980	Torquay United	1		
Varty TH	Tommy	02/12/1921	Hetton-le-Hole	2004	Darlington	4	1	
Vaughan CJ	Charlie	23/04/1921	Bermondsey	1989	Sutton United	2	1	
Veacock J	Jimmy	05/09/1919	Liverpool		Marine	4		
Veck R	Bobby	01/04/1920	Titchfield	1999	Southampton	3	1	
Viles J					Bromley	4		
Vinall EJ	Jack	16/12/1910	Witton	1997	Luton Town	2		
Vince					Trowbridge Town	2		
Vincent NE	Ned	03/03/1909	Prudhoe	1980	Grimsby Town	1		
Wade SJ	Joe	07/07/1921	Shoreditch	2005	Arsenal	2		
Wainwright WT	Bill	28/10/1917	Worksop		Aldershot	1		
Wainwright G					Wrexham	2		
Wakefield					Slough United	2		
Wakeman A	Alan	20/11/1920	Walsall	2002	Aston Villa	8		
Walker					Gainsborough Trinity	2		
Walker ERW	Dick	22/07/1913	Hackney	1988	West Ham United	4		
Walker GH	Harry	20/05/1916	Aysgarth	1976	Portsmouth	2		
Walker RG	Geoff	29/09/1926	Bradford	1997	Bradford Park Ave.	3		
Walker S	Steve	16/10/1914	Sheffield	1987	Exeter City	4	5	
Walker V	Vic	14/04/1922	Kirkby-in-Ashfield	1992	Nottingham Forest	2		
Wallace					Grantham	1		
Wallace P					Romford	2		
Wallace JM	Jock	13/04/1911	Deantown	1978	Blackpool	5		
Wallbanks H	Harry	27/07/1921	Chopwell	1993	Fulham	2		
Wallbanks J	Jimmy	12/09/1909	Platt Bridge	1979	Reading	1		
Waller HH	Harry	20/08/1917	Ashington	1984	Arsenal	1		
Walsh W	Billy	31/05/1921	Dublin		Manchester City	4		r
Walshaw K	Ken	28/08/1918	Tynemouth	1979	Sunderland	2	1	
Walton FH	Frank	09/04/1918	Southend-on-Sea	1986	Southend United	2		
Walton G	George	1911	Burnley		Walsall	1		
Walton J	Joe	05/06/1925	Manchester		Manchester United	2		
Wands AMD	Alex	05/12/1922	Cowdenbeath		Sheffield Wed.	6		
Warburton A	Arthur	1909	Whitefield	1972	Southport	1		
Ward B					Kettering Town	2		
Ward RA	Robert				Coventry City	1		
Ward RA	Ralph	05/02/1911	Oadby	1983	Tottenham Hotspur	2		
Ward TA	Tommy	06/08/1917	Wolsingham		Sheffield Wed.	2	1	
Ward TV	Tim	17/10/1918	Cheltenham	1993	Derby County	1		e
Wardlaw JC	John	1919	Scotland		Ipswich Town	3		
Wardle G	George	24/09/1919	Kibblesworth	1991	Exeter City	2		
Wardle W	Billy	20/01/1918	Houghton-le-Spring	1989	Grimsby Town	2		

Bert Turner

Billy Wardle

Don Welsh

Name		D.o.B	Place of Birth	Died	Club	Ap.	Gl.	Int
Ware H	Harry	22/10/1911	Birmingham	1970	Norwich City	1	1	
Warner J	Jack	21/09/1911	Tonyrefail	1980	Manchester United	4		w
Warner LH	Les	19/12/1918	Birmingham	1982	Coventry City	2		
Warnes G	George	04/12/1925	Worksop	2004	Rotherham United	8		
Warren RR	Ray	23/06/1918	Bristol	1988	Bristol Rovers	4		
Washington J					Bishop Auckland	2		
Watkins RB	Barry	30/11/1921	Bedlinog	2004	Bristol Rovers	4		
Watson JF	Jack	31/12/1917	Hamilton	1976	Bury	1		
Watson WJB	Jimmy	14/08/1910	Govan		Brighton & Hove A.	6		
Watson WT	Willie	11/06/1918	Swansea	1978	Preston North End	2		
Watt-Smith					Yorkshire Amateur	2		
Waugh WL	Billy	27/11/1921	Edinburgh		Luton Town	2		
Wayman C	Charlie	16/05/1922	Bishop Auckland	2006	Newcastle United	1		
Webb JA	Jack	19/05/1908	Southwick, County Dur.	1984	Newport County	2		
Webster R	Dick	06/08/1919	Accrington	1979	Accrington Stanley	4		
Webster WT	Billy	1909	Sunderland		Stalybridge Celtic	1		
Weightman W					Barnet	2		
Weir A	Alex	20/10/1916	Longridge		Watford	4		
Welsby					Marine	3		
Welsh A	Andy	1918	Annfield		Northampton Town	1		
Welsh D	Don	25/02/1911	Manchester	1990	Charlton Athletic	8	4	e
West N	Norman	1918	Walker		Hartlepool United	2		
West T	Tom	08/12/1916	Salford		Oldham Athletic	4	2	
Weston RH	Reg	16/01/1918	Greenhithe	1998	Swansea Town	2		
Westwood WR	Ray	14/04/1912	Kingswinford	1982	Bolton Wanderers	9	8	e
Wetter					Lovells Athletic	1		
Whalley H	Bert	06/08/1913	Ashton-under-Lyne	1958	Manchester United	4		
Wharton JE	Jackie	18/06/1920	Bolton	1997	Preston North End	6	1	
Wheatley HJ	Joe	09/05/1912	Eastham		Shrewsbury Town	2		
Whent JR	Jackie	03/05/1920	Darlington		Brighton & Hove A.	9		
Whitaker W	Billy	07/10/1923	Chesterfield	1995	Chesterfield	2		
White AL	Albert				Aldershot	1		
White F	Fred	05/12/1916	Wolverhampton		Sheffield United	1		
White J	Jack	17/03/1924	Doncaster		Aldershot	8	1	
White RBW	Ray	13/08/1918	Bootle	1988	Tottenham Hotspur	2		
White T	Tom	10/11/1924	High Hold	1998	Sunderland	3		
Whitehead WG	Billy	06/02/1920	Maltby		Queen's Park Rgs.	6		
Whitehouse					Lovells Athletic	6		
Whitelaw DL	Dave	09/08/1909	Anderston	1989	Wrexham	1		
Whitelum C	Cliff	02/12/1919	Farnworth	2000	Sunderland	6	2	
Whiteside A	Arnold	06/11/1911	Garstang	1994	Blackburn Rovers	2		
Whitfield W	Wilf 'Baggy'	17/11/1916	Chesterfield		Bristol Rovers	4		
Whitney					Cheltenham Town	2		
Whittaker WP	Bill	20/12/1922	Charlton	1977	Brentford	4		
Widdowfield E	Ted	1915	Hetton-le-Hole		Halifax Town	1		
Wightman JR	Jock	02/11/1912	Duns	1964	Blackburn Rovers	2		
Wildman FR	Frank	11/06/1908	South Kirkby	1994	Swindon Town	1		
Wilkins R	Ron	21/12/1923	Treherbert	1983	Newport County	3		
Wilkinson					Chorley	2		
Wilkinson					Gainsborough Trinity	2		
Wilkinson H	Bert	02/08/1922	Sunderland		Lincoln City	4		
Willemse SB	Stan	23/08/1924	Brighton		Brighton & Hove A.	4	1	
Williams					Chelmsford City	1		
Williams					Slough United	2		
Williams					Stalybridge Celtic	2		
Williams BF	Bert	31/01/1920	Bradley, Staffs		Wolverhampton Wan.	4		e
Williams CE	Cyril	17/11/1921	Bristol	1980	Bristol City	8	3	
Williams DT	Danny	20/11/1924	Maltby		Rotherham United	8		
Williams E	Emlyn	15/01/1912	Maesteg	1989	Preston North End	6		
Williams F					Torquay United	2		
Williams G					Ipswich Town	1		
Williams GG	Gordon	19/06/1925	Swindon	1996	Swindon Town	2		
Williams HO	Horace	04/10/1921	Laughton	1978	Rotherham United	8		
Williams R	Ron	23/01/1907	Llansamlet	1987	Lovells Athletic	6	4	
Williams RF	Reg	28/01/1922	Watford		Chelsea	6	1	
Williams S	Sydney				Darlington	2		
Williamson					Stalybridge Celtic	1		
Williamson SH	Stewie	07/04/1926	Wallasey		Tranmere Rovers	4	1	

Ray Westwood

Bert Williams

Ken Willingham

Name		D.o.B	Place of Birth	Died	Club	Ap.	Gl.	Int
Williamson T	Tommy	16/03/1913	Salford	1992	Oldham Athletic	4		
Willingham CK	Ken	01/12/1912	Sheffield	1975	Sunderland	6		e
Willis A	Arthur	02/02/1920	Denaby	1987	Tottenham Hotspur	2		e
Willsher					Chelmsford City	2		
Wilman					Netherfield (Kendal)	2		
Wilson A	Archie	04/12/1924	South Shields	1979	Gateshead	6		
Wilson A	Albert	28/01/1915	Rotherham	1998	Crystal Palace	3		
Wilson C	Charlie				Burnley	1		
Wilson J	Jock	29/10/1916	Airdrie		Chesterfield	2		
Wilson JA	Joe	23/03/1911	High Spen	1984	Brighton & Hove A.	10	1	
Wilson JW	Joe	29/09/1911	West Butsfield	1996	Barnsley	6	1	
Winter DT	Danny	14/06/1918	Tonypandy	2004	Chelsea	6		
Winterbottom					Stalybridge Celtic	1		
Winters IA	Ian	08/02/1921	Renfrew	1994	York City	7	4	
Witcomb DF	Doug	18/04/1918	Cwm	1997	West Bromwich Alb.	4		w
Witcombe					Lovells Athletic	1		
Wombwell DP	Douglas				Mansfield Town	6	5	
Wood					Bath City	1		
Wood					Grantham	3		
Wood AR	Alf	14/05/1915	Aldridge	2001	Coventry City	2		
Wood C	Cyril				Accrington Stanley	1		
Wood E	Eric	13/03/1920	Bolton	2000	Rochdale	4	1	
Wood EJ	Jackie	23/10/1919	Canning Town	1993	West Ham United	4	2	
Wood S	Stan	01/07/1905	Winsford	1967	Halifax Town	2		
Wood TL	Terry	03/09/1920	Newport		Cardiff City	2		
Woodcock A	Arthur				Stockport County	1		
Woodgate JT	Terry	11/12/1919	East Ham	1985	West Ham United	4		
Woodley VR	Vic	26/02/1910	Cippenham	1978	Derby County	3		e
Woodman DWM	Douglas				Swindon Town	2		
Woodruff A	Arthur	12/04/1913	Barnsley	1983	Burnley	2		
Woods					Bath City	2	1	
Woods					Netherfield (Kendal)	2		
Woods PB	Paddy				Hartlepool United	1		
Woods W	Billy	12/03/1926	Farnworth	1980	Rochdale	2	1	
Woodward T	Tom	08/12/1917	Westhoughton	1994	Bolton Wanderers	8		
Woodward V	Vivian	20/05/1914	Troedyrhiw		Fulham	2		
Wookey KW	Ken	23/02/1922	Newport	2003	Newport County	6	2	
Woolacott H	Harold		Wales		Carlisle United	3		
Wooldridge J	Jim	28/09/1918	Rossington		Doncaster Rovers	2		
Wootton L	Len	13/06/1925	Stoke-on-Trent	1990	Port Vale	1		
Worrall FJ	Fred	08/09/1910	Warrington	1979	Portsmouth	2		e
Worrall J	Joseph				Stockport County	2		
Wort					North Shields	1		
Wragg S					Kettering Town	2		
Wrigglesworth WH	Billy	12/11/1912	South Elmsall	1980	Manchester United	4	2	
Wright GA	George	04/02/1920	Sheffield		Cardiff City	2		
Wright R	Reg				Walthamstow Avenue	3		
Wright WA	Billy	06/02/1924	Ironbridge	1994	Wolverhampton Wan.	4	3	e
Wroe E	Edward	1922			Lincoln City	4	1	
Wyles TC	Cec	01/11/1919	Gosberton Clough	1990	Blackburn Rovers	2	1	
Yarker F	Frederick				Northampton Town	4		
Yates R	Dick	06/06/1921	Queensferry	1976	Chester	2		
Young					Sutton United	2		
Young A	Alf	04/11/1905	Sunderland	1977	York City	5		e

Doug Witcomb

Vic Woodley

Billy Wright

THE FOOTBALL LEAGUE 1945-46

Because many players were still in the armed forces the Football League declared that 1945-46 was a "transitional season" and guest players were allowed. Players' appearances and goals this season are not included in their formal career records.

Clubs that would have formed Divisions One and Two in a normal season were split geographically into Leagues North and South. A full programme of 42 games was arranged for the two divisions. Two points were awarded for a win, and goal average (goals for divided by goals against) was used to separate clubs level on points.

Clubs that would have formed Division Three (North) were split into two divisions of 10 clubs each, labelled East and West. Hull City and New Brighton did not participate. In the first half of the season, the clubs played a full league programme of 18 games. In the second half of the season, the clubs played for a League Cup. Firstly, the 10 clubs in each group played home and away fixtures against 5 other clubs in the group. From the final league table, the top 8 clubs from each division went forward into a knockout tournament, with games played over two legs. In parallel with the knockout stage, the four clubs that had been omitted, and those that were later knocked out, competed for a further League title, labelled as the Division Three (North) second competition. The results of the knockout games were counted towards the League table, so it is not surprising that the League Cup (North) winners, Rotherham United, also won the second competition. Three cup games went to extra time; the score at 90 minutes was used for the League table.

Clubs that would have formed Division Three (South) were also split into two divisions, this time labelled North and South. In the first half of the season, the clubs played a full league programme of 20 games. As with the northern clubs, a League Cup competition filled the second half of the season. Firstly, the clubs played 7 or 8 other clubs from their own division, home and away. Also, 8 clubs from each division played home and away games against a club from the other southern division, with the result counting towards their own table. At the end of this process, each club had played 16 games. The top two from each division then met in semi-finals and the final.

In the pages that follow, month names are abbreviated as follows:

A	August	J	January
S	September	F	February
O	October	M	March
N	November	A	April
D	December	M	May

To "read" the grids, remember that the home club is in the column and the away club is in the row. Not all fixtures were played in some of the divisions.

Birmingham City, League South winners (back row left to right): Fred Harris, Ted Duckhouse, Gil Merrick, Don Dearson, Arthur Turner, Frank Mitchell. (front): Ambrose Mulraney, Dennis Jennings, Neil Dougall, Charlie Wilson-Jones, Harold Bodle, George Edwards.

Sheffield United, League North champions. The club flew to Berlin in May 1946 to play a Combined Services team. Left to right: Doug Livingstone (coach), Fred White, Charlie Thompson, Harold Brook, Alec Forbes, Fred Furniss, Walter Rickett, Albert Cox, Albert Nightingale, Colin Collindridge, Bobby Reid, Stan Machent, Eddie Shimwell, Harry Latham, Dick Lawrence (director)

SOUTH

Results grid (home team in rows; for each fixture the score is on the upper line and the match-date code on the lower line). Column order: Arsenal, Aston Villa, Birmingham City, Brentford, Charlton Athletic, Chelsea, Coventry City, Derby County, Fulham, Leicester City, Luton Town, Millwall, Newport County, Nottingham Forest, Plymouth Argyle, Portsmouth, Southampton, Swansea Town, Tottenham Hotspur, West Bromwich Alb., West Ham United, Wolverhampton Wan.

```
Arsenal
  -   2-4 0-3 1-1 1-2 1-2 0-0 0-1 2-0 1-2 0-2 4-0 7-0 2-2 3-0 4-3 1-1 1-1 2-0 2-1 3-2
      S22 F02 a29 O20 M09 S01 a22 N10 a20 S08 M30 D26 D15 N17 D08 a06 O06 F09 J12 m04 D29
Aston Villa
  5-1  -  2-2 1-1 0-2 0-3 0-0 4-1 3-0 3-0 7-1 2-0 5-2 3-1 4-2 3-2 2-0 6-3 5-1 3-3 2-2 1-1
  S29     J12 a17 O13 M27 a20 a06 O20 a22 S01 m01 D19 D01 N10 N17 M30 S08 F02 S05 D29 D26
Birmingham City
  0-1 3-1  -  1-0 1-0 5-2 2-0 1-0 2-0 6-2 3-2 4-0 3-2 3-1 0-1 1-0 4-0 5-0 8-0 4-0 0-1 0-1
  M13 J19     O27 F16 M03 D29 D22 F23 D25 S03 N24 a19 a13 M16 a10 D08 S29 O06 S08 D25 a27
Brentford
  6-3 0-1 2-1  -  1-1 4-4 1-2 0-0 1-2 1-2 6-1 7-0 2-1 5-1 3-2 0-2 1-4 2-2 1-3 2-0 1-1 0-0
  F23 F16 O20     M16 D01 J19 S13 M23 S06 a24 D15 A25 a27 a13 a19 D25 N24 N10 O13 S22 S15
Charlton Athletic
  6-2 0-0 0-0 4-3  -  0-0 3-1 2-1 4-2 2-1 5-1 2-3 2-0 2-0 4-0 2-0 3-0 1-0 3-4 1-2 7-4 1-1
  O27 O06 a29 a10     M30 S08 a20 N17 S01 S29 a06 D29 D26 D01 D15 a22 N03 a17 F02 J12 M04
Chelsea
  1-2 2-2 2-3 4-2 0-1  -  2-1 3-0 0-0 4-0 2-1 3-0 2-0 0-4 2-0 3-0 1-0 3-4 1-2 7-4 1-1 1-1
  M16 F23 N10 D08 a03     a10 S19 a13 J19 F16 D25 S15 A25 a19 a27 S12 D22 N17 O20 O13 S22
Coventry City
  2-0 2-2 2-3 1-0 1-1 2-0  -  3-1 3-1 0-1 0-3 7-2 7-1 1-4 3-1 3-1 0-1 2-2 0-1 3-2 2-5 1-0
  A25 a17 S17 J12 S15 F02     M14 S22 M30 a22 F09 N15 N10 O06 O20 M02 a06 m04 D26 D15 D08
Derby County
  1-1 0-1 0-2 3-2 3-1 1-1 3-0  -  5-2 4-1 4-3 8-1 4-1 3-2 3-1 3-1 8-1 2-1 2-0 3-3 5-1 2-0
  a19 a13 D15 D29 m01 m04 M16     A25 a10 a03 J12 O20 O13 S15 S22 F02 F16 D26 D08 N17 N10
Fulham
  5-2 1-4 3-2 2-2 2-4 3-2 2-0 2-1  -  1-1 4-1 7-0 3-1 3-3 4-0 5-2 3-1 5-2 1-1 1-4 0-1 3-0
  N03 O27 a15 M30 N24 a06 S29 S01     S08 O06 a22 m04 D29 D15 D26 a20 D01 M09 F09 F02 J12
Leicester City
  4-5 0-1 0-1 1-3 2-3 1-7 1-3 1-1 0-1  -  0-2 2-6 2-0 0-3 2-3 2-2 1-2 0-2 4-0 1-3 4-1 1-2
  J26 a23 D26 m04 A25 J12 M23 F23 S15     a13 F02 N10 O20 S29 O13 F09 M16 D29 D15 D08 N17
Luton Town
  1-2 1-1 0-3 1-4 1-4 3-1 1-2 1-1 2-2 2-1  -  0-1 1-0 1-4 0-0 1-1 4-2 3-1 3-1 1-2 1-4 1-0
  S15 A25 m04 F02 S22 M23 a19 M30 O13 a06     F02 N10 O20 S29 O13 F09 M16 D29 D15 D08 N17
Millwall
  1-1 2-2 5-1 3-1 2-2 0-8 1-1 1-2 0-1 2-2 2-0  -  4-0 2-1 6-1 4-0 5-3 5-1 3-2 1-0 2-0 0-0
  M23 M16 M17 D22 a13 D26 F16 J19 a19 a15 F23     M02 N17 O27 N10 M09 a20 J12 D29 D26 D15
Newport County
  1-2 0-4 0-1 0-5 2-1 1-3 1-4 1-5 2-0 4-0 3-1  -  2-4 2-6 3-1 1-4 2-3 1-1 4-2 1-3
  D25 D22 a22 S01 S13 S08 N22 O27 A30 N03 D01 S29 O16 J19 J26 O06 F22 a20 a06 M30 M09
Nottingham Forest
  3-2 1-3 1-0 2-0 0-2 0-1 0-0 1-1 1-1 1-1 0-2 2-2 7-2  -  2-0 3-0 4-0 2-2 0-2 0-2 1-1 0-0
  D22 D08 a06 a20 D25 S01 N03 O06 S12 O27 N24 S08 a23     S17 J19 J26 O06 F22 a20 a06 M30 M09 M02
Plymouth Argyle
  0-4 0-3 2-3 1-1 1-5 1-4 1-1 0-4 0-2 2-3 1-1 1-2 0-3 3-2  -  1-3 0-3 1-3 0-1 0-4 1-2 3-2
  N24 N03 a01 a06 D08 a22 O13 S08 D22 S22 O20 a27 J12 m04     D29 S01 D35 M30 M02 F09 F02
Portsmouth
  1-1 2-3 3-4 2-0 0-3 3-0 1-1 3-0 2-2 2-0 2-1 1-1 2-3 2-2 6-1  -  3-2 5-0 0-3 2-3 0-2
  D01 N24 M30 a22 D22 a20 O27 S29 D25 O06 N03 S01 F02 J12 S12     S08 A29 a06 M09 M02 F09
Southampton
  1-1 3-5 1-1 3-4 7-0 4-3 4-2 1-1 3-1 2-2 2-4 0-0 5-2 5-5 3-1  -  5-2 3-2 1-2 3-3 2-4
  a13 M23 D01 D26 a19 D29 F23 a29 a27 F16 M16 m04 O13 S22 A25 S15     J19 D15 N17 N10 O20
Swansea Town
  3-2 5-4 2-4 4-1 1-1 5-3 3-2 2-3 2-2 4-3 2-0 5-0 3-3 0-0 4-1  -  4-2 2-4 2-3 2-5
  O13 S15 S22 N17 N10 D15 a13 F21 D08 M09 a27 D29 M02 D26 m04 J12 O20 S01 a19 M23
Tottenham Hotspur
  2-0 3-0 0-1 1-0 2-1 3-2 2-0 2-5 1-3 6-2 2-3 5-1 1-0 3-2 2-0 2-0 4-3 3-1  -  4-2 2-3 1-4
  F16 F20 O13 N03 F23 N24 J26 D25 M16 S12 J19 D01 a27 a19 M23 a13 D22 O27 S29 S15 A25
West Bromwich Alb.
  0-1 1-0 0-0 3-4 2-5 8-1 2-2 2-3 3-1 3-1 6-0 1-0 5-2 2-0 5-2 4-1 5-0  -  1-2 1-1
  J19 A29 S15 O06 a15 O27 D24 D01 F16 D22 S12 N03 a13 M23 F23 M16 N24 A25 S22 a27 a23
West Ham United
  1-1 1-2 3-2 0-2 2-0 6-3 2-3 3-5 2-2 3-4 4-1 1-3 7-0 3-1 3-1 3-0 1-1 1-1  -  2-1
  a27 S10 S01 S29 J19 O06 D22 N24 a29 D01 D25 O27 M23 M16 F16 F23 N03 a22 S08 a20 a13
Wolverhampton Wan.
  1-1 1-2 3-3 1-0 1-2 1-0 1-0 1-0 2-0 3-0 3-0 1-2 5-2 4-0 1-1 4-0 3-2 1-0 4-2 0-0 3-3  -
  S03 D25 a20 S08 A27 S29 D01 N03 J19 N24 D22 O06 M16 F23 M29 O16 O27 M30 S01 a22 a06
```

	p	w	d	l	f	a	w	d	l	f	a	tf	ta	pts
Birmingham City	42	17	0	4	56	14	11	5	5	40	31	96	45	61
Aston Villa	42	13	6	2	61	28	12	5	4	45	30	106	58	61
Charlton Athletic	42	14	6	1	50	17	11	4	6	42	28	92	45	60
Derby County	42	16	3	2	67	26	8	4	9	34	36	101	62	55
West Bromwich Alb.	42	13	3	5	60	29	9	5	7	44	40	104	69	52
Wolverhampton Wan.	42	13	5	3	44	20	7	6	8	31	28	75	48	51
West Ham United	42	10	4	7	53	38	10	7	4	41	38	94	76	51
Fulham	42	13	4	4	60	35	7	6	8	33	38	93	73	50
Tottenham Hotspur	42	15	0	6	51	33	7	3	11	27	48	78	81	47
Chelsea	42	11	3	7	44	29	8	3	10	48	51	92	80	44
Arsenal	42	9	5	7	41	28	7	6	8	35	45	76	73	43
Millwall	42	11	6	4	51	33	6	2	13	28	72	79	105	42
Coventry City	42	11	3	7	45	32	4	7	10	25	37	70	69	40
Brentford	42	8	6	7	46	33	6	4	11	36	39	82	72	38
Nottingham Forest	42	7	8	6	31	24	5	5	11	41	49	72	73	37
Southampton	42	9	7	5	61	46	5	2	14	36	59	97	105	37
Swansea Town	42	12	4	5	61	43	3	3	15	29	69	90	112	37
Luton Town	42	7	5	9	29	37	6	2	13	31	55	60	92	33
Portsmouth	42	9	5	7	45	30	2	1	18	21	57	66	87	28
Leicester City	42	4	3	14	30	47	4	4	13	27	54	57	101	23
Newport County	42	7	1	13	33	55	2	1	18	19	70	52	125	20
Plymouth Argyle	42	2	3	16	19	56	1	5	15	20	64	39	120	14

NORTH

Cross-table of results (home team listed down the left; score shown above, match-reference code below):

```
                    Ba  BR  Bk  BW  BP  Bu  By  Ch  Ev  GT  HT  LU  Li  MC  MU  Mi  NU  PN  SU  SW  SC  Su

Barnsley            -   4-0 1-1 0-3 3-0 2-0 1-3 2-2 2-0 1-0 3-2 1-0 2-0 2-2 2-2 1-3 1-5 3-5 4-0 3-3 4-2 ...
                        m04 D15 a27 J12 a06 D29 M30 a19 D08 M16 S15 D26 F02 S22 O10 F16 A25 O20 M02 O17 O13

Blackburn Rovers    3-1 -   1-1 0-1 1-2 4-2 2-3 0-7 2-1 3-2 1-6 0-0 0-5 0-0 1-3 3-3 1-2 0-2 0-0 2-1 5-1 2-1
                    J01     S15 F20 N10 O20 O06 S17 J12 O25 D25 F23 S22 N24 M16 a19 D01 F16 a13 D15 a20 M23

Blackpool           1-1 5-2 -   1-1 0-1 2-1 3-1 0-1 5-2 5-3 1-0 4-2 1-1 5-4 1-5 3-1 1-1 6-3 1-2 5-1 2-1 4-0
                    D22 S08     S12 S29 a22 S01 D01 D25 a13 N24 J19 a20 O06 M27 M16 O27 A27 F23 N03 M30 F16

Bolton Wanderers    2-0 1-2 1-1 -   0-0 2-0 1-0 1-0 3-1 0-0 2-1 6-0 1-0 3-1 1-1 2-1 0-1 0-0 1-4 2-1 2-2 1-2
                    a20 F02 D29     M13 S08 J12 a22 S01 J01 a06 O13 a29 M27 O20 D08 a10 S22 N17 M30 D15 N10

Bradford Park Ave.  2-1 2-1 3-0 0-5 -   7-0 6-0 1-0 1-2 2-3 2-2 9-4 0-2 2-3 2-1 1-1 5-3 3-1 0-4 3-2 1-0 1-0
                    J19 N03 S22 F16     N17 O20 A27 a03 S15 S12 M16 O13 D01 M23 a27 M27 F23 a19 D25 A25 a13

Burnley             3-2 1-4 1-1 2-2 2-1 -   2-3 3-1 1-0 1-2 4-3 2-3 1-3 1-0 2-2 8-1 3-2 0-0 0-1 2-2 1-0 2-3
                    a13 O27 a19 S15 N24     S22 M16 a27 M30 J26 N10 A25 D15 D08 F02 D29 O13 m04 J12 a01 D26

Bury                1-1 3-2 1-4 0-2 2-3 1-0 -   2-3 3-1 1-1 2-1 3-1 2-1 1-3 1-1 1-1 2-1 1-1 2-2 1-2 2-4 3-0
                    S12 O13 A25 J19 O27 S29     D25 m04 a27 N24 F23 a13 N24 F02 a13 N24 F02 M23 D01 a19 M16

Chesterfield        1-1 4-0 0-3 1-2 2-0 3-0 3-1 -   1-1 0-2 0-0 3-1 1-1 0-1 1-1 1-0 2-0 1-0 0-0 1-1 1-1 3-0
                    M23 D29 D08 a19 m04 M09 D26     a13 N17 M02 A25 D15 J12 S15 O20 F02 a27 O13 F20 N10 S22

Everton             0-4 4-1 7-1 3-2 0-0 2-0 3-1 4-0 -   2-1 5-2 0-2 2-2 4-1 1-1 3-0 4-1 2-0 0-3 0-2 4-1
                    a22 J19 a26 A25 F02 a20 J01 a06     D15 M30 S22 D29 F09 O13 N17 M02 S15 N10 M09 D08 O20

Grimsby Town        0-0 2-0 4-2 0-2 2-1 1-1 1-1 3-3 1-2 -   5-3 3-2 1-1 0-2 1-1 1-0 1-6 1-2 0-2 4-1
                    D01 S01 a06 D25 S08 M23 a20 N24 D22     N03 J26 a20 S29 J19 F23 O06 m04 F16 O27 M16 F16

Huddersfield Town   2-1 0-2 2-4 1-1 1-1 4-2 3-0 1-2 0-1 3-2 -   3-2 3-1 3-0 3-2 7-0 1-4 2-0 1-4 3-2 3-1 4-1
                    M09 D26 N17 a13 D29 F16 D15 F23 M23 N10     a27 D08 m04 A25 O13 J12 a23 S22 F02 O20 S15

Leeds United        1-2 1-4 1-2 2-1 3-1 1-2 3-3 1-2 2-0 4-1 1-1 -   3-0 1-3 3-3 1-0 0-3 2-1 2-4 0-1 0-0 4-2
                    S08 M02 J12 O06 m01 N03 F09 S01 S29 M09 a20     F02 M30 N17 D25 a06 O20 D15 a22 D29 D01

Liverpool           5-2 4-0 4-0 2-2 4-1 2-3 1-1 2-2 2-1 2-0 4-1 1-1 -   0-5 0-5 1-2 3-0 4-2 0-3 0-2 4-1 2-2
                    D25 S29 a27 A29 O06 S01 S08 D22 S12 a19 D01 a10     O27 F16 M23 N03 J12 M16 N24 a13 F23

Manchester City     2-3 4-2 1-4 1-0 6-0 1-2 4-1 1-0 1-3 0-2 3-2 5-1 1-0 -   1-3 2-1 4-3 3-0 2-1 1-5 0-2 0-2
                    M13 N17 O13 F23 D08 D22 N10 J19 F16 S22 J01 M23 O20     a13 A25 D25 M16 a27 S12 S15 a19

Manchester United   1-1 6-2 4-2 2-1 4-0 3-3 1-1 0-2 0-0 5-0 2-3 6-1 2-1 1-4 -   4-1 4-1 6-1 2-3 4-0 2-1 2-1
                    S29 M09 F02 O27 M30 D01 M02 S08 O06 J12 S01 N24 F09 a06     D29 a22 N03 D26 a20 m04 D15

Middlesbrough       2-5 5-1 4-2 1-0 3-0 2-1 3-0 0-0 3-1 2-8 4-1 2-5 2-2 2-1 0-6 -   0-1 3-4 2-0 9-1 4-1
                    N03 a22 M09 D01 a20 a10 a06 O27 N24 M02 O06 D26 M30 S01 S12     S08 D15 J19 S29 m01 J01

Newcastle United    1-0 8-1 2-2 3-4 4-0 0-1 4-2 3-2 1-3 6-2 4-1 1-1 6-2 1-1 0-1 1-1 -   2-1 6-0 2-0 2-4 1-1
                    m01 D08 O20 M16 D15 S12 N17 J26 F23 O13 J19 a13 N10 D26 a19 S15     M23 A25 J01 S22 a27

Preston North End   2-3 3-1 5-0 1-2 4-6 4-0 1-2 1-0 0-2 1-2 2-0 8-2 2-1 3-1 2-2 0-1 3-1 -   5-2 0-1 2-4 1-1
                    S01 M21 S03 S29 a11 O06 S17 a20 S08 D29 a22 O27 J19 M09 N10 D22 M30     D08 a06 D26 N17

Sheffield United    1-1 2-1 4-2 2-3 1-1 5-1 2-1 1-1 4-0 7-1 4-1 2-3 1-3 1-0 2-7 3-0 2-0 2-1 -   1-0 6-3
                    O27 a06 M02 N24 a22 J01 M30 O06 N03 F09 S29 D22 M09 a20 D25 J12 S01 D01     S08 F02 S13

Sheffield Wed.      0-3 1-1 3-2 0-0 3-0 1-1 2-0 1-0 0-0 4-1 3-0 2-0 2-1 1-1 2-3 3-1 6-0 0-3 3-0 -   0-0
                    F23 D15 N10 a01 D26 J19 D08 F16 M16 O20 F04 a23 N17 D29 a27 S22 m04 a13 S15     O13 A25

Stoke City          4-0 5-0 6-3 4-1 3-0 0-0 2-0 6-1 2-3 4-2 6-2 2-1 0-1 2-0 1-2 1-4 3-1 6-0 0-3 3-0 -   0-0
                    N24 a27 M23 D22 S01 F23 a22 N03 a15 O27 S13 a06 S08 S20 F16 S29 D25 a08 O06        J19

Sunderland          1-0 2-2 3-1 1-0 1-0 1-1 2-1 0-5 0-4 2-0 0-2 5-1 0-2 4-0 4-2 0-1 1-0 0-1 1-2 1-0 4-2 -
                    O06 M30 M13 N03 a06 D25 M09 S29 O27 F02 S08 D08 M02 a22 D22 m04 a20 N24 D29 S01 O17
```

	p	w	d	l	f	a	w	d	l	f	a	ff	ta	pts
Sheffield United	42	14	3	4	61	29	13	3	5	51	33	112	62	60
Everton	42	14	5	2	58	23	9	4	8	30	31	88	54	55
Bolton Wanderers	42	11	6	4	32	18	9	5	7	35	27	67	45	51
Manchester United	42	13	4	4	61	29	6	7	8	37	33	98	62	49
Sheffield Wed.	42	13	5	3	39	20	7	3	11	28	40	67	60	48
Newcastle United	42	13	4	4	68	27	8	1	12	38	43	106	70	47
Chesterfield	42	9	8	4	29	16	8	4	9	39	33	68	49	46
Barnsley	42	11	5	5	44	33	6	6	9	32	35	76	68	45
Blackpool	42	13	4	4	56	34	5	5	11	38	58	94	92	45
Manchester City	42	12	0	9	43	37	8	4	9	35	38	78	75	44
Liverpool	42	10	5	6	47	36	7	4	10	33	34	80	70	43
Middlesbrough	42	12	2	7	44	43	5	7	9	31	44	75	87	43
Stoke City	42	14	2	5	60	24	4	4	13	28	55	88	79	42
Bradford Park Ave.	42	13	2	6	53	35	4	4	13	18	49	71	84	40
Huddersfield Town	42	13	2	6	50	33	4	2	15	40	56	90	89	38
Burnley	42	9	5	7	42	36	4	5	12	21	48	63	84	36
Grimsby Town	42	8	6	7	32	34	5	3	13	29	55	61	89	35
Sunderland	42	12	2	7	33	27	3	3	15	22	56	55	83	35
Preston North End	42	10	2	9	50	34	4	4	13	20	43	70	77	34
Bury	42	8	6	7	35	35	4	4	13	25	50	60	85	34
Blackburn Rovers	42	7	5	9	31	44	4	2	15	29	67	60	111	29
Leeds United	42	7	4	10	36	42	2	3	16	30	76	66	118	25

Div 3 North (West)

	Accrington Stanley	Barrow	Chester	Crewe Alexandra	Oldham Athletic	Rochdale	Southport	Stockport County	Tranmere Rovers	Wrexham
Accrington Stanley	-	4-1 D01	5-2 N03	0-1 J01	1-1 S29	4-2 D26	1-0 O27	3-0 O06	2-3 S01	2-1 S08
Barrow	0-4 D29	-	1-3 S29	0-0 O20	3-2 D25	2-1 N10	3-3 S15	2-3 S01	0-2 O13	1-0 J01
Chester	3-3 N10	3-1 S22	-	0-0 O13	2-2 D22	3-3 O27	5-3 S01	4-2 D25	5-1 S08	4-1 D01
Crewe Alexandra	1-2 D22	7-0 O27	2-0 O06	-	0-0 S01	1-4 D01	3-0 S29	1-2 S08	5-3 N03	2-1 D25
Oldham Athletic	0-3 S22	3-1 D26	2-3 D29	4-2 A25	-	2-1 S15	3-0 J01	4-1 N03	1-2 O27	0-0 O13
Rochdale	2-0 D25	3-0 N03	3-1 O20	3-2 D29	4-2 S08	-	5-0 O13	4-2 S29	0-0 a19	3-1 S01
Southport	0-0 O20	2-1 S08	3-5 A25	2-7 S22	3-0 D01	1-2 O06	-	0-4 D22	0-1 D20	2-2 O10
Stockport County	0-0 O13	2-3 A25	1-1 D26	4-5 S15	3-1 N10	7-0 S22	1-1 D15	-	2-1 D29	1-2 O20
Tranmere Rovers	1-3 A25	1-1 O06	3-0 S15	4-1 N10	2-1 O20	3-2 D22	1-2 D26	3-1 D01	-	2-3 S22
Wrexham	1-0 S15	1-1 D22	2-0 D24	2-3 D26	1-1 O06	4-1 A25	3-0 N03	3-2 O27	2-0 S29	-

	p	w	d	l	f	a	w	d	l	f	a	tf	ta	pts
Accrington Stanley	18	6	1	2	22	11	4	3	2	15	8	37	19	24
Rochdale	18	8	1	0	27	8	2	1	6	16	27	43	35	22
Crewe Alexandra	18	5	1	3	22	12	4	2	3	21	19	43	31	21
Chester	18	5	4	0	29	16	3	1	5	15	22	44	38	21
Wrexham	18	6	2	1	19	8	2	2	5	11	17	30	25	20
Tranmere Rovers	18	5	1	3	20	14	4	1	4	13	17	33	31	20
Stockport County	18	3	3	3	21	14	3	0	6	17	24	38	38	15
Oldham Athletic	18	5	1	3	19	13	0	4	5	10	19	29	32	15
Barrow	18	3	2	4	12	18	1	2	6	9	26	21	44	12
Southport	18	2	2	5	13	22	1	2	6	9	25	22	47	10

Div 3 North (East)

	Bradford City	Carlisle United	Darlington	Doncaster Rovers	Gateshead	Halifax Town	Hartlepools United	Lincoln City	Rotherham United	York City
Bradford City	-	2-3 D29	2-5 N10	3-3 O06	5-1 a20	5-1 S01	2-0 S29	5-1 S08	0-4 O27	6-0 D26
Carlisle United	2-2 D01	-	3-3 J01	2-4 O27	3-2 D26	4-1 S15	1-3 O06	4-3 S29	3-2 N03	0-2 S01
Darlington	3-2 N03	7-1 D22	-	2-1 S15	2-4 A25	1-2 O20	5-2 D26	6-1 D01	6-1 O13	3-1 S29
Doncaster Rovers	3-1 O13	3-0 O20	1-2 S08	-	2-2 N10	3-0 D15	2-0 S01	3-1 D25	0-3 S22	1-1 D01
Gateshead	3-2 D22	3-1 D25	4-2 S01	3-1 N03	-	3-3 S29	3-1 O29	6-1 O06	4-1 D01	1-3 S08
Halifax Town	0-0 A25	5-2 S08	6-5 O27	2-3 D22	1-4 S22	-	3-2 D01	6-2 N03	1-4 D25	3-1 O13
Hartlepools United	3-2 S22	3-2 O13	0-0 D25	1-1 A25	0-2 O20	0-0 D08	-	1-4 J01	2-4 S15	0-2 N03
Lincoln City	2-3 S15	5-0 S22	1-3 D29	4-0 D26	1-4 O13	1-2 N10	4-2 D22	-	1-1 A25	2-2 O27
Rotherham United	4-1 O20	5-0 N10	1-2 O06	7-1 S29	3-1 J01	6-3 D26	3-0 S08	3-0 S01	-	3-2 D22
York City	2-2 D25	3-3 A25	3-4 S22	1-2 D29	2-1 S15	0-0 O06	5-2 N10	3-0 O20	1-1 F20	-

	p	w	d	l	f	a	w	d	l	f	a	tf	ta	pts
Rotherham United	18	8	0	1	35	10	4	2	3	21	18	56	28	26
Darlington	18	7	0	2	35	15	5	2	2	26	21	61	36	26
Gateshead	18	7	1	1	30	15	4	1	4	21	19	51	34	24
Doncaster Rovers	18	5	2	2	18	10	3	2	4	16	25	34	35	20
York City	18	3	4	2	20	15	3	2	4	14	19	34	34	18
Halifax Town	18	5	1	3	27	23	2	3	4	12	23	39	46	18
Bradford City	18	5	1	3	30	18	1	3	5	15	22	45	40	16
Carlisle United	18	4	2	3	22	22	1	1	7	12	36	34	58	13
Lincoln City	18	3	2	4	21	17	1	0	8	13	37	34	54	10
Hartlepools United	18	2	3	4	10	17	1	0	8	12	28	22	45	9

Div 3 North (West) Cup

	Accrington Stanley	Barrow	Chester	Crewe Alexandra	Oldham Athletic	Rochdale	Southport	Stockport County	Tranmere Rovers	Wrexham
Accrington Stanley	–	5-3 M16	2-1 M09	–	3-3 F02	–	4-0 F23	–	1-0 J26	–
Barrow	0-5 J12	–	–	0-3 F16	–	0-3 M09	1-2 J26	4-0 F02	–	–
Chester	4-1 M02	–	–	8-3 F02	2-0 J19	–	1-2 J12	–	4-2 F16	–
Crewe Alexandra	–	–	5-5 F09	–	3-1 J12	3-1 F23	1-1 J19	3-2 M02	–	–
Oldham Athletic	2-1 F09	0-0 F23	–	1-1 J05	–	–	–	–	1-2 M09	2-1 J19
Rochdale	–	–	6-1 J26	2-2 F16	–	–	1-3 J12	2-3 F02	–	1-2 M02
Southport	3-0 F16	4-2 M02	–	2-1 J26	0-2 M16	–	–	–	–	3-1 F09
Stockport County	–	5-2 J19	2-0 J19	4-1 D08	–	2-2 F09	–	–	4-0 F23	–
Tranmere Rovers	1-2 M06	2-1 F09	–	–	3-3 M02	–	3-0 F16	–	–	3-2 M16
Wrexham	–	–	2-0 F23	–	1-2 J26	2-1 M09	1-1 F02	–	7-3 J12	–

	p	w	d	l	f	a	w	d	l	f	a	tf	ta	pts
Stockport County	10	4	1	0	17	5	3	0	2	9	10	26	15	15
Southport	10	4	0	1	12	6	2	2	1	8	7	20	13	14
Accrington Stanley	10	4	1	0	15	7	2	0	3	9	10	24	17	13
Oldham Athletic	10	2	2	1	6	5	2	2	1	12	10	18	15	12
Crewe Alexandra	10	3	2	0	15	10	0	2	3	8	17	23	27	10
Wrexham	10	3	1	1	13	7	1	0	4	8	13	21	20	9
Chester	10	4	0	1	19	8	0	1	4	7	17	26	25	9
Tranmere Rovers	10	3	1	1	12	8	1	0	4	5	17	17	25	9
Rochdale	10	1	1	3	12	11	1	1	3	6	9	18	20	6
Barrow	10	1	0	4	5	13	0	1	4	8	16	13	29	3

Div 3 North (East) Cup

	Bradford City	Carlisle United	Darlington	Doncaster Rovers	Gateshead	Halifax Town	Hartlepools United	Lincoln City	Rotherham United	York City
Bradford City	–	3-2 F02	4-5 J12	–	–	–	6-2 M02	–	5-1 M09	0-0 F09
Carlisle United	6-2 J26	–	5-1 M09	–	3-0 F23	–	1-3 F16	–	–	3-1 J19
Darlington	2-1 J19	1-3 J05	–	–	3-1 F09	–	3-1 J26	7-2 F23	–	–
Doncaster Rovers	–	–	–	–	4-2 J26	1-1 F16	–	0-0 J19	3-1 F23	M16
Gateshead	–	0-2 M02	3-1 F16	3-3 M09	–	2-2 J12	–	–	6-4 F02	–
Halifax Town	–	–	4-1 F09	0-1 J19	–	–	2-5 J05	1-3 J26	–	0-1 F23
Hartlepools United	0-0 F23	5-3 F09	5-1 F02	–	1-1 M09	–	–	–	2-3 J19	–
Lincoln City	–	–	6-2 M02	2-3 J12	–	2-3 F02	–	–	1-5 F09	2-2 M13
Rotherham United	2-4 M06	–	1-3 M02	1-3 M16	–	1-1 J12	6-1 F16	–	–	–
York City	2-2 F16	1-2 J12	1-3 F02	–	1-1 M02	–	6-2 M09	–	–	–

	p	w	d	l	f	a	w	d	l	f	a	tf	ta	pts
Doncaster Rovers	10	3	2	0	11	4	3	1	1	13	11	24	15	15
Carlisle United	10	4	0	1	18	7	3	0	2	12	10	30	17	14
Bradford City	10	3	1	1	18	10	1	2	2	9	12	27	22	11
Hartlepools United	10	2	2	1	13	8	2	1	2	12	13	25	21	11
Gateshead	10	2	2	1	14	12	2	0	3	7	11	21	23	10
Darlington	10	4	0	1	16	8	1	0	4	10	23	26	31	10
Rotherham United	10	1	1	3	11	12	2	1	2	13	14	24	26	8
York City	10	1	2	2	11	10	1	2	2	5	8	16	18	8
Halifax Town	10	1	0	4	7	11	1	4	0	8	7	15	18	8
Lincoln City	10	1	1	3	13	15	1	0	4	8	23	21	38	5

The top eight clubs in each division went forward to the knock-out phase

DIVISION THREE (NORTH) CUP: KNOCKOUT ROUNDS

The score at 90 minutes in all these games also counted towards the Second Championship, except for the First Round replay.

FIRST ROUND, FIRST LEG March 23 1946

Accrington Stanley	v	York City	1-0
Carlisle United	v	Tranmere Rovers	5-1
Chester	v	Bradford City	3-0
Crewe Alexandra	v	Hartlepools United	1-2
Darlington	v	Southport	2-1
Doncaster Rovers	v	Stockport County	2-2
Oldham Athletic	v	Gateshead	2-2
Rotherham United	v	Wrexham	4-0

FIRST ROUND, SECOND LEG Mar 30 1946

Bradford City	v	Chester	2-2		2-5
Gateshead	v	Oldham Athletic	3-0		2-5
Hartlepools United	v	Crewe Alexandra	3-3		5-4
Southport	v	Darlington	3-1	aet	4-3
Stockport County	v	Doncaster Rovers	2-2	aet	4-4
Tranmere Rovers	v	Carlisle United	2-1		3-6
Wrexham	v	Rotherham United	0-2		6-0
York City	v	Accrington Stanley	3-1		3-2

FIRST ROUND REPLAY April 3 1946

Docaster Rovers	v	Stockport County	4-0

SECOND ROUND, FIRST LEG April 6 1946

Carlisle United	v	Gateshead	1-2
Chester	v	York City	4-0
Doncaster Rovers	v	Rotherham United	0-0
Hartlepools United	v	Southport	1-2

SECOND ROUND, SECOND LEG April 13 1946

Gateshead	v	Carlisle United	2-1	aet	4-2
Rotherham United	v	Doncaster Rovers	2-0		2-0
Southport	v	Hartlepools United	1-1		3-2
York City	v	Chester	1-0		1-4

SEMI-FINALS, FIRST LEG April 19 1946

Chester	v	Southport	3-0
Gateshead	v	Rotherham United	2-2

SEMI-FINALS, SECOND LEG April 22 1946

Rotherham United	v	Gateshead	3-1	5-3
Southport	v	Chester	2-4	2-7

FINAL, FIRST LEG April 27 1946

Rotherham United	v	Chester	2-2

Rotherham United: Warnes, Selkirk, Hanson, Edwards, H Williams, Mills, Guest, J Shaw, Ardron, Burke (Luton Town), Dawson. Scorer: J Shaw (2)
Chester: Scales, James (Bradford PA), McNeil, Marsh, Walters, Lee, Bett (Sunderland), Leahy, Burden (Wolves), Astbury, Hamilton. Scorers: Bett, Hamilton
Att: 12,000

FINAL SECOND LEG May 4 1946

Chester	Rotherham United	2-3

Rotherham United won 5-4 on aggregate

Chester: Scales, James (Bradford PA), McNeil, Marsh, Walters, Lee, Bett (Sunderland), Leahy, Burden (Wolves), Astbury, Hamilton. Scorers: Leahy, Bett
Rotherham United: Warnes, Selkirk, Hanson, Mills, H Williams, D Williams, Wilson (Crystal Palace), J Shaw, Ardron, Burke (Luton Town), Dawson. Scorers: Dawson, Burke, J Shaw
Att: 12,650

Div 3 North (2)

	Accrington	Barrow	Bradford C	Carlisle U	Chester	Crewe Alex.	Darlington	Doncaster R	Gateshead	Halifax T	Hartlepool U	Lincoln C	Oldham Ath.	Rochdale	Rotherham U	Southport	Stockport Co	Tranmere R	Wrexham	York C
Accrington Stanley	–	–	3-1 a19	–	–	–	2-2 a06	–	–	–	2-1 a27	–	–	–	–	–	–	–	–	1-0 M23
Barrow	–	–	2-0 a13	–	–	–	–	–	2-3 a27	–	2-1 a22	–	–	1-2 M30	–	–	–	–	–	–
Bradford City	2-0 a22	2-3 a06	–	2-2 M30	–	–	–	–	–	–	–	–	–	–	–	–	–	–	4-2 m04	–
Carlisle United	–	–	–	–	3-1 a27	4-0 a19	1-2 a06	–	–	–	–	–	–	–	–	–	–	5-1 M23	–	–
Chester	–	–	3-0 M23	–	–	–	–	–	–	–	–	–	–	2-3 m04	3-0 a19	–	–	–	–	4-0 a06
Crewe Alexandra	–	–	–	2-1 a27	–	–	–	–	1-2 M23	–	–	–	–	–	–	4-2 a19	–	–	2-1 a06	–
Darlington	4-3 a13	–	–	2-2 a22	–	–	–	–	4-1 a20	–	–	–	–	–	–	–	2-1 M23	2-3 m04	–	–
Doncaster Rovers	–	–	–	–	–	–	–	–	–	–	5-1 m04	–	–	0-0 a06	–	–	2-2 M23	–	–	1-1 a22
Gateshead	–	4-2 m04	–	0-1 a13	–	–	–	–	–	–	3-0 M30	–	–	–	2-2 a19	–	–	–	–	–
Halifax Town	–	–	–	–	–	–	–	–	–	–	2-3 M30	1-0 a06	–	–	–	0-1 a20	–	–	–	–
Hartlepools United	–	3-1 a19	–	–	2-3 M30	–	–	–	–	–	–	–	–	–	–	1-2 a06	–	–	–	6-2 m04
Lincoln City	5-1 m04	–	–	–	–	–	–	–	1-1 M23	–	–	–	–	1-2 a13	–	–	–	–	3-0 a20	–
Oldham Athletic	–	–	–	–	–	2-1 a27	2-2 M23	–	1-1 a13	–	–	–	–	0-4 a22	–	–	–	–	–	–
Rochdale	–	2-1 M23	–	–	–	–	–	–	–	–	2-3 a06	3-1 a20	–	–	–	–	2-1 m04	–	–	–
Rotherham United	–	–	–	2-2 a27	–	2-0 a13	3-1 a22	–	–	–	–	–	–	–	–	–	–	–	4-0 M23	–
Southport	–	–	–	2-4 a22	2-1 M30	–	–	–	–	–	1-1 a13	–	–	2-0 a27	–	–	–	–	–	–
Stockport County	–	–	–	1-2 m04	–	0-1 a22	2-2 M30	–	3-2 a27	–	–	–	–	–	–	–	–	–	6-1 a13	–
Tranmere Rovers	–	–	–	2-1 M30	3-0 a27	–	–	–	–	–	3-0 a22	–	–	–	–	–	3-0 a06	–	–	–
Wrexham	–	–	3-1 a27	–	0-0 a13	–	–	–	–	–	1-1 a22	–	–	–	–	–	0-2 M30	–	–	–
York City	3-1 M30	–	–	–	1-0 a13	–	5-1 a19	–	–	–	2-3 a27	–	–	–	–	–	–	–	–	–

	p	w	d	l	f	a	w	d	l	f	a	tf	ta	pts
Rotherham United	8	3	1	0	11	3	2	2	0	7	4	18	7	13
Rochdale	8	3	0	1	9	6	3	0	1	8	4	17	10	12
Carlisle United	9	3	0	1	13	4	2	1	2	7	7	20	11	11
Crewe Alexandra	8	3	0	1	9	6	2	1	1	5	5	14	11	11
Chester	8	3	0	1	12	3	1	2	1	8	7	20	10	10
Gateshead	8	2	1	1	9	5	2	1	1	8	8	17	13	10
Tranmere Rovers	8	4	0	0	11	1	1	0	3	5	16	16	17	10
Lincoln City	8	2	1	1	10	4	2	0	2	7	9	17	13	9
Hartlepools United	9	2	0	2	12	8	2	1	2	8	10	20	18	9
Stockport County	9	2	1	2	12	8	1	1	2	5	9	17	17	8
Darlington	9	3	1	1	14	10	0	1	3	3	11	17	21	8
York City	8	3	0	1	11	5	0	1	3	3	12	14	17	7
Southport	8	2	1	1	7	6	1	0	3	4	8	11	14	7
Accrington Stanley	8	3	1	0	8	4	0	0	4	5	14	13	18	7
Barrow	8	2	0	2	7	6	1	0	3	7	11	14	17	6
Doncaster Rovers	8	1	3	0	8	4	0	1	3	4	11	12	15	6
Halifax Town	7	1	0	2	3	4	0	3	1	5	6	8	10	5
Bradford City	8	2	1	1	10	7	0	0	4	2	11	12	18	5
Wrexham	7	1	2	1	4	4	0	0	3	3	10	7	14	4
Oldham Athletic	8	1	2	1	5	8	0	0	4	2	12	7	20	4

Div 3 South (North)

	Clapton Orient	Ipswich Town	Mansfield Town	Northampton Town	Norwich City	Notts County	Port Vale	Queen's Park Rgs.	Southend United	Walsall	Watford
Clapton Orient	-	2-1 O27	0-0 S01	1-0 N03	3-0 D29	3-3 D20	1-1 O06	0-2 S05	2-2 S08	2-0 S29	4-0 J10
Ipswich Town	3-1 O20	-	1-1 F20	2-1 S22	0-0 D19	1-0 S08	0-1 S01	2-1 O13	3-1 D26	5-3 D29	4-2 O10
Mansfield Town	2-2 A25	1-2 D22	-	2-0 D25	4-1 O13	2-3 O27	1-2 D01	2-6 S12	2-2 N03	6-1 S19	1-2 S15
Northampton Town	6-1 N10	3-3 S29	4-0 D26	-	4-1 J01	1-2 O06	1-0 S08	0-2 O20	6-2 D29	1-0 S01	3-0 S18
Norwich City	3-0 S13	4-0 D01	5-1 O06	2-1 D22	-	5-1 S29	3-4 A30	1-1 D25	6-1 O27	2-1 N03	8-1 A25
Notts County	1-0 D01	1-1 S15	1-0 O20	7-1 O13	2-2 S22	-	3-1 S19	0-1 N10	4-1 O05	2-0 D24	1-2 D26
Port Vale	4-0 O13	3-2 A25	2-0 D24	0-0 S15	2-2 S03	3-0 D29	-	0-0 S22	1-1 J01	0-1 D26	2-1 O20
Queen's Park Rgs.	3-0 S19	2-0 O06	3-2 D29	4-1 O27	1-2 D26	6-0 N03	4-1 S29	-	4-1 S01	4-0 S08	1-1 J01
Southend United	1-1 S15	2-0 D25	1-1 N10	0-1 S05	1-4 O20	7-3 S12	2-0 D22	1-2 A25	-	0-1 D01	6-2 S22
Walsall	5-3 S22	3-0 S12	2-0 S28	1-1 A25	1-2 N10	3-3 D22	1-5 D25	1-1 S15	6-0 D08	-	0-3 O13
Watford	5-2 D22	4-3 N03	2-1 S08	4-2 A27	2-1 S01	7-2 D25	2-2 O27	0-2 D01	0-1 S29	2-1 O06	-

	p	w	d	l	f	a	w	d	l	f	a	tf	ta	pts
Queen's Park Rgs.	20	8	1	1	32	8	6	3	1	18	7	50	15	32
Norwich City	20	8	1	1	39	11	3	3	4	15	20	54	31	26
Port Vale	20	5	4	1	17	7	4	2	4	17	18	34	25	24
Watford	20	7	1	2	28	17	3	1	6	14	30	42	47	22
Ipswich Town	20	7	2	1	21	11	1	2	7	12	25	33	36	20
Notts County	20	6	2	2	22	9	2	2	6	17	38	39	47	20
Northampton Town	20	7	1	2	29	11	1	2	7	8	23	37	34	19
Clapton Orient	20	5	4	1	18	9	0	2	8	10	33	28	42	16
Walsall	20	4	3	3	23	18	2	0	8	8	24	31	42	15
Southend United	20	4	2	4	21	15	1	3	6	12	34	33	49	15
Mansfield Town	20	3	2	5	23	21	0	3	7	6	21	29	42	11

Div 3 South (South)

	Aldershot	Bournemouth	Brighton & Hove A.	Bristol City	Bristol Rovers	Cardiff City	Crystal Palace	Exeter City	Reading	Swindon Town	Torquay United
Aldershot	-	2-2 S15	4-2 N10	2-1 O20	3-2 D29	1-5 S29	2-5 S01	3-5 S05	1-3 D26	1-1 a10	3-0 O06
Bournemouth	7-0 S08	-	3-0 O13	8-1 S22	3-5 J05	1-5 S01	2-1 D26	3-1 O20	4-1 D08	2-4 O24	0-2 D29
Brighton & Hove A.	4-2 N03	4-2 O06	-	4-3 S19	3-4 S08	2-3 O27	7-3 S22	3-2 D19	1-0 S01	4-3 D29	3-0 D01
Bristol City	3-0 O27	1-1 S29	3-1 S05	-	3-0 S01	3-2 O06	1-2 S08	5-1 D27	3-3 D29	4-1 D26	6-2 N03
Bristol Rovers	4-5 S10	2-2 D22	2-4 S15	0-3 A25	-	2-2 D25	1-1 D01	2-1 S22	3-3 N15	2-0 O20	3-0 j17
Cardiff City	4-1 S22	9-3 A25	4-0 O20	2-4 O13	4-2 D26	-	6-1 D29	0-0 N10	2-1 D15	3-0 D08	6-0 S08
Crystal Palace	0-0 A25	4-1 D25	5-1 S29	0-1 S15	1-0 D19	3-0 S12	-	2-1 O13	2-2 S05	10-1 N10	5-0 D22
Exeter City	1-4 S19	0-3 O27	3-2 D22	1-0 D01	2-2 S29	3-2 N03	0-1 O06	-	5-1 S08	1-1 S01	0-2 D26
Reading	2-4 D25	3-2 D01	1-2 A25	6-2 S12	2-2 N03	3-1 D22	3-4 S19	1-1 S15	-	1-2 O13	4-1 O27
Swindon Town	2-0 D22	2-1 N07	3-2 S12	4-3 D25	2-3 O27	1-2 D01	1-3 N03	1-4 A25	3-0 O06	-	1-1 S29
Torquay United	2-2 O13	3-2 S12	0-0 a27	0-1 N03	0-3 A29	0-7 S15	1-2 D15	3-1 D25	4-3 O20	0-2 S22	-

	p	w	d	l	f	a	w	d	l	f	a	tf	ta	pts
Crystal Palace	20	7	2	1	32	7	6	1	3	23	24	55	31	29
Cardiff City	20	8	1	1	40	12	5	1	4	29	19	69	31	28
Bristol City	20	7	2	1	32	13	4	0	6	19	27	51	40	24
Brighton & Hove A.	20	8	0	2	35	22	2	1	7	14	28	49	50	21
Bristol Rovers	20	3	4	3	21	21	4	2	4	23	23	44	44	20
Swindon Town	20	5	1	4	20	19	3	2	5	15	28	35	47	19
Bournemouth	20	6	0	4	33	20	1	3	6	19	30	52	50	17
Aldershot	20	3	3	4	20	27	3	2	5	18	29	38	56	17
Exeter City	20	4	2	4	16	18	2	2	6	17	23	33	41	16
Reading	20	4	2	4	26	21	1	3	6	17	28	43	49	15
Torquay United	20	3	2	5	13	23	2	2	6	9	29	22	52	14

Div 3 South (North) Cup

	Clapton Orient	Ipswich Town	Mansfield Town	Northampton Town	Norwich City	Notts County	Port Vale	Queen's Park Rgs.	Southend United	Walsall	Watford
Clapton Orient	-	0-2 F09	2-1 a13	2-1 J12		0-0 M09	0-0 a20	0-3 M30	0-1 F23	4-3 F02	
Ipswich Town	-	-	2-1 M09		4-0 F16	1-2 M30	1-0 F23	1-0 J19	2-1 F02	-	2-2 a13
Mansfield Town	1-2 F16	3-0 M16	-	3-1 M30		2-0 J19	2-1 a06	0-0 F23	-	1-2 F02	1-0 a22
Northampton Town	0-2 a06		1-1 M23	-	1-1 F02	2-1 M09	-	0-1 J19	1-4 a20	4-1 F16	
Norwich City	3-4 J19	1-0 F09		2-1 J26	-	2-1 a22	-	0-1 M02	1-1 a13	3-0 M30	
Notts County	-	1-0 M23	1-2 J12	1-2 M16	0-1 a19	-	3-2 F02	0-3 a13	-	1-0 F16	2-1 F23
Port Vale	2-2 M16	4-1 M02	0-0 a13	-	2-1 J26	-	-	0-2 M30	2-1 a20	1-0 J19	-
Queen's Park Rgs.	6-0 a22	4-1 J12	3-0 M02	-	3-1 a06	4-2 M23	-	-	4-0 F16	-	2-1 M16
Southend United	2-1 M23	2-1 J26	-	4-3 J15	1-0 F23	-	1-1 A22	0-0 a17	-	2-2 M09	-
Walsall	4-3 J05	-	2-2 J26	3-1 a22	4-2 a06	2-0 F09	3-1 J12	-	2-0 M16	-	-
Watford	2-0 a19	0-1 a06	0-3 a20	1-0 F09	2-1 M23	6-2 M02	-	1-3 O00	-	-	-

	p	w	d	l	f	a	w	d	l	f	a	tf	ta	pts
Queen's Park Rgs.	16	8	0	0	30	7	3	3	2	8	4	38	11	25
Walsall	16	7	1	0	23	10	3	3	2	11	8	34	18	24
Mansfield Town	16	5	1	2	13	6	3	3	2	11	9	24	15	20
Southend United	16	4	4	0	13	9	2	1	5	9	16	27	25	16
Norwich City	16	5	1	2	18	9	2	1	5	9	16	27	25	16
Ipswich Town	16	6	1	1	15	7	1	0	7	4	17	19	24	15
Clapton Orient	16	3	2	3	8	11	3	1	4	14	20	22	31	15
Port Vale	16	5	2	1	12	7	0	2	6	9	18	21	25	14
Northampton Town	16	3	2	3	14	12	2	0	6	13	17	27	29	12
Watford	16	4	0	4	13	17	1	1	6	10	18	23	35	11
Notts County	16	4	0	4	9	11	1	0	7	8	20	17	31	10

Div 3 South (South) Cup

	Aldershot	Bournemouth	Brighton & Hove A.	Bristol City	Bristol Rovers	Cardiff City	Crystal Palace	Exeter City	Reading	Swindon Town	Torquay United
Aldershot	-	2-1 J19	2-2 m04	-		-	0-3 a03	5-3 a20	2-7 F23	1-3 M09	1-1 a06
Bournemouth	3-0 J12	-	4-0 a19	3-2 a20	3-3 M09	-	4-0 M02	1-1 a06	3-2 M30	6-1 F16	-
Brighton & Hove A.	4-6 F16	1-4 F02	-		1-3 a22	2-2 J17	2-2 M02	1-2 M16	-	-	4-0 M23
Bristol City	-	1-0 a22	-		1-2 M30	3-2 M09	2-2 a13	3-0 F16	-	2-1 J19	5-1 M02
Bristol Rovers	-	1-2 M16	6-1 a20	0-0 -	-	1-0 F23		2-1 J12	-	0-0 a06	3-1 a19
Cardiff City	-		3-2 M16	3-0 M02	-	-	3-0 a22	5-1 F02	5-2 a13	2-0 M30	3-0 F16
Crystal Palace	6-0 F02	2-1 F23	6-1 J19	1-2 a06	-	1-1 a20	-	3-3 M23	3-0 F09	-	1-1 -
Exeter City	1-0 a22	3-1 a13	0-0 F23	3-0 F09	0-1 J19	2-1 J26	2-3 M30	-	-	-	M09
Reading	5-1 M02	1-1 M23	4-1 M09	-	-	3-2 a06	0-2 F16	-	-	5-0 F02	6-0 J19
Swindon Town	4-0 M16	0-0 F09	-	1-1 J12	2-1 a13	3-2 M23	-	3-2 J26	-	-	0-0 a22
Torquay United	1-1 a13	-	1-0 M30	4-2 F23	1-0 J26	1-0 F09	-	0-2 M16	3-1 J12	4-1 a20	-

	p	w	d	l	f	a	w	d	l	f	a	tf	ta	pts
Bournemouth	16	6	2	0	27	9	2	2	4	10	11	37	20	20
Bristol Rovers	16	5	2	1	17	7	3	1	4	10	12	27	19	19
Reading	16	6	1	1	26	7	2	1	5	20	22	46	29	18
Crystal Palace	16	4	2	2	24	11	3	2	3	13	19	37	30	18
Cardiff City	16	7	0	1	24	7	1	1	6	15	15	39	22	17
Bristol City	16	6	1	1	19	8	1	2	5	11	19	30	27	17
Torquay United	16	6	1	1	15	7	0	3	5	4	23	19	30	16
Exeter City	16	4	2	2	12	7	1	2	5	10	21	22	28	14
Swindon Town	16	4	3	1	14	10	1	1	6	7	25	21	35	14
Aldershot	16	2	3	3	14	21	1	1	6	9	27	23	48	10
Brighton & Hove A.	16	1	3	4	17	21	0	3	5	6	24	23	45	8

The top two clubs in each division played off for the Cup:

Semi-finals April 27 1946

Bournemouth	v	Queen's Park Rgs	1-1
Bristol Rovers	v	Walsall	1-3

Semi-final replay May 1 1946

Queen's Park Rgs	v	Bournemouth	0-1 a.e.t.

Final at Stamford Bridge, May 4 1946

Bournemouth	v	Walsall	1-0

Bournemouth: Bird, Marsden, Sanaghan, Woodward, Wilson, Gallacher, Currie, Paton, Kirkham, Tagg, McDonald. Scorer: McDonald
Walsall: Lewis, Methley, Shelton, Crutchley, Foulkes, Newman, Hancocks, Talbot, Mullard, Wilshaw (Wolves), Alsop
Att. 19,715

Inter-division games, counted in both final tables:

Watford	v	Cardiff City	1-7	J12
Cardiff City	v	Watford	0-2	J19
Bristol City	v	Queen's Park Rgs.	2-0	F02
Port Vale	v	Bristol Rovers	1-0	F16
Bristol Rovers	v	Port Vale	4-2	F19
Swindon Town	v	Northampton Town	1-4	F23
Northampton Town	v	Swindon Town	5-1	M02
Crystal Palace	v	Norwich City	2-3	M09
Norwich City	v	Crystal Palace	6-1	M16
Aldershot	v	Walsall	1-1	M23
Walsall	v	Aldershot	3-1	M30
Brighton & Hove A.	v	Southend United	2-2	a06
Southend United	v	Brighton & Hove A.	1-1	a13
Queen's Park Rgs.	v	Bristol City	4-2	a19
Reading	v	Ipswich Town	2-0	a20
Ipswich Town	v	Reading	2-1	a22

1945-46 INTERNATIONAL MATCHES

Victory international. Saturday September 15, 1945 at Windsor Park, Belfast. Att. 45,061
Ireland (0) 0
England (0) 1 (Mortensen)
Ireland: T Breen (Linfield); W McMillan (Belfast Celtic), JM Feeney (Linfield); J Todd (Blackpool), J Vernon (Belfast Celtic), S Jones (Blackpool); J McKenna (Linfield), JW Sloan (Tranmere), S McCarthy (Belfast Celtic), PD Doherty (Manchester City) *capt*, P Bonnar (Belfast Celtic)
England: FV Swift (Manchester City); L Scott (Arsenal), TH Kinsell (West Bromwich); FC Soo (Stoke), C Franklin (Stoke), J Mercer (Everton) *capt*; S Matthews (Stoke), HS Carter (Sunderland), T Lawton (Everton), SH Mortensen (Blackpool), LGF Smith (Brentford)
Referee: P Craigmyle (Aberdeen)

Victory international. Saturday October 20, 1945 at The Hawthorns, West Bromwich. Att. 54,611
England (0) 0
Wales (1) 1 (Powell)
England: BF Williams (Wolves); L Scott (Arsenal), TH Kinsell (West Bromwich); FC Soo (Leicester), C Franklin (Stoke), J Mercer (Everton) *capt*; S Matthews (Stoke), M Fenton (Middlesbrough), A Stubbins (Newcastle), MW Barrass (Bolton), W Watson (Huddersfield)
Wales: C Sidlow (Wolves); DT Winter (Bolton), WM Hughes (Birmingham) *capt*; DJ Dearson (Birmingham), RG Davies (Nottm Forest), WAR Burgess (Tottenham); A Powell (Leeds), TA Astbury (Chester), G Lowrie (Coventry), WH Lucas (Swindon), G Edwards (Birmingham)
Referee: G Reader (Hampshire)

Victory international. Saturday November 10, 1945 at Hampden Park, Glasgow. Att. 97,000
Scotland (1) 2 (Waddell, Dodds)
Wales (0) 0
Scotland: R Brown (Queen's Park); J McPhie (Falkirk), J Shaw (Rangers) *capt*; W Campbell (Morton), A Paton (Motherwell), GD Paterson (Celtic); W Waddell (Rangers), G Smith (Hibernian), E Dodds (Blackpool), J Deakin (St Mirren), WB Liddell (Liverpool)
Wales: C Sidlow (Wolves); DJ Dearson (Birmingham), WM Hughes (Birmingham) *capt*; DF Witcomb (West Bromwich), RG Davies (Nottm Forest), WAR Burgess (Tottenham); WEA Jones (Swansea), F Squires (Swansea), G Lowrie (Coventry), HR Cumner (Arsenal), G Edwards (Birmingham)
Referee: MC Dale (Glasgow)

Victory international. Saturday January 19, 1946 at Wembley Stadium, London. Att. 85,000
England (2) 2 (Brown, Pye)
Belgium (0) 0
England: FV Swift (Manchester City); L Scott (Arsenal), GFM Hardwick (Middlesbrough); WA Wright (Wolves), C Franklin (Stoke), J Mercer (Everton) *capt*; S Matthews (Stoke), J Pye (Notts Co), T Lawton (Chelsea), RAJ Brown (Charlton), J Mullen (Wolves)
Belgium: F Daenen (Tilleur); R Paverick (Antwerp) *capt*, J Pannaye (Tilleur); A Puttaert (Union St Gilloise), M Vercammen (Lyra), R Devos (Beerschot); V Lemberechts (Malinois), H Coppens (Malinois), A Declyn (Malinois), J Mermans (Anderlecht), F Sermon (Anderlecht)
Referee: G Reader (Hampshire)

Victory international. Wednesday January 23, 1946 at Hampden Park, Glasgow. Att. 46,000
Scotland (0) 2 (Delaney 2, 1 pen)
Belgium (0) 2 (Lemberechts, D'Aguilar)
Scotland: R Brown (Queen's Park); J McGowan (Partick), J Shaw (Rangers) *capt*; J Campbell (Clyde), A Paton (Motherwell), GD Paterson (Celtic); G Smith (Hibernian), AN Baird (Aberdeen), J Delaney (Celtic), J Deakin (St Mirren), J Walker (Hearts)
Belgium: F Daenen (Tilleur); R Paverick (Antwerp) *capt*, J Pannaye (Tilleur); A Puttaert (Union St Gilloise), M Vercammen (Lyra), R Devos (Beerschot); V Lemberechts (Malinois), H Coppens (Malinois), A Declyn (Malinois), FC d'Aguilar, F Sermon (Anderlecht)
Referee: J Jackson (Glasgow)

Victory international. Saturday February 2, 1946 at Windsor Park, Belfast. Att. 53,000
Ireland (2) 2 (Walsh 2)
Scotland (1) 3 (Hamilton, Liddell 2)
Ireland: T Breen (Linfield); W McMillan (Belfast Celtic), JM Feeney (Linfield); J Todd (Blackpool), J Vernon (Belfast Celtic), T Aherne (Belfast Celtic); KP O'Flanagan (Arsenal), AE Stevenson (Everton) *capt*, DJ Walsh (Linfield), JJ Carey (Manchester Utd), P Bonnar (Belfast Celtic)
Scotland: R Brown (Queen's Park); J McGowan (Partick), J Shaw (Rangers) *capt*; W Campbell (Morton), A Paton (Motherwell), GD Paterson (Celtic); W Waddell (Rangers), G Hamilton (Aberdeen), E Dodds (Blackpool), KM Chisholm (Queen's Park), WB Liddell (Liverpool)
Referee: D Maxwell (Belfast)

Victory international. Saturday April 13, 1946 at Hampden Park, Glasgow. Att. 139,468
Scotland (0) 1 (Delaney)
England (0) 0
Scotland: R Brown (Queen's Park); D Shaw (Hibernian), J Shaw (Rangers) *capt*; W Campbell (Morton), F Brennan (Airdrie), J Husband (Partick); W Waddell (Rangers), C Dougall (Birmingham), J Delaney (Manchester Utd), G Hamilton (Aberdeen), WB Liddell (Liverpool)
England: FV Swift (Manchester City); L Scott (Arsenal), GFM Hardwick (Middlesbrough); WA Wright (Wolves), C Franklin (Stoke), J Mercer (Everton) *capt*; WB Elliott (West Bromwich), LF Shackleton (Bradford PA), T Lawton (Chelsea), J Hagan (Sheffield Utd), DCS Compton (Arsenal)
Referee: P Craigmyle (Aberdeen)

Victory international. Saturday May 4, 1946 at Ninian Park, Cardiff. Att. 45,000
Wales (0) 0
Ireland (1) 1 (Sloan)
Wales: WW Shortt (Plymouth); AT Sherwood (Cardiff), WM Hughes (Birmingham) *capt*; J Warner (Manchester Utd), TG Jones (Everton), WAR Burgess (Tottenham); A Powell (Leeds), W Morris (Burnley), T Ford (Swansea), WH Lucas (Swindon), RJ Clarke (Cardiff)
Ireland: T Breen (Linfield); W McMillan (Belfast Celtic), T Aherne (Belfast Celtic); JJ Carey (Manchester Utd), J Vernon (Belfast Celtic), PM Waters (Glentoran); KP O'Flanagan (Arsenal), JW Sloan (Tranmere), DJ Walsh (Linfield), PD Doherty (Derby) *capt*, J McKenna (Linfield)
Referee: GO Hancock (Pottlottyn)

Victory international. Saturday May 11, 1946 at Stamford Bridge, Chelsea, London. Att. 75,000
England (0) 4 (Carter 2, Lawton, Brown)
Switzerland (0) 1 (Friedländer)
England: FV Swift (Manchester City); L Scott (Arsenal), GFM Hardwick (Middlesbrough); WA Wright (Wolves), C Franklin (Stoke), WH Johnson (Charlton); S Matthews (Stoke), HS Carter (Derby), T Lawton (Chelsea) *capt*, RAJ Brown (Nottm Forest), LGF Smith (Aston Villa)
Switzerland: E Ballabio; R Gyger, W Steffen; H Springer, F Andreoli, J Courtat [sub: F Rickenbach]; A Bickel, W Fink, L Amadò *capt*, HP Friedländer, J Fatton
Referee: M Delasalle (France)

Victory international. Wednesday May 15, 1946 at Hampden Park, Glasgow. Att. 113,000
Scotland (3) 3 (Delaney, Liddell 2)
Switzerland (1) 1 (Aeby)
Scotland: R Brown (Rangers); D Shaw (Hibernian), J Shaw (Rangers) *capt*; W Campbell (Morton) [sub: GL Young (Rangers) 46], F Brennan (Airdrie), J Husband (Partick); W Waddell (Rangers), W Thornton (Rangers), J Delaney (Manchester Utd), T Walker (Hearts), WB Liddell (Liverpool)
Switzerland: E Ballabio; R Gyger, W Steffen; F Rickenbach, F Andreoli, R Bocquet; L Amadò *capt*, W Fink, HP Friedländer, R Maillard, G Aeby
Referee: P Stevens (Luton)

Victory international. Sunday May 19, 1946 at Colombes Stadium, Paris. Att. 58,481
France (0) 2 (Prouff, Vaast)
England (0) 1 (Hagan)
France: J Darui (Roubaix); A Grillon (Stade Francais), M Salva (Racing Club de Paris); J Prouff (Stade Rennais), A Cuissard (St Etienne), L Leduc (Red Star); A Aston (Red Star) *capt*, O Heisserer (Strasbourg), P Sinibaldi (Rheims), L Ben Barek (Stade Francais), E Vaast (Racing Club de Paris)
England: BF Williams (Wolves); JD Bacuzzi (Fulham), GFM Hardwick (Middlesbrough); WA Wright (Wolves), C Franklin (Stoke), WH Johnson (Charlton); S Matthews (Stoke), HS Carter (Derby), T Lawton (Chelsea) *capt*, J Hagan (Sheffield Utd), LGF Smith (Aston Villa)
Referee: M Scherz (Switzerland)

UNOFFICIAL HOME INTERNATIONAL CHAMPIONSHIP 1945–46

	P	W	D	L	F	A	Pts
Scotland	3	3	0	0	6	2	6
Northern Ireland	3	1	0	2	3	4	2
England	3	1	0	2	1	2	2
Wales	3	1	0	2	1	3	2

MOSCOW DYNAMO TOUR OF BRITAIN, NOVEMBER 1945

13 November 1945
Stamford Bridge, Chelsea   *est. 85,000*
Chelsea (2) 3 *(Goulden, Williams, Lawton)*
Moscow Dynamo (0) 3 *(Kartsev, Archangelski, Bobrov)*
Chelsea: Woodley; Tennant, Bacuzzi (Fulham), Russell, Harris, Taylor (Fulham), Buchanan, Williams, Lawton, Goulden, Bain.
Moscow Dynamo: Khomich; Radikorsky, Stankevitch, Blinkov, Semichastny, Soloviev L, Archangelski, Kartsev, Beskov, Bobrov, Soloviev S.

17 November 1945
Ninian Park, Cardiff   *40,000*
Cardiff C (0) 1 *(Moore)*
Moscow Dynamo (3) 10 *(Bobrov 3, Beskov 4, Archangelski 3)*
Cardiff C: McLoughlin; Lever, Raybould, Hollyman, Stansfield, Lester, Moore, Carless, Gibson, Wood, Clarke.
Moscow Dynamo: Khomich; Radikorsky, Stankevitch, Blinkov, Semichastny, Soloviev L, Archangelski, Kartsev, Beskov, Bobrov, Soloviev S.

21 November 1945
White Hart Lane, Tottenham   *54,620*
Arsenal XI (3) 3 *(Rooke, Mortensen 2)*
Moscow Dynamo (2) 4 *(Bobrov 2, Beskov, Kartsev)*
Arsenal XI: Griffiths (Cardiff C) [sub: Brown (QPR)]; Scott, Bacuzzi (Fulham), Bastin, Joy, Halton (Bury), Matthews (Stoke C), Drury, Rooke (Fulham), Mortensen (Blackpool), Cumner.
Moscow Dynamo: Khomich; Radikorsky, Stankevitch, Blinkov, Semichastny, Soloviev L [sub: Oreshkin], Trofimov [sub: Archangelski], Kartsev, Beskov, Bobrov, Soloviev S.

28 November 1945
Ibrox Park, Glasgow   *90,000*
Rangers (2) 2 *(Young, Smith)*
Moscow Dynamo (2) 2 *(Kartsev 2)*
Rangers: Dawson; Gray, Shaw, Watkins, Young, Symon, Waddell, Gillick, Smith [sub: Duncanson], Williamson, Johnstone.
Moscow Dynamo: Khomich; Radikorsky, Stankevitch, Blinkov, Semichastny, Oreshkin, Archangelski, Kartsev, Beskov, Bobrov [sub Demetriev], Soloviev S.

FA AMATEUR CUP ROUNDS PROPER 1945-46

Round One (January 19 1946)

Abbey United v Hitchin Town	3-5
Bishop Auckland v Ferguson Pailin	7-1
Bournemouth Gasworks v Totton	2-5
Bromley v Barking	1-0
Chippenham Town v Slough United	1-5
Clapton v Enfield	2-1
Crook Colliery Welfare v Evenwood Town	5-3
Erith & Belvedere v Sutton United	2-2
Golders Green v Ford Sports	2-1
Guiseley v Billingham Synthonia	4-3e
Hastings & St Leonards v Eastbourne	1-2
Hayes v Wealdstone	3-0
King's Lynn v Cambridge Town	4-1
Kingstonian v Wycombe Wanderers	1-1e
Leyton v Tufnell Park	4-0
Marine v Basford United	5-2
Metropolitan Police v Letchworth	4-0
Moor Green v Bournville Athletic	2-0
Norton Woodseats v ICI Alkali	6-1
Oxford City v Maidenhead United	5-2
Raleigh Athletic v Rawmarsh Welfare	2-5
Romford v Leytonstone	0-0e
St Albans City v Ilford	0-3
Southall v Grays Athletic	3-1
South Bank v Yorkshire Amateur	3-0
Stanley United v Shildon	9-0
Walthamstow Avenue v Dulwich Hamlet	3-0
Walton & Hersham v Corinthian Casuals	3-2
Willington v Ferryhill Athletic	3-3*
Wimbledon v Crittall Athletic	3-1
Woking v Finchley	2-1
Wood Green v Barnet	3-4
r Leytonstone v Romford	3-5
r Sutton United v Erith & Belvedere	2-4
r Willington v Ferryhill Athletic	1-3
r Wycombe Wanderers v Kingstonian	10-1

Round Two (February 2 1946)

Barnet v Walton & Hersham	4-0
Bishop Auckland v Stanley United	3-0
Clapton v Erith & Belvedere	1-2
Eastbourne v Erith & Belvedere	5-2
Ferryhill Athletic v Crook Colliery Welfare	5-1
Golders Green v Leyton	1-3
Hayes v Bromley	0-4
Hitchin Town v King's Lynn	5-3
Ilford v Metropolitan Police	5-1
Marine v Rawmarsh Welfare	4-2
Moor Green v Norton Woodseats	4-1
Oxford City v Slough United	2-3
Southall v Romford	4-2
South Bank v Guiseley	3-1
Wimbledon v Woking	5-2
Wycombe Wanderers v Walthamstow Avenue	1-1e
r Walthamstow Avenue v Wycombe Wanderers	7-5

match abandoned in extra time

Round Three (February 16 1946)

Bromley v Walthamstow Avenue	0-0e
Eastbourne v Erith & Belvedere	2-3
Hitchin Town v Barnet	2-5
Leyton v Southall	2-4e
Marine v Ferryhill Athletic	4-1
Moor Green v Slough United	2-1
South Bank v Bishop Auckland	1-3
Wimbledon v Ilford	1-2
r Walthamstow Avenue v Bromley	2-1

Round Four (March 9 1946)

Barnet v Southall	4-3
Bishop Auckland v Moor Green	4-1
Ilford v Walthamstow Avenue	2-3e
Marine v Erith & Belvedere	2-1

Semi-finals (March 30 1946)

Barnet v Marine	1-0N
Bishop Auckland v Walthamstow Avenue	2-1N

Final (April 20 1946)

Barnet v Bishop Auckland	3-2N

At Stamford Bridge, Chelsea. Att. 53,832

*Barnet: H Powell, G Wheeler, E Bunker, JC Gerrans,
L Pullen, W Weightman, AJ Jordan, D Kellerer,
RW Phipps, LC Finch (capt), P Reilly*

*Bishop Auckland: J Walshington, K Humble (capt),
L Farrer, JW Longstaff, AT Hadfield, JD Fairs,
WR Shergold, F Richardson, H Teasdale, J Tait,
R Anderson.*

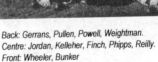

*Back: Gerrans, Pullen, Powell, Weightman.
Centre: Jordan, Kelleher, Finch, Phipps, Reilly.
Front: Wheeler, Bunker*

FA CUP QUALIFYING ROUND 1939-40

Extra Preliminary Round (September 2 1939)

1	Amble v Chopwell Colliery	8-4
	Annfield Plain v Gosforth & Coxlodge	5-0
	Ashington v Whitley & Monkseaton	2-1
	Birtley v Trimdon Grange Colliery	2-1
	Crookhall CW v Newcastle West End	1-1
	Reyrolle (Hebburn) v Shankhouse	5-2
	Throckley Welfare v Scotswood	1-2
2	Birtley v Trimdon Grange Social	2-1
	Holiday's Sports (Cornsay) v Brandon Social	2-0
	Usworth Colliery v Dawdon Colliery Recreation	5-1
	Washington Chemical Works v Chilton Colliery Rec.	2-1
7	Wilmslow Albion v Buxton	0-4
	Moultonians (Northwich) v Middlewich Athletic	
	Willaston White Star v Cheadle	
	Nantwich v Haslingden Villa	5-1
10	Armthorpe Welfare v Rossington Main	5-0
	Meltham Mills v Bentley Colliery	1-1
	Brodsworth Main Colliery v Bradford Rovers	4-3
	Goole Town v Luddendenfoot	8-1
	Grimethorpe Rovers v Ossett Town	4-2
	Guiseley v Rawmarsh Welfare	1-3
	Upton Colliery v South Kirkby Colliery	3-5
	Pilkington Recreation v Worksop Town	0-1
	Ravensthorpe v Farsley Celtic	
16	Norwich Electricity Works v Norwich YMCA	
17	Clapton v Dagenham Town	4-2
	Esso (Purfleet) v Harwich & Parkeston	
18	Berkhamsted Town v Barnet	1-2
	Epping Town v Ware	1-3
	Harrow Town v Finchley	0-3
	St Albans City v Bishop's Stortford	6-1
	Wealdstone v Old Johnians	7-3
	Bushey United v Stevenage Town	
	Saffron Walden Town v Leavesden	
	Kings Langley v Hertford Town	
	Harlow Town v Welwyn Garden City	2-3
	Enfield v London Caledonians	
	Tufnell Park v Pinner	
	Wood Green Town v Old Lyonians	
19	Hounslow Town v Wycombe Wanderers	0-3
	Maidenhead United v Yiewsley	4-0
	Uxbridge v Redford Sports	0-4
	Osberton Radiator (Oxford) v Pressed Steel (Cowley)	5-3
	Newbury Town v Bicester Town	1-2
	Oxford City v Headington United	
	Slough v Marlow	
	Civil Service v Lyons Club	
20	Egham v Woking	0-12
	Walton-on-Thames v Leyland Motors (Kingston)	2-1
	Camberley & Yorktown v PO Engineers (Wallington)	
	Kingstonian v Banstead Hospital	
	Vickers Armstrong (Byfleet) v Guildford	
	Wimbledon v Venner Sports	

21	Gravesend United v Bexley v Gravesend United	3-1
	Maidstone United v Margate	2-2
	RM Deal v Whitstable	
23	Thornycroft v Winchester City	
	Hamworthy v Sherborne Town	
	Bournemouth Gasworks Ath. v Bournemouth	4-0
	Trafalgar Sports v Osborne Athletic	
	Fareham v Gosport	
	HMS Victory v East Cowes	
24	Calne & Harris United v Pewsey Y.M.	

The competition was cancelled on the outbreak of war

We know that many of the games shown with no result were cancelled when one or both clubs withdrew. Other fixtures may have been played but we have been unable to find the results.

APPENDIX: THE BOLTON DISASTER

33 people lost their lives and some 500 were injured at Burnden Park Bolton on March 9 1946. In the immediate aftermath, the Home Secretary, Mr J. Chuter Ede, commissioned an inquiry into the incident and the Mayor of Bolton opened an appeal fund. The council of the Football Association immediately donated £2,000 to the appeal and allowed member clubs to take collections at games.

After the enquiry, a report by Mr R. Moelwyn Hughes K.C. was presented to the Home Secretary. The causes of the disaster were stated to be:

That the crowd was far larger than was expected;

That too many were admitted to the enclosure;

That means were taken to decide when the enclosure was full were defective, and, when taken, were slow and unorganized;

Unauthorised entry, a contributory but not a main factor;

The siting of crush barriers.

The disaster was unique, according to the report. "There was no collapse of a structure; it was the first example in the history of football following of serious casualties inflicted by the crowd upon itself". It was stated that "the ground officials should have taken more interest in the state of the crowd awaiting admission to the enclosure. They could have realized in advance the necessity for closing the turnstiles. The responsible police officers stationed outside should also have appreciated this necessity would arise and so informed the club authorities."

"The total number admitted was not known until some time after turnstiles had ceased to admit people. The enclosure was full at 2.35 pm. At that time illegal entry had not begun. The turnstiles admitted 2000 more in the next 10 minutes." Mr Hughes said "Had they closed at 2.35 pm the safety figure would not have been exceeded and I do not think the disaster would have happened."

Evidence had been given by Mr James Austin, checker at turnstile number 1, that he had closed it at 2.40 pm because he had complaints from spectators inside the ground that they could not see. At this stage, an exit gate was opened by someone inside the ground. 11 year-old William Farringdon told the inquiry that because of the crush he and his friend decided to leave. While standing near the exit gate he noticed four men, one of whom did something to the padlock before giving the gate a shove. The gate opened, and the man told him to get out first, which he did. A big crowd outside the gate made a move, and he was caught in the crush. Mr Norman Crook, a cotton comber overlooker, came forward following an appeal by the police. He and his 12 year-old son decided to leave at 2.30; the ground was full and the crowd began swaying. He realized his son would not see the game and decided to leave the ground. Finding the gate padlocked, he took his keys from his pocket and opened the padlock with an ordinary screw key. He pushed the gate open 12" and squeezed out. There was a sudden rush, and when he turned round, people were jammed in the door. A padlock was produced in court, and sure enough, Mr Crook's key unlocked it. Gateman James Austin estimated that 300 people came into the ground through the gate before a mounted constable and two other officers succeeded in closing the gate. However, people then began climbing over the fencing leading to the railway and some of it was pulled down. It was estimated that another 500 or 600 people got over that way before the mounted man and other policemen were able to stop them.

The exact situation in the enclosure was appreciated by two constables at the crucial point when the need to close the turnstiles became apparent. The report said: "One failed to find any appropriate club official, and the other met the club's head checker (turnstile attendant) by accident."

A Home Office forensic scientist examined the damaged crash barriers. Two had given way and one had been bent forward. The broken uprights of one barrier were found to be corroded at ground level. The scientist reported that other barriers which must have been subjected to more than the usual pressure had withstood it without distortion.

Other conclusions in the report were:

That, on the information they had, the steps taken by the club were on the whole proper;

On their information the police allocated and placed a reasonable force;

The ground officials left too much to the police and were not easily available;

Cooperation between police inside and outside the ground was defective; the so-called "reserve" in the police disposition was illusory, and the collection of additional police help to the danger point was haphazard.

The Mayor of Bolton's appeal fund for the dependents of those killed raised a total of £52,000 before it closed in August 1946. A concert was arranged for the fund at the Adelphi Theatre in London on April 4 1946. It featured, amongst others, Tommy Trinder, Arthur Askey, Jack Buchanan and the Charlton Athletic team. £12,000 was raised by a representative match between England and Scotland, played at Maine Road Manchester on August 24 1946 before a gate of 70,000:

England (2) 2 (Welsh 2)
Scotland (1) 2 (Thornton 2)
England: FV Swift (Manchester City) *capt*; J Walton (Manchester Utd), GFM Hardwick (Middlesbrough); WA Wright (Wolves), LH Leuty (Derby), FR Mitchell (Birmingham); S Matthews (Stoke), D Welsh (Charlton), R Lewis (Arsenal), WA Fielding (Everton), C Mitten (Manchester Utd)
Scotland: W Miller (Celtic); D Shaw (Hibernian), J Shaw (Rangers) *capt*; W Campbell (Morton), F Brennan (Newcastle), J Husband (Partick); W Waddell (Rangers), C Dougall (Birmingham), W Thornton (Rangers), G Hamilton (Aberdeen), WB Liddell (Liverpool)
Referee: G Dutton (Warwick)

THE AUTHORS

Jack Rollin arrived in 1932, so recalls ducking World War Two bombs and the machine guns of stray enemy planes. A long career in journalism with Soccer Star, the Sunday Telegraph and other newspapers led Jack to write pioneering works on soccer statistics and the 'you wouldn't believe it' side of the beautiful game. Jack has been editor of the *Sky Sports (formerly Rothmans) Football Yearbook* since 1988 and also edits the *Playfair Football Annual*. His many books on football include *Soccer at War, The Essential History of England,* and *The Guinness Record of the World Cup.* He is soccer correspondent to the *Encyclopaedia Britannica*.

Tony Brown is 12 years Jack's junior and (as far as he knows) never got closer to a bomb than the crater left in his back garden from a raid three years before he was born. Unfortunately the ones that fell on the County Ground in Meadow Lane during the same raid made a bit of a mess, causing Notts to miss the 1941-42 season. After a professional career in computing and telecoms, Tony was forcibly retired in 1994, at which point he set up a publishing business specialising in soccer books and databases. Tony's SoccerData imprint has now published nearly 100 books on football topics, including acclaimed reference works such as the *Match by Match* series that will soon have covered Football League history from 1888 to 1970. His databases of results and dates are used by many media groups and work is progressing towards the ultimate goal of including the line-ups and goalscorers of every game.

ACKNOWLEDGEMENTS

The authors are indebted to many of their colleagues for help and support in compiling the book. We would particularly like to mention the late Don Aldridge, Kit Bartlett, John Brodie, Colin Cameron, Denis Clarebrough, Michael Joyce, Gerald Mortimer and John Treleven. Also, our thanks go to Arthur Turner and Reg Harrison, veterans of the 1946 FA Cup final, for kindly responding to our request for a foreword.

Photographs are from the authors' collections or have kindly been loaned by our colleagues. Copyright holders are acknowledged in the text. If we have overlooked a credit to a copyright holder, please contact the publisher so that the mistake can be rectified in any future editions.

Derby welcomes home the victorious team